FIGHTER PILOT

HELEN DOE

AMBERLEY

To unexpected heroes

First published in 2015
This edition published 2016

Amberley Publishing
The Hill, Stroud,
Gloucestershire, GL5 4EP

www.amberley-books.com

ISBN 978 1 4456 6012 7 (paperback)
ISBN 978 1 4456 4612 1 (ebook)

British Library Cataloguing in Publication Data.
A catalogue record for this book is available from the British Library.

Typesetting and Origination by
Amberley Publishing.
Printed in the UK.

CONTENTS

ACKNOWLEDGEMENTS

This book arose from several conversations with my father. As I grew up he was still a serving RAF officer and in those days he rarely mentioned his wartime experience, apart from the occasional reference. He was then, in general, not very approving of those who rushed out memoirs or books that glorified war. Many years later he was persuaded to write his memoirs, and when I later became an academic historian we discussed another book using the many newly released documents. It has taken me several years and has been a steep, but very worthwhile, learning curve. During my research I came to an even greater appreciation of the achievements of those who served during the war, and there are many unsung heroes; ordinary people doing extraordinary things.

When I began I was asked by one serving officer whether I planned to destroy any myths. It was a good question; myths do need testing, and in this book they have been checked wherever possible and also put into context. As my research journey continued it raised a host of questions about why, who, where and when, so what is reflected in this book is also a part of my education about aspects of the RAF in the Second World War. I also had a key question in my mind regarding leadership. My father's highest decoration, the DSO, was for outstanding leadership. So who and what influenced his leadership? He was also certain that there were those who had never had due credit. He was a great admirer of the part played by Dowding and Park, in particular, but was equally determined that men like Pat Hughes, and other lost colleagues, should be remembered for their significant contribution. I have tried to make sure that they are remembered here and I thank my brother, Robert, who inspired me at my father's funeral by ensuring that the congregation recalled those who did not come back from war.

In my research I soon found that mentioning my father's name brought a smile to many people, and he is valued not just for his wartime actions but for the man he was. But being his daughter also brought some potential limitations as there was a risk of familial bias. Luckily I stumbled on Eddie Sparkes and his memoirs. Eddie comes across as a fascinating, if unconventional character, and it was clear he did not get on with his commanding officer, Bob; he did not get on with any of his COs. But he did provide that opposite view, which was helpful.

Thanking all the people who have helped me in my research is not easy as there have been so many who have been more than generous with time, material and enthusiastic encouragement. My colleagues at the University of Exeter, and in particular Dr Michael Duffy, were helpful supporters of my mission. Archivists are wonderfully patient and helpful people and I am indebted to Sebastian Cox at the RAF Historical Branch, Nick Mays of News International, the team at Surrey Record Centre, archivist Peter Capon at the Museum of Army Flying, the team at the RAF Museum and the staff at the National Archives. Sir Emsley Carr's grandchildren Sarah, Richard and William, shared memories and photographs with me. Professor Murray Meikle of University of Cambridge discussed maxillofacial injuries and coped with all my layman's questions and very kindly let me see drafts of his book. Jagan Pillarisetti sent me copies of 10 Squadron IAF operations record books. Professor Harry Bennett of Plymouth also sent early drafts of his work on the French pilots and Dr Jeremy Crang shared some unpublished research data with me. Professor Richard Overy encouraged me despite his busy schedule and Stephen Bungay read the early chapters and made some very helpful comments. Friends and family were roped in at various stages. Tony and Jan Wright provided medical information, my niece Julie Weston sent me information on her grandmother, and my sister, Susan, and my brother, Robert, have been strong supporters. A thank you to Sheryll Murray MP and Anna Soubry MP who supported my project and unlocked doors. Various people helped in location research – Mary Pollack at Kings Somborne and Lieutenant Colonel Chris Ion, Army Air Corps Regimental Secretary, who put me up in Middle Wallop officers' mess in late August and spent much time showing me around the base. Kristen Alexander shared information and gave great long-distance support from Australia. Sally Bryant encouraged and made useful comments on early drafts. Wing Commander Erica Ferguson and Keith Arnold of Bentley Priory were most kind. 234 Squadron Association members, especially Derek Colbourne, Group Captain Nigel Walpole and Air Commodore Tim Thorn, have been more than helpful and welcomed me to the group. Ray and Effie Stebbings and Lois and Hugh Pihlens were wonderfully kind. Air Marshal Dick Garwood helped in many ways to open doors for me. Group Captain John Jupp provided me with material and some very useful comments on leadership. Sir Erik Bennett, Dickie Dicken, Tim Elkington, Terry Kane, Keith Lawrence and Tony Pickering were generous with their memories and time. Many more people were very generous with photographs and I have credited them where possible.

I owe a special debt to Air Vice-Marshal John Feesey, who read several versions of the drafts, patiently listened to my wittering, gently educated me, saved me from errors on many occasions and proofread the final document.

I am well aware that I have dared to venture into a specialist territory which has an army of knowledgeable and enthusiastic researchers. My errors are all my own and are no reflection on those who assisted me so kindly.

My most important thank you is to my husband, Michael, who has been infinitely patient, helpful and forbearing during the gestation of this book.

Helen Doe

ABBREVIATIONS

ACSEA	Allied Command South East Asia
AOC	Air Officer Commanding
AP/O	Acting Pilot Officer
AuxAF	Auxiliary Air Force
Bf 109	Messerschmitt Bf 109
Bf 110	Messerschmitt Bf 110
CAS	Chief of Air Staff
CFI	Chief Flying Instructor
CGI	Chief Ground Instructor
C-in-C	Commander-in-Chief
CID	Criminal Investigation Department
COS	Chiefs of Staff
DFC	Distinguished Flying Cross
Do 17	Dornier 17
Do 18	Dornier 18
DSO	Distinguished Service Order
E/A	Enemy aircraft
ENSA	Entertainments National Service Association
FAFL	Forces Aériennes Françaises Libres
FLS	Fighter Leaders School
He 111	Heinkel 111
He 113	Heinkel 113 (Note: this aircraft was a hoax)

IAF	Indian Air Force
Ju 87	Junkers 87
Ju 88	Junkers 88
LMF	Lack of Moral Fibre
Me 109	Messerschmitt Bf 109
Me 110	Messerschmitt Bf 110
ORB	Operations Record Book
OTC	Officer Training Corps
OTU	Operational Training Unit
RAAF	Royal Australian Air Force
RAFA	Royal Air Force Association
RAFVR	Royal Air Force Volunteer Reserve
RCAF	Royal Canadian Air Force
RFC	Royal Flying Corps
RNAS	Royal Naval Air Service
RNVR	Royal Naval Volunteer Reserve
RNZAF	Royal New Zealand Air Force
SFTS	Service Flying Training School
UAS	University Air Squadron
USAAF	United States Army Air Forces
VAD	Voluntary Aid Detachment
VCP	Visual Control Post
WAAF	Women's Auxiliary Air Force

I

EARLY YEARS AND EARLY INFLUENCES

The *Telegraph* obituary hailed Bob Doe as the third-highest-scoring ace in the Battle of Britain, listed his decorations (DSO, DFC and Bar) and noted that he had been 'a shy, sickly boy' who 'left school at fourteen to work as an office boy at the *News of the World*'.[1] A similar story unfolded in *The Times*.[2] It is good journalism, the ordinary lad with an unpromising start who battles against the odds and becomes a hero. We like the unconventional hero and this background challenged the popular view of the middle- and upper-class fighter pilots of the battle. Few office boys get national attention in this way and the 'shy, sickly' tag had become part of the Bob Doe myth.

Bob first spoke publicly of his early childhood to John Willis, the documentary maker. Willis, at the time, interviewed Bob for the Yorkshire Television documentary *Churchill's Few*, which went on air in 1985 and was accompanied by a book.[3] There was a positive public response to the documentary and many people, some of whom were old comrades, contacted Bob. Encouraged by this and urged on by many, Bob wrote his memoirs with the help of Leslie Dawson and these were published in 1991. In his own book, Bob did not dwell on his early life and summarised it in just a few pages.[4] The book of the programme, *Churchill's Few*, and Bob's memoirs gave the description that would stay with Bob for the rest of his life, culminating in the shortened version that appeared in the obituaries. The reality is slightly different and this chapter looks at the early influences on Bob and reveals a rather more complex story.

Bob was the only child of James and Linda Doe and he was born in Reigate, Surrey. James and Linda had married during the First World War just before James volunteered. James came from an agricultural family and was the only child of a late second marriage. He grew up with his half-brother and sister in Snailwell, a small village near Newmarket, which is on the border between Cambridgeshire and Suffolk. James' father, Thomas, was an agricultural labourer, as so many of his ancestors had been before him. James' fate might have seemed to be to follow his father, but something changed, and both James and his father broke out of the agricultural labourer mould and became domestic gardeners. This was a position with more potential. Domestic gardener was a role in which a man, if he were prepared to move, could make progress up the promotional ladder. By 1901 James was living with his parents and widowed grandfather in Exning, Suffolk. In the countryside around Newmarket there was no shortage of gentlemen's residences requiring gardeners.

Ten years later the family had moved away from their traditional East Anglia base to Surrey. James had a job as a live-in gardener in a very elegant house, Tadworth Court, owned by Charles Morton. Here, James was one of a large domestic team of staff. Tadworth Court, once the country base for Great Ormond Street Children's Hospital, is today owned by The Children's Trust, a charity for severely disabled children. Pevsner, the great architectural scholar of historic buildings in England, noted Tadworth Court's seventeenth-century origins and described it as 'one of the most elegant in the whole country'. The gardens were extensive and required a large team to manage them. James was able to observe elegant country living at a respectful distance.[5]

Bob's mother, Linda, also came from a rural family. Linda Caroline Coster was born in Wiltshire in the small village of Wroughton, today mainly a dormitory village for Swindon. Linda's family also had a strong agricultural background, which is hardly surprising as agricultural labour was the male occupation for the vast majority of the rural working class. It was a label that was all-encompassing and included both unskilled and highly skilled alike. By the mid-nineteenth century there was a major shift in occupational groupings. In 1852 there were 1.7 million men classed as agricultural labourers and this fell to 1 million by 1921, the fastest fall being between 1861 and 1881.[6] By 1901, Linda's father, Charles, was working for the Great Western Railway in Swindon as a storekeeper. For both sides of Bob's family the end of the nineteenth century brought new occupations to provide ways out and off the land, James in his role as a domestic gardener and Linda in service working in Berkshire. Before the war, the major employment sector for young women was still domestic service.

James and Linda were married in 1915 at Reigate church. James was thirty-three and Linda twenty-seven. They worked together as cook and gardener on a small estate in Reigate and lived in a four-roomed cottage on the estate, Broadfield Cottage, with James' parents.[7] Linda was a forceful personality, a dominant woman with a close connection to the church. She was a fierce disciplinarian while her husband, James, was a gentle, quiet, unassuming man with little conversation.

Robert Francis Thomas Doe was born on 10 March 1920 after his father's return from war. He was named Robert after his maternal grandfather and Thomas after his paternal grandfather, but his second name, Francis, is a bit of a mystery. Bob, known as Bobbie as a young boy, had rickets in early childhood and recalled going up to London with his mother to see a specialist.[8] Little was then known about rickets, which stems from a vitamin D deficiency and is generally associated with inner-city children with little access to sunlight and a poor diet. A gardener's child living on a small estate would not be restricted in either way, but it can also be associated with late breastfeeding. A change of diet and plenty of fresh air would soon have resolved the problem and the pictures of him as young child show a sturdy toddler with no sign of any ill effects.

In Bob's interview with Willis, Bob, then sixty-five, cited the early illness as the reason he started school late at the age of seven.[9] It may have had more to do with a house move. His father, James, had a big change in his career in 1927 when he was appointed to a prestigious job as head gardener of a country house at Walton-on-the-Hill, still in Surrey but a few miles to the north. The family moved into a semi-detached cottage in

Meadow Walk in the village owned by the estate. The butler lived in the other semi-detached cottage, a clear measure of the comparative status of both positions.

Walton-on-the-Hill is an archetypal English village with a large pond, a green, a small primary school and two public houses. In 1931 the population was under 2,000. In the long list of local businesses there were auctioneers, firms of motor engineers and one garage with cars for hire, a cycle repairer, a music teacher, grocers, newsagents and, of course, essential for small boys, a confectioner. The area had many large houses, several of which were located close to the famous Walton Heath Golf Club with its thirty-six-hole course. The club was famed for the well-known golfers who frequented it during the First World War. Established in 1904, it had as its golf professional James Braid, who was a very well-known golfer. The golf club was a big attraction for many; Lloyd George was a regular player and had a house nearby, and it has been said that the First World War was fought on its golf links.[10]

The family settled in to their new home in Meadow Walk and Bob attended the local Church of England primary school in Walton-on-the-Hill. Typical of all village schools, it was a small red-brick building with four classrooms and outside toilets.[11] It was not a beacon of education for the young as by any standards it was failing its pupils. An inspection in 1928, when Bob had been there just one year, highlighted a series of problems:

The Headmaster has recently been absent ill for 3 months, the Senior Assistant taking his place with 3 supply teachers in succession. Allowance was made for this in judging the conditions of the school. Much the best work being done is in the second class where the senior assistant is teaching firmly and capably, with the result that the children are compelled to work, make steady progress and retain what they learn. Arithmetic however is not strong the ground work not being well enough known. In the rest of the school though some very fair work was seen in all classes, there is a need of much more determined & stimulating teaching, & for the children to acquire habits of industry & self-reliance. At present they appear to take only a moderate interest in their work, & to lack the desire to apply themselves closely to it.[12]

One problem was the grouping of the children with a wide age range, which gave real difficulties in focusing on developmental needs. In his discussion with the headmaster, the inspector placed special stress on the need for a better grading of the children. On the day of inspection there were seventeen children over twelve 'below Standard VI, while the ages of the children in the 2nd class ranged from 8 to 14'.[13] However, in the extensive criticism there was one positive note as sport was a strength: 'The school is to be congratulated on its success in the district football & cricket leagues.' But four years later there was still concern:

Since the last report was written in 1928 there have been many changes in the staff of this school, and the work in consequence suffered. In January 1932 when the present Head Master was appointed the school was in a state bordering on inefficiency, and since that date further changes in the personnel of the Assistant staff have greatly interfered with the progress of the school towards recovery.

The report continued, noting that the older children had lost the 'jollity and spontaneity that were characteristic of their behaviour in the infants' class'. The senior class, led by the headmaster, was good, but 'arithmetic is still weak and speech is hurried, careless and indistinct'. In the middle class he found the 'teaching failed to secure the attention and interest of the children, who frequently became noisy and fidgety. Firmer control and more stimulating teaching are an immediate necessity in this class.'[14] This poor teaching was reflected in the attendance figures for the school. From 1925 to 1934 the number of pupils had steadily declined, from 192 to 170, and attendance had slipped from 94 per cent to 89 per cent.[15] The school was not providing a good start for any child's education and particularly not for a boy entering his early teens.

Bob had good memories of life in the village, although his primary school was never mentioned, and he recalled joining the local church choir and, as boys do, shooting the heads off flowers:

When I was a child one of the first things I was given when I was old enough was an air gun. I remember getting into awful trouble 'cause I went round the garden one day shooting all the heads off the tulips ... most satisfying to see this tulip suddenly fall off after you shot at it. I became a natural shot I think.[16]

If he caused damage at home he was rather more in awe of the gardens at the big house, Wonford, for which his father was responsible. James worked for Sir Emsley Carr, who was the majority owner and editor of the *News of the World*. James had a team of eight gardeners working for him. The grounds were extensive and there was a large conservatory attached to the house. James and his team grew a variety of plants with herbaceous borders and he had one border dedicated to tulips and another to carnations. The garden also featured a sunken garden, a rockery that had been brought stone by stone from an exhibition in Kew and a pond. James was a very successful award-winning plantsman with a Royal Horticultural Society gold cup for his carnations. There were, of course, plenty of vegetables and fruits to supply the household and Bob recalls eating what to him at the time seemed exotic fruit.[17] There are also photographs of 'young Bobbie', as he was known then, sitting in the garden at Wonford. Also in the extensive grounds were good sports facilities. The Carr family included two daughters and six sons (the eldest of whom died at Passchendaele) and they were keen on sports. Carr was 'a proud family man ... not unusual to have twenty or more members of the family to sit down to lunch or dinner ... those attending had much to occupy their leisure time: there were squash and tennis courts, a putting green and cricket pitch in the grounds and the Walton Heath golf course nearby'.[18]

Bob's parents, or rather his mother, were ambitious for him. His mother sent him for violin lessons since the ability to play an instrument was seen as a measure of social progress. But his primary school was clearly not helping to engage this young man in his studies. If his parents wanted him to get a better education they needed to remove him from the Church school. The challenge was a financial one: either he could stay at the failing school until the age of fourteen, or they could pay for him to go to a secondary school (typically a grammar school) if he could qualify (a very big question in view of the state of his tuition) and if they could afford it. The education system suffered massive cuts from 1922, and by 1931 the proportion of children aged fifteen to eighteen who remained in a school stood at only 6 per cent.[19] There was an inherent class bias in the secondary school system. State-aided grammar schools were training an elite and gave an education patterned on that offered in the public schools. For the lucky few who got there, a grammar school education could lead to university and professional career, and this could also lead to a complete change in social identity in the class-ridden interwar years.[20] For those who were not seen as having the potential to go to a grammar school the choices were limited. Bob, with his poor early educational start, was in that group.

However, Bob was fortunate; while he could have remained at his inadequate primary school until fourteen, someone had other ideas for him. There was one positive measure to assist adolescent education in the interwar period and this was a move to allow local education authorities to develop an expanded and more advanced curriculum than that available at the standard primary school. London county authorities introduced the central school in 1911. Its four-year curriculum had a broad academic basis and a general vocational orientation. It gained popularity and the London County Council alone had 140 such schools by 1927.[21] In April 1932, one month after his twelfth birthday, he was admitted to the Leatherhead Central School.[22] It was an odd time to join a school, midway in the school year, but it was a very good move.

Previously known as the Upper Mixed School, the school in Kingston Road in Leatherhead became a central school in 1926. The headmaster,

Stephen King, was an energetic and visionary man who had worked hard to change the school since his arrival in 1923. He introduced outside speakers to let fresh ideas into their minds and arranged excursions to places of interest. By 1935 the school had 400 pupils, both boys and girls, and around fourteen staff, which gave a reasonable teacher–pupil ratio. If Bob and the other primary school children in Walton had been let down by a succession of poor teachers, his move to Leatherhead was a major change. Stephen King's hard work was rewarded in a glowing inspection report in 1938:

> The school is outstandingly good. One simple proof of this is that, on March 31st last, out of 484 children 72 were between 14 and 15 years of age and 23 over 15, and that in addition to a normal two stream organisation, the school has six leavers' classes, each with a different objective. Though several external examinations are successfully taken, in no case did it appear that the curriculum was unduly biased or the breadth of the children's education limited thereby.[23]

Stephen King was singled out for praise as the 'success of the school and its peculiar quality are due primarily to the Head Master'. The report recognised that he took a personal interest in every child in the school even after they had left. He kept in close touch with them through an 'Evening School which has 270 members, and also through the Old Scholars' Association', which 'takes an active interest in its members' occupations and employment'.[24] King had a flair for organisation and was totally devoted to the life of the school, and this enthusiasm was shared by his staff, who reportedly

> make every possible effort for the children's welfare. The children know this and respond accordingly, so that the school exerts an influence far beyond its own boundaries and that of the ordinary leaving age. The school, in short, is an active and intelligent community, life in which must have a permanent effect for good on all its members. It reflects the highest credit on all concerned.[25]

King was an extraordinary teacher and a superb leader who knew how to get the best out of his pupils. He visited the 'Contributing Junior Schools', the feeder schools, and perhaps this is where he first encountered Bob. King's pupils may not have been destined for university but they were going to get all the advantages he could possibly offer them as a preparation for their working lives. Bob thrived in this environment and found his natural place as a sportsman. He was good at cricket and athletics and this apparently shy boy was picked aged thirteen to represent not just his school but his county as a hurdler in the All-England Schoolboys' Championship. A newspaper clipping shows Leatherhead Central School Athletics Team, with Bob in the front row on the right. This was a school that encouraged aspirations from all its pupils and developed their abilities.[26] While Bob may not have taken any examinations, academic study was not completely neglected as he later admitted to a liking for mathematics.[27]

The headmaster's drive led to school plays and these were performed in public to an audience of proud parents and friends. In 1934 the programme for the school's production of *The Merchant of Venice* ran for three nights from 21 March to 23 March and was announced as the school's second dramatic performance. As extra encouragement to the public the programme enthusiastically exclaimed that 'those who saw the first pronounced it a surprising and gratifying success'. Public performances of Shakespearean plays were standard events in grammar schools and public schools, and King saw no reason why his school should be any different. Such performances display a school to advantage and encourage pupils to grow in stature by speaking in public. Choosing the actors is a tricky task; the starring parts need to be taken by those who can cope with the pressure. The rest of the cast also has to be chosen with care. Among the cast was R. Doe as Tubal, a Jewish friend of Shylock. Tubal has just eight lines to say in the play but this seems a big step for the apparently shy Bob. But the bigger surprise, and challenge to his later image of his youthful self, is that on the night he did not play Tubal. He was, for whatever reason, propelled into the leading role of Antonio. For the sake of the school, the cast and the young person, ambitious headmasters do not put the least confident and shyest boy into the leading role at late notice. The main actors have to provide a lead for the whole cast. Bob's athletic prowess and dramatic ability at the Leatherhead Central School lays to rest the shy, sickly child image.[28]

Bob mistakenly recalled leaving school at fourteen; in fact he remained one more year. The 1918 Education Act fixed obligatory school attendance to fourteen but local education authorities could require attendance until the age of fifteen.[29] There were interwar concerns about adolescent unemployment, which led to calls to raise the school leaving age.[30] By remaining one more year, there was one final highlight for Bob before leaving school. Stephen King was keen to expand his pupils' horizons and in 1935 he arranged a cruise to Scandinavia for a select group. Among the twenty-eight boys selected for this special trip was Bob.[31]

It was the first excursion abroad for pupils from the school. Twenty-eight boys were selected to go to Scandinavia and a party of girls to Bruges.[32] It was also a departure for the association that organised the trips. The School Journey Association was a voluntary body of teachers that had organised such trips for some years for public and secondary schoolboys. This was the first time that elementary schoolboys were taken and the opportunity was widely reported in the local press. Demand was expected to be high from across Britain for the 800 places.[33] The Secretary of the Association announced that the plan was 'to go to Oslo and Copenhagen and spend three days at each place'.[34]

In the end, 840 schoolboys sailed from Tilbury on Monday 12 August on a 2,000-mile cruise to Scandinavian countries, 'the first of its kind ever arranged for elementary schools'.[35] It was not luxurious. The specially chartered vessel was the *Nevasa*. The 9,000-ton ship was built in 1912 and originally carried passengers to and from India. She accommodated 128 first-class and 98 second-class passengers. During the war she had served as a troopship, and as a 660-bed hospital ship. By 1925 she was rebuilt as a permanent troopship with capacity for 1,000 men.[36] Except for five days visiting Oslo and Copenhagen the boys were kept busy on board ship. They spent 'most of their time learning about navigation and the life of sailors. Relaxation will be provided by concerts, films and games.'[37] During the cruise the boys slept in hammocks between decks while the accompanying 300 adults had cabins.[38] This was a big opportunity for the small group of boys from Leatherhead Central School.

A trip to Scandinavia may broaden the mind but it was not going to solve the big decision about Bob's future. Unemployment among juvenile boys was a particular concern in the 1930s.[39] For many working-class boys in the interwar period the majority still followed their fathers' occupations and as a head gardener, James could probably have provided his son with a start.[40] This, however, does not appear to have been a favoured route and the cruise does not seem to have engendered a sudden wish for a nautical life; perhaps the North Sea put paid to that. Bob was keen, like so many young men of his generation, on flying, but in 1935 this was out of the question as there were simply no opportunities for a young man with no money and no qualifications. So, at a loss to know what to do for his son, Bob's father went to his employer for advice.

James Doe's employer was a man of very considerable influence. Carr was the chairman, part-owner and joint managing director, with H. H. Aldridge, of the *News of the World*. Carr had formed a highly successful partnership with Riddell, later Lord Riddell, which had consolidated the success of the newspaper. On Riddell's death in 1934 Carr gained a majority share and he remained the editor for fifty years.[41] It was a highly competitive newspaper world, with circulation wars being fought by promotional gimmicks and door-to-door canvassing.[42] The paper's journalists rushed to be the first to get the news of murders, sexual confessions and lurid memoirs. Stars such as Gracie Fields, Ivor Novello, George Robey, Robert Donat, Clark Gable, Sam Goldwyn and Walt Disney were featured, together with sports personalities of the day, boxers, jockeys and famous cricketers like Don Bradman.[43] Carr described the paper as 'a human document representing the daily life of the average man – not neglecting the more serious problems, but also touching upon the lighter forms of life, bringing humour, brightness and humanity into everyone's existence'.[44] Under his leadership the paper's circulation figures rose from 40,000 to a record-breaking 4.5 million. It was the biggest-selling Sunday paper in the world and the only Sunday paper to have its own printing press.[45]

Despite the paper's more lurid journalism, Carr kept himself above the gossip-mongering and was noted as both a major influence in newspaper circles and a considerable philanthropist. His knighthood in 1918 recognised his wartime charitable efforts supporting 'Welsh troops, particularly those captured by the enemy'. He was a great encourager of sport, particularly athletics and golf. There was a Carr cup in cricket and golf, and not forgetting horticulture as there was the Sir Emsley Carr cup for carnations. The Emsley Carr Mile, an annual athletics running race, was later created in his name by his son, William, in 1953. Sir Emsley was very involved with many press organisations and was a key figure in the parliamentary reporters' circles. When he was appointed as chairman of Walton Heath Golf Club he amazed the members by announcing that the Prince of Wales had agreed to become captain. The dukes of York and Gloucester also became members. James Braid, the golf professional, was credited with helping the Prince of Wales get his handicap down to single figures. The prince would fly in and land his aeroplane near a big house in Kingswood nearby.[46] Carr was indeed well connected at the top of the British establishment.

Bob's father was not inhibited by the prospect of asking his employer for help. Carr was known as a man of great kindness. His obituary described him as possessed of 'all the human virtues and more abundantly those of kindliness, generosity and forbearance'.[47] Sir Emsley Carr it was said was an 'easy going man who preferred events to flow smoothly along with a minimum of disturbance'.[48] That cannot have been easy to achieve in the newspaper world. Faced with his head gardener's dilemma over his only child, Carr agreed to find an opening for Bob at his newspaper.

On 13 January 1936 Bob arrived in central London to start work as an office boy in the *News of the World*. This was a new and sophisticated environment of journalists and scoops, but Bob was not a part of that; he was in the share transfer department. Under Carr the 'first limited attempts at diversification were made'.[49] The business owned several local newspapers, some property and even 13 per cent of Walton Heath Golf club.[50] If Bob's new job was not glamorous, working in the City did have benefits for an adolescent; there were girls and plenty of them.

His job entailed him moving around the City taking letters and packages from different parts of the *News of the World* business. Working in the heart of London he was part of a rapidly changing social scene. The world of work had changed remarkably in the interwar years. Young men and women emerged during these years as prominent consumers of clothes and leisure pursuits including dance halls, magazines and the cinema. One aspect that cannot have escaped the notice of a teenage boy in central London was the emergence of independently minded, fashion-conscious young women. Young women represented over 45 per cent of the female workforce.[51] Before the First World War, many of them were destined for domestic service but now opportunities in the better-paid retail and clerical sectors expanded. Dance halls targeted young consumers and the Palais or Mecca were well established across the country. This change had been noted by the *News of the World*, which introduced a women's features page in 1929.[52] Young workers between the wars experienced a greater amount of leisure than their parents, although for young women there were still strong social restrictions on their freedom in leisure time.[53] For entertainment there were cinemas, which increased dramatically, due to demand, from 3,000 in 1926 to nearly 5,000 in 1939.[54] While Bob may not have had much money left over to spend, he and his friends could chat to the young women they met on their errands around the city. This was a far more sophisticated environment than Walton.

The newspaper was also an influence. Staff at the time were encouraged to move temporarily to try out in different departments.[55] Bob later said that he worked on the women's page and he also suggested to some early RAF colleagues that he had been a journalist, albeit a very junior one.[56] The newspaper was not all scoops, gossip and scandal. One leading commentator who was writing for the paper in the challenging times that included the rise of Hitler in Germany and the Spanish Civil War was

Winston Churchill. From January 1935 he was commissioned to write twelve articles for the paper, starting with his autobiography. In May 1935 Winston asked how the readers had received it. The answer was that it had been a great success and the deputy editor, Davies, wanted more contributions and suggested a series, to be called 'Great Men I have known'.[57] In January 1936 Churchill wrote a tribute to King George V, who had just died. It was also highly praised by many commentators.

Sir Emsley Carr and Churchill developed a close working relationship to mutual benefit; this was the period when Churchill was out of office and often a lone voice. Churchill was also a member of Walton Heath Golf Club, as was his wife, Clementine. Carr personally motored down to see Churchill at his Chartwell home to discuss the next series, to be known as 'Great Men of All Time'.[58] As events on the Continent continued to cause concern this series was scrapped; a new series entitled 'Great Events of Tomorrow' was commissioned and Churchill committed to several 3,000-word articles up to 1939. They included 'How Future Wars Will Be Waged' and 'The Effect of Aerial Transport on Civilisation'. As the likelihood of war grew, it was decided to promote these more strongly and move them from the feature page to the leader page.[59] On 13 May 1939 Churchill sent an article, 'Will There Be a War?', and on Sunday 18 June 'Air Raids and the Population' was published. All of these showed the prevailing view that the war would be dominated by bombing. Churchill wrote, 'It is a great pleasure to have the long pleasant and profitable association with the *News of the World*.' [60]

It is a measure of the very close link between Carr and Churchill that the next year, in May 1940, when Churchill had just been made Prime Minister and the war was at its most worrying stage, he took time out to attend Carr's retirement dinner and give the main speech. The king even sent a message. Bob had a very well-placed supporter indeed. Even a junior employee such as Bob would have noticed the articles by Churchill, but he may have missed the last as he resigned from the *News of the World* in 1939. His staff card shows his last day of work as 17 March and notes the refund to him of his death benefit contributions, £3 11s.[61] Bob had achieved his ambition: he was joining the RAF.

2

PREPARATION FOR BATTLE

The 1930s are well known as a period of recession, mass unemployment (reaching a peak in 1933 at 3 million unemployed) and headline events such as the Jarrow March. But it was also a time when people flocked to the new entertainment available in the cinemas and became consumers of a wide range of new and exciting goods and the nation discovered a taste for speed records on land, sea and in the air. Malcolm Campbell was knighted in 1931 in recognition of his many world-beating land-speed records, and there were the endurance races such as the Italian Mille Miglia and the French twenty-four-hour Le Mans race.

For the air-obsessed, the headline news in 1931 was Britain winning the Coupe d'Aviation Maritime Jacques Schneider, popularly known simply as the Schneider Trophy. The trophy was awarded to the fastest seaplane over a set three-kilometre course and it attracted huge crowds. The win by George Stainforth at Lee-on-Solent in 1931 was a milestone, as winning it three years in a row meant Britain retained the cup permanently.[1] Stainforth, who was a serving officer in the Royal Air Force, reached 655 kilometres per hour in his Supermarine 6 with Rolls-Royce engines. The aeroplane was designed by Reginald Mitchell, later famous as the designer of the iconic Spitfire.

While his parents and most certainly his father's employer, Sir Emsley Carr, were aware of the depression and its impact, Bob was more interested in Biggles' daring exploits. As with many young boys of his age, Bob was fascinated by aeroplanes and the Biggles books were essential reading. He later recalled, 'Before I joined the Air Force I used to spend a lot of time reading the W. E. Johns books, *Biggles* ... I read every book that was written about him. So, really, I had been indoctrinated to a war by reading *Biggles*.'[2] The author and journalist W. E. Johns retired from the RAF in 1931. Biggles made his first appearance in a short story in the magazine *Popular Flying* and a collection of them became the first Biggles book, *The Camels are Coming*, published in August 1932. Johns was a prolific writer, publishing fifteen Biggles books between 1932 and May 1938 aimed at an enthusiastic audience of young boys. He continued to write Biggles stories until his death in 1968.[3]

If Bob wanted to emulate his fictional hero it was not going to be easy. An ambition to fly was a difficult one to achieve for a young man with no income, and parents were notoriously unkeen about letting their sons risk their lives in the dangerous machines. But his diet of Biggles' books and flying magazines was trumped by the chance encounter with the real thing:

> To me, aeroplanes were very romantic things when I was young. I used to cycle six miles each a day to school. And there is a long downhill one way and uphill the other way. And one afternoon I was coming home and an RAF bi-plane fighter, one of the early ones, had to force land in a field close to where my road was and I stopped and walked round this thing and I really think that was where the start of fascination with flying began with me. From that moment onwards I used to keep a big cuttings book. I cut out pictures of every aeroplane I could find and stuck it in there and kept on doing it until I was actually started flying.[4]

Less than ten miles by road from Walton was Kenley aerodrome, which at the time was the base for 23 Squadron. It was to Kenley that Douglas Bader was posted in 1930, and it was while serving here that Bader had the air accident in which he lost his legs.[5] It was also Kenley where Winston Churchill tried unsuccessfully to fly until begged by his wife to give it up before he killed himself. It is not possible to pin down exactly which aeroplane the young Bob witnessed but it is likely to have come from Kenley, where the squadrons were equipped with Bristol Bulldog and Gloucester Gamecock biplanes.

A glance at the contemporary newspapers shows why so many parents were concerned about flying as a career. Crashed aeroplanes, both civil and military, were regular news items. A search of newspaper articles from 1930 to 1934 in Surrey shows a large number of aircraft crashes, including near misses and accidents due to fog, lack of fuel or pilots unable to recover from spins. The stories in the Surrey press and others were repeated in newspapers across the country.

Plane disaster

Fatal accident involving a bomber machine which crashed near Guildford, 3 men died, Virginia aircraft of No 55 (Bomber) Squadron Worthy Down.[6]

Air Crash at Kingston

A Royal Air Force single-seater aeroplane was wrecked in a field close to Kingston by Pass, Kingston Vale, Surrey to-day when the pilot had to make a forced landing owing to shortage of petrol. The pilot had a remarkable escape from injury. The machine narrowly missed an oak tree and went a few yards over the hedge and crashed in a field. The pilot just before the crash was able to jump clear. He landed safely in a field. The plane was smashed.[7]

The Prince of Wales' aeroplane made the news in 1933 when, piloted by Flight Lieutenant Fielden, it was forced to land on returning after delivering the Prince to Le Bourget. Fielden 'decided to make a landing at Redhill instead of continuing to Croydon, on account of low clouds and bad visibility. He came down in a field at Ham Farm, Nutfield. The field is being prepared as an aerodrome by British Air Transport Limited but has not yet been levelled.'[8] Redhill was just a few miles south of Bob's village of Walton and he would later come to know that aerodrome well.

The Air Council was alarmed about the adverse effects of the extensive newspaper and newsreel reports of flying accidents and the negative images being portrayed, so in 1936 they asked for restraint in reporting such incidents.[9] Meanwhile, the RAF was promoting itself vigorously. The first Empire Air Day was held in 1934 when forty RAF stations were opened to the public with demonstrations of bombing. The following year the air day was extended and was advertised as being bigger and more comprehensive. Civil aerodromes and flying clubs were also opened to visitors.[10] These events were hugely popular and drew large crowds. Kenley was one of the airfields open to the public. All of this made the RAF an exciting prospect for air-minded boys and the RAF had little difficulty in recruiting compared to the Army and Navy.[11]

The glamour of flying was a strong pull and was strengthened by the negative influence on Bob of his father's wartime experience. James Doe volunteered for the Army at the comparatively late age of thirty-six and enlisted on 6 June 1915 in the County of London Regiment, just two days after his marriage.[12] For his first two years James was based in England but on 16 January 1917 he and his comrades embarked for Salonika, where he spent six months before moving on to Egypt. James remained a private, except for one period when he was paid as lance corporal during the journey to Salonika. He returned from Egypt just over one year later via France, arriving in England in January 1919, and was discharged one month later. Altogether, like many others he was one small cog in a vast army, unremarkable and unnoticed, and his character was noted as 'very good'.[13]

So what was it in this apparently unremarkable war that persuaded his son to avoid the Army? Salonika is one of the forgotten campaigns of the First World War and was invisible to the British public, focussed as they were on the sufferings of the men in northern France and Belgium. Salonika was a theatre of war in which the British were reluctant agents. French and British troops had been sent to Greece in 1915 to provide assistance to the Serbs who were attacked by German, Austro-Hungarian and Bulgarian troops. In the event the defence was unsuccessful and the troops fell back to Salonika. The British priority at the time in the

Mediterranean was Egypt and they wished to withdraw from Salonika but France, Russia, Italy and Serbia insisted on a presence remaining in the Balkans. However, during 1916 offensive operations began, with a second offensive in April and May of 1917. It was for this second phase that fresh troops, including Private James Doe, arrived from England. This new offensive did not change the front line and trenches were established. The reinforcements were badly needed as casualties were high, due not just to war but to malaria. There were over 160,000 cases of the disease and over 500,000 non-battle casualties. Due to the low priority given by the War Office, for whom Egypt was a higher priority, and also to enemy submarine action, equipment and manpower lagged behind France and Flanders in both quality and quantity.[14] The morale of the men was not helped by the lack of awareness of the British public to the campaign; a posting to Salonika was literally seen as a holiday compared to Flanders. To the men suffering in the conditions in the disease-wracked camps in Salonika it was a cruel joke that 'if you want a holiday go to Salonika'.[15]

As with so many of his contemporaries Bob was determined that flying was for him, but getting into the RAF was not going to be easy for a young man with no academic record. There were several routes into the RAF in the 1930s and there were commissioned or non-commissioned places and plenty of non-flying roles. The key target for a Biggles fan was to be a commissioned pilot. However the build-up to war came to the assistance of an impecunious clerk on Fleet Street, it was still not going to be easy and would require determination and sponsorship.

Bob's entry into the RAF was one he enjoyed retelling:

The Air Ministry in those days was at the end of Kingsway, just above Bush House and just below Fleet Street, and one lunchtime I walked in to the Air Ministry and said, I want to be a pilot please. I was directed to various offices and every time they found out I hadn't passed an exam, I was passed on to another office. I ended up in an office with quite an elderly bloke. I was nineteen and he was probably in his thirties. He had his hat on the desk which had scrambled egg round the edge of it. He seemed to like me and I stayed talking to him for about half an hour. At the end of that time he said 'Well, because of your lack of education, you're going to have to sit an exam here at the Ministry.' He arranged the exam for the Wednesday of the following week. He took a book out of the drawer and marked a paragraph and told me to learn that paragraph by heart. That was the moment of the arm, which is how you put your foot on the pedal and the power is applied. I learnt this by heart and the only difficult question at all in this exam was 'What is the moment of the arm?' Which I had verbatim! That's how I became an officer in the Royal Air Force.[16]

But it was not quite that easy, even in the immediate pre-war period, and there is some date confusion. What is being described is his entry into the RAFVR, which did eventually lead to him becoming an officer. Between 1934 and 1939 there were increasing ways of becoming an RAF pilot as the Air Ministry built up its recruits. These can be divided into two categories, regular and direct-entry reserve forces. The latter were those who flew in their spare time such as the University Air Squadrons (UAS) and the Auxiliary Air Force (AuxAF). The University Air Squadrons comprised undergraduates and graduates, many of whom were scientists, lawyers and academics. Many went on to hold high office, such as Keith Park. If the UAS represented an academic elite, the weekend flyers who formed the AuxAF were a social elite and were 'characterized by the most extreme kind of social exclusiveness to be found in Britain of the 1920s and 1930s'.[17] Particular examples were 600 and 601 Squadrons, based on Whites Club and the City of London. 'It enshrined materialism as a cult. To be an AuxAF squadron was to belong to a jealously guarded elite, access to which was barred by social and financial hurdles which were impassable for many who might have wished to fly with them.'[18] For the aspiring pilots such as Bob, with little income, a lower-class background and no secondary education qualifications, there was no chance.

However, it was clear to the Air Council that existing recruitment channels alone would not supply the needs of a wartime RAF. Rapid expansion was needed; the net had to be cast wider and in this way the 'democratic reserve' was established, with a new plan for recruiting and training pilots. In a memorandum written by a civil servant called Scott, the general lines on which these reserves could be recruited and trained were laid out. Social and academic qualifications were still deemed important and the recruits had to be 'of secondary and public school type in order that they should have the education and ability to be satisfactorily trained'. As a service the RAF had different needs. While the Army could take on large numbers of recruits with just an elementary education, the technical needs of the RAF required an alternative recruitment policy.[19] Scott believed that successful recruitment depended on sensible demands on the volunteers' time by limiting training to weekends and evenings, with one full-time fortnight per year. The centres had to be reasonably close by, there had to be a financial inducement, and the cooperation of the employers was essential. Finally, he recognised the importance of an enjoyable social scene, so that 'reservists enjoy themselves and look forward to attendance at the centres'.[20]

This social side was heavily emphasised:

> While the desire to fly, patriotism, and retaining fees large enough to count in a young man's yearly budget will be the means of attracting our reservists, no permanent success can be attained unless the scheme is a social success. The young men must enjoy their evening meetings and their weekends. The Air Ministry cannot create a social life; it can only organise so the reservist can create it for themselves.[21]

An ideal vehicle for this expansion might have been the AuxAF, as it was already established as a part-time reserve, but it was not in favour of sacrificing its 'exclusive character to serve wider interests'. Even the mild suggestion that it form a reserve of accountants and stores officers was violently rejected. So a wholly new body needed to be established. Although there was some resistance to Scott's plans, mainly from a concern about a strain on resources, particularly instructors, it did eventually come into being much as he envisaged. There would be a common entry in one rank, that of airman pilot. Officer requirements were to be filled by a combination of selection and competition after the age of twenty-one.[22] The scheme was put in place on 27 August 1936 and recruiting began in December 1936. It took time to sort out contracts with the civilian firms who would deliver the training. As had been anticipated, the big challenge was the shortage of suitable instructors. This was overcome by using both full-time and part-time staff and working weekends and evenings, a situation that assisted the recruits. The first fifty recruits were attested in January 1937.[23]

From March 1937 the new volunteer reserve was promoted through national and local newspapers. Candidates had to be between eighteen and twenty-five, be physically fit and have an education up to the standard of the School Certificate.[24] The RAFVR was the democratising factor. Young men were to come from all walks of life, 'their sole criterion for their acceptance being their competence to perform the role required of them'. The RAFVR became the 'portal of entry through which the majority of men who flew during the war were to pass'.[25] Advertisements were widely placed in local newspapers, such as this one in Derby:

Ground instruction in subjects associated with flying given at the Derby Centre and flying training at Derby (Burnaston) Aerodrome. Which may be taken in your spare time. It will not interfere with your daily occupation. What is more a retaining fee of £25 a year and extra emoluments, including travelling allowances are granted. Grasp this exceptional opportunity.[26]

There was no shortage of young men wanting to grasp the opportunity. Each recruit under twenty-one, then the age of majority, required their parent's permission. While the young men were keen to join the 'best flying club in the world', it did not find favour with some parents, who viewed it as a risky career.[27] But for the potential recruits, such as Bob, parental anxieties had to be overcome in the face of such an amazing opportunity.

Bob was eighteen on 10 March 1938 and keen to apply as soon as possible. Applicants were required to apply to Hendon. Bob, however, was working in central London and so he walked into Kingsway House, close to Fleet Street. The scheme had been in place for a year by this time. Training started in April 1937 at thirteen civil flying schools and the total intake into RAFVR was 1,122 pupils. The next year the Treasury approved an expansion of the scheme from 2,400 pilots to 7,000 and the number of centres doubled. By August 1938 the RAFVR had risen to 1,870 pilots, of which approximately half were qualified to fly solo on service aircraft.[28] With this second expansion of the successful scheme some chances could be taken with recruits such as Bob. He met the requirements in fitness, keenness and sporting ability and, while he had not passed any specific examinations, he was obviously bright, so some assistance was given to help him with the entry examination. Volunteers were recruited and selected by a board of officers and medically examined and taken on a five-year engagement. The recruitment form also required two references; the RAF was not going to open its doors and spend valuable funds on all and sundry. He needed his application to be completed by 'two responsible persons excluding relatives but including preferably a recent employer'.[29] They had to state how long they had known him and testify to his good moral character and suitability for service in the RAFVR.[30] He did have two men who could provide suitable references: his old headmaster and Sir Emsley Carr. Just as his headmaster had seen and encouraged his talent, so too did the anonymous RAF officer in Kingsway. The rest was now up to Bob.

Ground instruction was given in town centres, and in Bob's case this was in a building at the top of Charing Cross Road. Here after work he learned the theory of flight, airmanship, navigation, and aircraft and engine maintenance and then made the long journey home across London. The really important part for him was the flying plan, which would be a total of sixty hours per year, twenty-eight at weekends, twelve on summer evenings and twenty during the fortnight of annual training. After reaching a standard of proficiency he would be paid £25 per year, with a training allowance for weekends and evenings of one shilling per hour and all his travelling expenses refunded.[31] For his eagerly anticipated first flying experience Bob was told to report to Hanworth aerodrome.

One of the original thirteen RAFVR schools, the aerodrome was a grass airfield situated in Hanworth Park. Known as London Air Park, it had been a centre for private flying in the early 1930s and the *Graf Zeppelin* airship arrived there in 1932. Amelia Earhart flew to Hanworth after landing in Ireland at the end of her 1932 crossing of the Atlantic.[32] With the introduction of the RAFVR, air displays were given to encourage recruitment. *Flight* magazine reported on such a display at Hanworth in June 1937 where the demonstrations included a first-class ten minutes of close-formation flying by the reserve instructors in Blackburn B2 Trainers. 'Mr Ken Waller gave a perfectly finished exhibition of aerobatics in a Tiger Moth, and Messrs Louis Rowley and Mickey Jennings put up a very spectacular dual aerobatics show in B2 trainers mostly at low altitude.'[33] Exactly one year later, Flight Lieutenant Louis Rowley had a new pupil.

Bob stepped out of Hanworth underground station on Saturday 4 June 1938 and walked down the long road to the centre of the airfield. After being shown how to put on his parachute he was handed over to Rowley, who was a tall, large man, topping Bob's six-foot frame by a few more inches. Rowley's career impressed Bob; he had been in the RAF and after leaving had continued flying with Alan Cobham's Flying Circus. Sir Alan Cobham, a First World War flying ace and entrepreneur, had pioneered national aviation days in 1932. He recruited skilled pilots, put on dazzling displays of aerobatics and gave many people their first experience of flying.

Bob flew for fifty minutes in two sessions with Flight Lieutenant Rowley at the controls of a B2 and flew again on Sunday. The initial flight was scary; 'the side of the cockpit was so thin, how was I going to be stopped falling out?' pondered Bob.[34] Bob did not have a head for heights, which had made the anticipation of flying more than a little nerve-wracking, but flying was a completely different experience. Once separated from the ground there is no sensation of height. From that moment he loved flying and he had to go back to work on Monday and wait until Thursday evening for his next flight. But then he had his two full weeks from 12 June to 26 June, when he flew almost every day, and went solo on 16 June in just under ten hours. The second week was intensive flying, clocking up nearly forty hours, and then after such heady times it was back to flying at weekends or on Thursday evenings. On 3 July 1938 he flew solo from Hanworth to Cambridge, which was real independence in the air.[35] This first long flight tested his navigation skills.

Travelling to Hanworth after work, he made the long journey from Fleet Street to the airfield and then at the end of the evening the long journey home by bus. This restricted his ability to enjoy the social scene envisaged by the scheme's originators. From now his flying time was limited and there were some weeks when he did no flying at all. In December 1938 he flew a Hart Trainer and then on 30 January 1939 he was rated by the chief flying instructor. He was noted as average, with the stern comment 'Rather overconfident'.[36]

As a sergeant in the RAFVR, Bob could continue flying at weekends but he now wanted more; he wanted to join up. The RAF had two ranks for pilots; they could be a commissioned officer or a sergeant pilot. RAFVR candidates were entered as airmen pilots with the rank of sergeant and usually joined the RAF in that rank. But early advertising had also hinted at the possibility of greater things by suggesting that 'later they will have opportunities of promotion to commission rank on merit'.[37] Something or someone persuaded Bob to apply for a commission, but entry to the RAF at most levels required good qualifications. Halton apprentices came from a 'mixture of secondary, elementary and continuation schools' and took an exam similar to the School Certificate but with more emphasis on mathematical and scientific aspects as opposed to literary subjects.[38] A lucky few could then apply to become sergeant pilots. Applying to be an officer was very ambitious for Bob, with his complete lack of educational qualifications.

There were several routes to becoming an officer. Cranwell was for those aiming for a permanent commission and high rank in the service. Entry requirements and cost tended to rule out those without a public school background. Between January 1934 and September 1939, 70 per cent of Cranwell cadets were from public schools.[39] Another option was to apply for a short service commission, but here, too, the right background and educational ability were essential.[40] From 1919 the RAF were not looking for 'a particular degree of wealth or a particular social position, but a certain character' in their officers.[41] Sporting or athletic ability was highly desired but so too was level of education, and here they required pilots to have a School Certificate. A university education was highly prized. But while this may appear highly democratic a public school background was still seen as crucially important.[42] In Sir John Slessor's view the 'public school system ... does, and I believe always will, produce a very high proportion of the best leaders of men in Britain'.[43]

With a war imminent some relaxation of entry requirements might be thought necessary but this did not appear to be required in the case of the RAF. A paper written in October 1937 on 'Entry and Promotion of Personnel in War' estimated a need for 2,000 recruits per month for flying crews, 50 per cent of which would be pilots. The War Office anticipated recruiting from universities with a 'strong preference for those who have obtained OTC [Officer Training Corps] certificates', and recognised that 'a large proportion will have no enthusiasm for the Army; indeed it may be anticipated that a considerable majority will prefer the Air Force'.[44] The 'requirement for flying crews of 12,000 could obviously be satisfied several times over out of the total field of 600,000 even with the most rigorous selection. Given moderate standard of intelligence and education the criterion for selection will be simply character; in comparison with steady nerves and stout heart other qualities will fade into insignificance in the conditions under which the next war will be fought.'[45] Nevertheless, 'a high standard of physical fitness and intelligence was required of air crew recruits, and in the early part of the war the equivalent of a secondary education was also demanded'. This educational standard was not altered until mid-1940 when, recognising that this 'debarred many excellent recruits otherwise suitable', it was modified to admit men with an elementary education. They were, however, helped to improve their general schooling during the preliminaries of service training.[46]

For those with the right background and qualifications the next step was the air crew selection board. The board made recommendations for duties as pilot, observer, air gunners or wireless operators (air crew). For those candidates considered suitable as pilots or observers, the board also stated whether they were recommended for commissioned rank. 'In addition to the general attributes expected of an officer, recommendations will not be confined to those who have served in an OTC. It will be appreciated that a high standard is required from candidates recommended for pilot and observer duties.'[47] RAF publications made it clear that selection was stringent and 'for every boy who achieved his wings, there were a dozen who did not'.[48] The board could make recommendations but final selection for commissioned rank depended on medical fitness, the result of passing out of initial training (at which point selection will be made by the officer in charge of the ground training school) and the result of passing out at the flying or observer courses.[49]

For those who, like Bob, were applying via the Volunteer Reserve, there was no requirement to go to a board. Reserve Command made a recommendation on commissioned rank for pilots and observers who were sent to initial training wings. But it was still a conditional recommendation and progress through further training would be the ultimate deciding factor.[50] It was a contentious issue within the RAF and even after the outbreak of war there were conflicting views on who should make the officer recommendation. Certainly not the chief flying instructors (CFI) at Elementary Flying Schools, since these were civilian schools and such reports on fitness for commission were therefore not deemed reliable. In Sir John Slessor's view, 'Not until the final month of a pilot's training at an FTS should the decision as to commissioning be taken.'[51] At the time of Bob's application in early 1939 it was clear that the numbers of men from the RAFVR who might be recommended for a commission would be limited in number. Only 100 men were recommended out of the many thousands of reservists and even then, reports received on their further flying training 'will provide a check on previous recommendations'.[52]

So while his entry to the RAFVR had been assisted by a benign officer, Bob's chance of getting a commission were slim. Even during the worst year of the war in 1940 some candidates were rejected for flying duties in the RAF on the grounds of a lack of a school certificate.[53] This inconsistency, bearing in mind Bob's lack of a certificate, suggests that rejections may have been made for other reasons but education was an easy one to cite. Bob must have been seen as an outstanding candidate. So as an applicant from the RAFVR, with suitably positive recommendations from his chief flying instructor and despite no school certificate, Bob was accepted into the RAF on 20 March 1939 as a pupil pilot and began his full time training at Redhill.

15 Elementary and Reserve Flying Training School Redhill was formed in July 1937 and was operated by British Air Transport Ltd.[54] From the expansion in 1935 civilian Reserve Schools also provided the *ab initio* training for pilots entering the RAF.

A course lasted two months giving twenty five hours each of dual and solo flying, with lectures and ground training in addition. From there, if he made the grade, the pupil went on to a Service school where he qualified on a service type and worked on formation, gunnery, navigation and so on before being posted to his squadron.[55]

The first aeroplane Bob flew was a Magister. One of his instructors was Flight Lieutenant Coleman. 'Pop' Coleman was then age thirty-one and a highly experienced flyer. Bob was taught instrument flying, slide slipping, low flying and aerobatics. Bob hated aerobatics; he never liked flying upside down.[56] The rest of the flying he very much enjoyed and now he was doing it full time. Socialising while in the RAFVR had been difficult since his time was limited due to his commute home. At Redhill, there were no such limitations and Bob, whom seems to have become a gregarious soul at this stage, made some good friends. One was Douglas Triptree. Triptree's home was in Bournemouth and he could not easily get there at the weekend, so Bob's parents invited him to spend his free weekends with them in Walton-on-the-Hill.[57] On 15 April 1939, at the end of their training course, Bob and Douglas Triptree had passed and were accepted for short-service commissions into the RAF as Acting Pilot Officers.[58]

The next stage was a spell at No 1 RAF Depot, Uxbridge. Here all recruits were introduced to the delights of square bashing under the eagle eye of a drill warrant officer whose physique and style of walking earned him the nickname of the 'pregnant pheasant'.[59] At Uxbridge the potential officers had to undergo an intensive course of drill, RAF administration and officers' mess etiquette.[60] One recruit recalled, 'We didn't see an aeroplane but spent two weeks "square bashing" physical training, being lectured on Air Force Law and being fitted for uniforms.'[61] For Bob the fitting of the uniform was a challenge. There was a grant of fifty pounds and those that could afford to do so increased the amount to ensure a suitably tailored uniform that fitted well. Bob did not have such extra money and selected the cheapest tailor on the recommended list. Despite five or six fittings supervised by the officer in charge he concluded that his uniform 'looked just what it was – cheap and nasty'.[62]

From Uxbridge the next step was to the Service Flying Training School, which in Bob's case was to 6 SFTS Little Rissington in Gloucestershire, where he joined forty-one officers and eight airmen on the course. He was now an acting pilot officer (AP/O) but it meant just that; they were trainees and still had much to learn:

> On arrival at the FTS the potential officer pupils, for administration reasons, will be accommodated in the officer's mess and wear a white armband on the left arm ... it must be clearly understood by all concerned that the fact that they are accommodated in the officer's mess does not imply that they will necessarily be passed as officers.[63]

Being trained together on the courses with the AP/Os were airmen pilots. Bill Wilkinson was one of the latter group and was at Little Rissington at much the same time as Bob. Like Bob, he left school with little in the way of qualifications and managed to join the RAF as an Aircraft Hand in 1934. By hard work, application and a bit of luck he was one of the very few selected from the ranks for training as a potential sergeant pilot. His cricketing skills also featured in his selection. Bill recalled the welcoming address from the station commander, Group Captain Al Ellis, in 1939. With Ellis was the chief flying instructor and the chief ground instructor (CGI). The CGI was Flight Lieutenant Colin Scragg, an ex-sergeant pilot who was held up to the men as an example 'of what one could achieve by hard work and devotion to duty.' He later became Air Vice-Marshal Sir Colin Scragg.[64] After a few words the airmen were dismissed as the station commander wanted to speak to the AP/Os, among whom was Bob. To them he described the airmen as 'the elite of the RAF and the AP/Os were less than dust and heaven help them if their behaviour, at any time, left anything to be desired'. The AP/Os were, recalled Wilkinson, with the 'odd exception an extremely pleasant crowd'.[65]

An earlier trainee, Fenton, recalled his Flying Training School at Sealand, Cheshire, with a curriculum divided between 'classroom, barrack square and flying. In our opinion, far too much of the first two and not enough of the last.'[66] Fenton's course began with forty-two pupils and one year later only twenty-one passed out. The remainder had 'fallen by the wayside for a variety of reasons ranging from death, inability to fly (quite a few), bouncing cheques and so on'.[67] Fellow trainees were quietly assessed and 'Dizzy' Allen summed up his entry of pupil pilots quickly into two categories, 'thieves and gents'.[68] Twenty-five per cent of Allen's course did not pass out. The hurdles were getting higher to jump.

Learning about life in an RAF officers' mess was part of the course. Not all trainee pilots found this easy and one historian suggests that having a school certificate did not presuppose that they had 'the sort of social conditioning which would make its products fit easily into mess life'. The RAF mess in the 1920s and 1930s was in building designed by Sir Edwin Lutyens and combined the atmosphere and etiquette of a 'gentleman's club with that of a first class hotel.'[69] This aspect does not appear to have fazed Bob, his recollection of this period related more to a lack of money:

> During the period of our training we were also being trained as officers, which meant dining in mess in either mess kit or dinner jacket five nights of the week. So however mean you were the mess bill came to about £13, which out of our monthly salary of £18 didn't leave a lot.[70]

For someone who expressed his social inferiority, settling in to a mess does not seem to have been the uphill challenge it might appear. He was after all the son of the head gardener to a very wealthy man, and in the (probably unlikely) event of requiring any social tips, his parents lived next door to the butler, a man whose role ensured he was even more superior than his employers on etiquette.

Flying was, of course, the key skill to be developed and in Bob's case this was not to be as a fighter pilot but in bombers. His dislike of aerobatics had ruled him out as a suitable fighter pilot. 'On arrival we stood in awe and looked at the planes we were to fly. They seemed very large and daunting with turrets which carried guns and two engines instead of one ... Half way through the course we were paired off, quite arbitrarily I think. I know I was paired off with the other largest person on the course.'[71] Bob at six foot was above average height which for a man in the 1930s was around five feet eight inches. The aeroplane was an Avro Anson and he was trained in low flying, night flying and bomb aiming.[72]

For two months Bob's instructor was Pilot Officer Wight Boycott. Cathcart Wight Boycott would himself go on to earn a DSO and Bar and retire as an air commodore. A good instructor could make a very significant difference not just to what was learned but to the enjoyment of the course. Fenton recalled a good teacher, Tom Pike, who had been a successful night fighter pilot during the First World War and later became Chief of Air Staff. Pike was

well-mannered and unruffled, just the qualities which helped me most. I never responded to sarcasm and abuse. Not many people do! It was a pleasure, still remembered, to fly with him and an important influence on my own attitude to teaching in the years when I was a flying instructor myself.[73]

Bill Wilkinson recalled the lectures that took up half the day and that flying took up the rest of the day.[74] There was limited time for other things such as writing up lecture notes and completing problems given by the ground instructor. He was not fortunate in one of his instructors. He was handed over to a newly arrived instructor who had a short service commission from the Commonwealth. The officer in question turned out to be a 'poor instructor and certainly did not have the right temperament for the job' and he never gave any pre or post-flight briefing.[75] After two serious incidents in the air when the aeroplane went into an unexpected dive, there was an inquiry. Wilkinson was called before the chief instructor (CI) and the rest of the most senior instructors. The CI decided he would take Wilkinson flying. 'What a difference. The CI came into the crew room about half an hour before we were due to fly, thoroughly briefed me and expertly explained what we were going to do and, in so doing, gave me all the confidence in the world.' After two joint flights Wilkinson went solo night flying and afterwards the CI came to the crew room with some 'words of encouragement and advice'.[76]

Training also included the Link Trainer, which was an early flight simulator and was intended to assist with instrument flying. 'This was a very clever but diabolical machine which recorded the course flown and altitude of a make believe aeroplane on graph paper.'[77] It was an 'exacting machine which demanded to be flown accurately, because it recorded every movement that was made and, of course, every mistake'.[78]

There were ways to escape and to let off steam. Good friends were essential and one of them was Geoffrey Gout:

Geoffrey and I knew each other from the start of training in early '39 until his death. He was one of our quiet colleagues and if my memory serves me right he had a dark green touring car which we all envied. A group of young embryo pilots we did everything together. The usual things at the time, out to the pub, any party that would have us, working out crazy schemes to annoy the instructors, just being devilish and very stupid. But in the process we built up an understanding between us that would stand by us later on.[79]

Having independent transport was critical in order to escape the base. Bob clubbed together with three other trainee pilots and bought a car for £20 in order to get to Cheltenham which was fifteen miles away. The car was distinctly stylish; it was a 1920 Hispano Suiza Barouche.[80]

Bob was awarded his wings on 5 August 1939. This was a great moment, one for which he had been working hard. It was the badge of the military elite, but he was not yet a warrior knight. It was not awarded with any great ceremony, merely permission to get the cloth wings from stores to sew on. It was at this point that the officer commanding the Flying Training School made the final decisions as to rank on passing out but its operation did not become effective until completion of the advanced training stage. This allowed sufficient time for gazetting of officer appointments and for posting arrangements to be made.[81]

From August came the signs of the impending war as reserves were called up. Aircraft now had war time markings, blackout was introduced, airmen had to wear their uniform at all times and gas masks were issued. On 1 September the Air Ministry broadcast that 'relations with a certain Power or powers have become strained', and on 3 September a handwritten note was added to the typed operations record for Little Rissington. 'PM announces on radio state of war between England and Germany 11:00 hrs.'[82] Bob was standing outside a hanger as Chamberlain's words were broadcast with, as he described it, his heart in his mouth.[83] On the same airfield Wilkinson was waiting for his flight commander to take him up on a progress test. The instructors were all in their office listening to the PM's broadcast. The flight commander then came out and said, 'War has been declared, Wilkinson, you and I must polish up our aerobatics', and promptly gave Wilkinson a long and thrilling lesson.[84] Across the country the nation paused and listened. That day Sir Emsley Carr, Bob's father's employer, wrote a personal letter to Winston Churchill from Wonford:

My dear Winston, I cannot say with what pride and satisfaction I heard of the decision of the Prime Minister to place you in full control of the Admiralty and my pride is shared by the entire British people. We know you are the right man in the right place.[85]

The appointment heralded the end of Churchill's contributions to, and earnings from, the *News of the World*. He wrote to Carr's editor, Major Davies, on the 24 September regarding the end of his contract and finished with words which a few months later might appear an exaggeration. 'Over the last three weeks I have not had a minute to think of anything but my task. They are the longest three weeks I have ever lived.'[86]

RAF reservists had now been called up for service and soon Little Rissington saw them arrive in great numbers. Many were wearing a variety of oddly shaped out of date and various shades of Air Force blue and 'a number wore their 1914-18 war ribbon'.[87] With the outbreak of war a popular navigation aid for pilots disappeared with the removal of place names from stations. 'No longer was it any help for us to descend until we were low enough to read the name of a country station when we were lost and we had to sharpen up our map reading skills rapidly.'[88]

Assessments were constant, although some avoided being rated as 'exceptional' since this 'destined you for flying training command'.[89] Bob, however, was rated as an average pilot and the next stage of his bomber training was at 9 Air Observer School at Penrhos, Wales. At Penrhos there was a training establishment of forty-five officers and 692 airmen and civilians. Among the officers on the staff was Wing Commander W. Wynter-Morgan, MC, as chief ground instructor, who was on a posting from the School of Technical Training at Cosford. He would later be closely involved in the Dambusters development. Also present was Wing Commander J. J. Williamson. Williamson had been the instructor and adjutant to the Oxford University Air Squadron at Manston in 1929.[90]

Bob flew on 20 October in an Anson from Little Rissington to Penrhos with a fellow AP/O, Redman.[91] Penrhos was located on the Irish Sea and at this stage in the war there was considerable uncertainty about the attitude of the Irish Government, which was certainly not pro-British. There was real concern that the Germans would land in Ireland assisted by a fifth column.[92] Three days after Bob's arrival there was a suspicious incident when a pilot flying on duty from the station in the early morning spotted the conning tower of a submarine two miles south of St Tudwals Islands. The submarine was submerging and the pilot suspected a fishing boat in the vicinity had given supplies to the submarine. The matter was reported to the local police and Coastal Command. Then at 02.00 hours on 26 October two white lights were observed at sea off Llanbedrog Head. The matter was reported and on investigation it seemed to have come from a merchant ship that had approached St Tudwal's Islands and moored there, subsequently moving towards Llanbedrog Head. A Battle aircraft was despatched to discover more. It located the ship, which turned out to be the *Eden Vale* from Wexford and was flying the Eire flags.[93] Nothing more was heard of the incidents but they were examples of the heightened early war alarms as the country faced the realities of war. It underlined the importance of their training which for Bob involved spending 'a lot of time shooting from the rear turret of an Anson'. This practice taught him deflection shooting, a skill he was going to need.[94]

On 3 November Bob's course finished and he and his fellow pilots returned to Little Rissington to his final assessment by the chief instructor. Bob had completed over eight hours instruction and the general instrument flying course on the link trainer. He had passed with a pass mark of 67.59 percent. He was assessed as 'Rather under confident and below average for navigation'.[95] It was not exactly a ringing endorsement. But he was through, he was a commissioned pilot, he was about to go on leave at the end of his training before his first proper posting and there was a war to fight.

3

THE BATTLE BEGINS AND LEADERSHIP LESSONS

On 6 November Bob, together with several other fellow pilot officers, travelled across England from South Gloucestershire to North Yorkshire. The words in his last assessment were perhaps meant as encouragement, but were unlikely to provide the nineteen year old with a positive sense of ability. Indeed he agreed with the rating and felt himself lacking. Such self-doubts, however, needed to be hidden from his fellow pilots.

Curious to know what type of squadron they were joining, they asked the driver of the lorry that met them at Hull. He didn't know and there was no further enlightenment when they arrived at the wooden hut that was the officer's mess.¹ Such uncertainty was hardly surprising as RAF Leconfield had only just been transferred from Bomber to Fighter Command on 25 October. Based at Leconfield were 616 Squadron, equipped with Spitfires, and 234 and 245 Squadrons equipped with 'unmodified Blenheim Fighters.'² 234 Squadron was formed officially just seven days before the new pilots arrived. It had originally been formed during the First World War in the Isles of Scilly as an RNAS/RAF unit with seaplanes and was disbanded in 1919.³ What the new arrivals were about to discover was that even in this short time they already had a replacement commanding officer. Squadron Leader Satchell was posted to Leconfield on 30 October to form the new squadron but had a car accident and was replaced by Squadron Leader Barnett. Barnett arrived to take up his post on the same day that fourteen young newly trained pilot officers and four sergeant pilots arrived. Bob already knew Crimp, Dewhurst, Elsdon, Hemingway, Gout, Hight and Hardy, who came with him from 6 FTS.[4] They were joined by Avery, Coysh, Gordon, Horton, Lawrence and Mortimer-Rose as the rest of the new officer pilots.[5]

The aircraft waiting for them in the hangers were an odd mix and distinctly limited. According to the operations record book (ORB) there were four Blenheims, three Magisters, two Tutors, three Gauntlets and one Battle with dual controls.[6] Bob's memory was of disappointment at such decrepit and ancient aircraft. Keith Lawrence and the rest of the pilots were similarly dismayed. This was their equipment, but what about the officers who would lead them? Their new CO, Barnett, was an experienced and decorated officer who had joined the RAF as a cadet at Cranwell in January 1930. After graduation he was posted to the Middle East and fought in Palestine. This fighting had been a highlight for the interwar RAF as it attempted to prove its value as a separate service. For his actions, Barnett had been made an MBE in the Coronation Honours List in 1937 together with two other officers who had also served in that theatre. Barnett joined 234 Squadron from Martlesham Heath, then the base for experimental aircraft.[7] Barnett had all the potential of a suitably awe inspiring figure for a group of young raw pilots.

Two days later Flying Officer Pat Hughes joined the squadron. Pat, soon to be promoted to flight lieutenant was a twenty-three year old Australian. He had joined the RAAF in 1935 and subsequently the RAF in 1937. The other flight commander was John Theilmann, who had joined the RAF on a short service commission in 1936 and had been with 41 Squadron at Catterick, where he had flown Spitfires.[8] These were the three leaders who needed to mould an inexperienced group of very recently qualified pilots, most of whom had been trained on bombers, into a fighting force.

Work began and if the new pilots anticipated plenty of flying this was soon dispelled as the lack of aircraft limited this. In many ways it was not far different from their training, limited flying and plenty of lectures. There were lectures on Fighter Command organisation and the use of wireless and the Link Trainer was well utilised. Gunnery was not forgotten as they headed for the range to fire guns. The operations record tersely noted; 'This is the first time most of them have fired a gun before'.[9] There would be much work to get this inexperienced group of young men operational. The two flight commanders assessed the pilots' flying skills while the squadron obtained aeroplanes from wherever possible. The pilots listened to lectures on armament, engines, rigging and signals, fired the Lewis guns and qualified on the Blenheim. Bob flew the Magister as co-pilot to Theilmann on 10 November, then subsequently as pilot on the following days. By the end of November he had flown the Tutor and the Gauntlet. In December, training continued with formation flying and both flight commanders took the controls of the Blenheim with Bob as co-pilot. By the end of December he had clocked up five hours in the Magister, three in the Blenheim and forty-five minutes in the Gauntlet.

The Magister was a two-seater monoplane with an open cockpit and was an excellent training aircraft, the Avro Tutor was a biplane two-seater for training, the Gloster Gauntlet was a single-seat biplane with an open cockpit and the Bristol Blenheim was a light bomber which carried three crew and was armed with a Browning and a Vickers gun. Keith Lawrence remembered the Magisters and Avro Tutors with affection as '1920 planes; lovely things to fly. To keep our hand in we did all hours on these odds and sods. Got up to all sorts of troubles.'[10]

Accidents were perhaps inevitable if costly and the squadron's official record reported a serious incident on 15 December:

P/O J. Hemingway (detailed as safety officer) and P/O C. B. Elsdon (carrying out the practises) engaged in instrument flying practise in Magister. It went into a spin and crashed both suffered fractured spines and detained in RAF Hospital Cranwell.[11]

On the face of it this is the report of an accidental but serious crash but it was carefully written up to disguise an unfortunate incident. Elsdon and Hemingway had decided to beat up a train between York and Darlington. They eventually overdid it and ended up in a field. Unluckily for them there was a Group Captain on the train who witnessed the event and who was called into the inevitable Court of Inquiry. Elsdon was posted away immediately to Bomber Command but Hemingway was removed from the RAF. Rather oddly, 'He continued living with the squadron as a civilian, believe it or not. He worked for admin. Most extraordinary.'[12] Hemingway appears in a squadron photograph in civilian clothes.

There were more incidents as the pilots tried out the aeroplanes. In December Gout crashed while taking off in a Blenheim after raising the undercarriage too soon. He was unhurt. Two months later Crimp wrote off the squadron's only Battle when force landing. He too was unhurt but was shortly posted out of the squadron to RAF Wick in Scotland. Pilot Officer Avery had also left the squadron for other duties. Avery was said by Lawrence to have been wholly unfitted for his role as a pilot.[13] Such was the early shakedown of the pilots in the new squadron and a lesson that their individual position as part of the team was not a given. By the end of January 1940 the squadron flying personnel consisted of one squadron leader, two flying officers (acting flight lieutenants) and twelve pilot officers. Of other ranks, there were eighteen senior NCOs, twenty-six corporals and 163 aircraftmen. The squadron was equipped with nine Blenheims, two Magisters, two Tutors and one Battle.[14]

Training continued with lectures in gun stripping on Vickers and Browning guns, together with lectures on Fighter Command attacks, battle orders, Fighter Command organisation, navigation and the organisation of the German Air Force. Eleven men were sent off to train as air gunners, presumably for service in the Blenheims with which the squadron was now being equipped. Those squadrons equipped with Blenheims, a twin-engined day-fighter that lacked manoeuvrability, were to suffer appalling losses against far superior German aircraft.[15] Bob was one of two pilots ordered up to Abbotsinch near Glasgow to collect two Fairey Battles. The Fairey Battle was a single-engine light bomber built in the late 1930s. Although it had a Rolls-Royce Merlin engine its performance was poor, being weighed down with a three-man crew and a bomb load. It was technically obsolete by 1940.[16] The trip turned out to be a bonus as Bob's aeroplane was not

ready and he had to remain for a week. By good fortune, he met someone
with whom he had trained at his elementary flying school in Redhill. The
officer concerned was very well connected socially. He was a member of
the Wakefield Oil family (they owned Castrol Oil) and he was engaged to a
titled lady who lived at Louden Castle. According to Bob's memoirs he was
introduced to a then very upmarket restaurant, Roganos, in Glasgow and
spent the weekend at the castle.[17] Presumably his friend was paying and
Bob does not appear to have been intimidated by staying in such socially
exclusive environs.

In one historian's view, 1939 ended on an uncertain note for the RAF
with some testing of tactics against the enemy by Bomber Command. Fighter
Command concentrated on training and building up its strength, but still, as
the men of 234 Squadron knew, with 'all too few of the modern types which
everyone knew it was going to need one day soon'.[18] As the pilots of 234
trained on their old aeroplanes they watched 616 Squadron with some envy.
616 had been posted to Leconfield at much the same time but they were
already being equipped with Spitfires, the sleek new wonder fighter plane
which represented the very latest in aircraft technology. However, there had
been much amusement in 234 as the 616 pilots got to grips with the new
aeroplanes; accidents were frequent, mainly caused by the nose tipping over.

We had seen them flying locally with 616. We shared the airfield with East
Riding squadron. We saw how difficult they were to fly. We came out one
morning and found 3 Spitfires on their noses. We took photographs and
called it '616 digging for victory'.[19]

While the Spitfire was a joy to fly in the air its design made it vulnerable
to accidents on the ground, with visibility when taxiing being a particular
challenge. Pilots learnt to zigzag in order to see where they were going. The
glee with which 234 watched the accidents was heightened by the difference
between the two squadrons. While 234 was made up entirely of newly
arrived pilots from the RAFVR who were still being squadron trained, 616
was not only fully operational but was an Auxiliary Air Force squadron with

all the inherent snobbery that this entailed at this early stage of the war. The Honorary Air Commodore was the Earl of Portland and until September 1939 its squadron commander had been the Earl of Lincoln. Probably of more significance and awe to Bob Doe, however, was the fact that the current CO, Walter K. Beisiengel, was a noted cricketer, who had successfully led both the RAF team and Leicestershire county cricket team in the 1930s.

On 21 February 616 Squadron had a very bad day. They had been scrambled that morning to escort a convoy off Flamborough Head. Flight Lieutenant Wilson, who was leading a section, 'descended through mist to locate convoy and not seen again. A very great loss to his flight and squadron.' That afternoon Yellow Section was scrambled at 14.15 and Flying Officer Bell, who was leading the section, had to avoid a Battle aircraft just before he was airborne and struck a Magister on the runway. Both aircraft were wrecked and Pilot Officer Coysh of 234 Squadron, who was flying solo in the Magister, was killed. Bell was uninjured. The funeral of Coysh, the first casualty of the squadron, was held three days later. Shortly afterwards two new pilots arrived in 234 as replacements for those lost or posted and they added a little more experience to the team. Sergeant Thompson reported from 603 Squadron and Pilot Officer Igglesden reported from 41 Squadron, where he had flown Spitfires alongside Theilmann.[20]

On 10 March, and after all their training on the Blenheims, the squadron watched as their Blenheims began to leave. It was also Bob's twentieth birthday, and his war was about to get very exciting as five days later a belated birthday present arrived. It was a never to be forgotten moment. 'A Spitfire landed, a solitary Spitfire. It taxied over to the hangar and we were told that it was ours. We sat in it, walked around it, it was so beautiful.'[21]

Fifteen more Spitfires arrived the next day, and conversion training commenced with no shortage of eager pilots ready to try out the Spitfire. This was a role for the two flight commanders, who now oversaw the conversion flights. Each pilot was issued with the pilots' notes for the Spitfire, and told to go off, read it and then report back to the flight office. The notes were read with great interest. Then they reported back to their relevant flight commander, who showed the young pilot around the cockpit, and off they went. 'It was just magic.'[22] On 25 March Bob had his first experience in P9365, the aircraft he was determined would remain 'his':

When I first got into Spitfires, the very early Spitfire Mark I before it had armour plating in fact, and you get into this thing and you taxi out and you can't see a thing in front of you 'cause the nose is right up in the air and you have to be very careful taxi-ing because if you put your brakes on at the same time, it'll stand on its nose. Which you don't want to have happen. So you have to keep it going side to side and on the way out you line up and you open the throttle and an almighty wuump hits you and this thing tears off across the airfield and you're air borne in no time at all. And you are then – you're not flying an aeroplane, you've got wings on your back and you're just flying. It is a dream. It's the most wonderful sensation I have ever known.[23]

This was tempered by the knowledge of a message that had arrived warning that anyone crashing a Spitfire would be posted immediately. This was a penalty that was generally agreed to be rather unfair in view of 616's accident rate.[24] But the Spitfire was too valuable and too critical as a war weapon. It was Mortimer-Rose who had the first accident, in a gust of wind that tipped his Spitfire on its nose, shortly accompanied no doubt by a telling off from the CO.[25] Morty was not posted.

It is at this time that an iconic photograph is taken of Bob standing in front of his Spitfire. It was a high point of his life to date. He stands with a solemn expression, staring into the camera. He is slim, fit, athletic and good-looking. He was tall (over six foot) and broad-framed, so he just fitted into the aircraft. What cannot be seen is that he was fair-haired, with steel-blue eyes. Bob was now a fighter pilot – not just a pilot, but a commissioned officer with one of the very latest aircraft. He was rubbing shoulders with men from superior social and educational backgrounds. By contemporary standards, the head gardener's son had come a long way in a very short time. Although he thought he was shy, this did not come across to his contemporaries, who recalled that Bob had something to say on most things.[26] His time in the newspaper world had given him much information across a range of topics.

When all the pilots had successfully gone solo, the next challenge was gunnery. The squadron had spent plenty of time on their Blenheims, including formation flying, but their gunnery instruction had been limited to firing guns on ranges at static targets. Deflection shooting, that crucial skill for a fighter pilot, who had to fire not just at a fast-moving target but from a fast-moving platform, was not included. This was where experience of game shooting was valuable. In Keith Lawrence's view, those who had such a background, and game shooting was an elite sport, were 'streets ahead of us'.[27] The pilots needed to fire the guns if only to see what it felt and sounded like, so they were invited to fire their guns into the North Sea, which Bob duly did:

> The only gunnery we did from a Spitfire was we were given 20 rounds for a gun each and told to go as far as the North Sea. You couldn't really miss the North Sea. And that's the only gunnery we did. And apart from that we knew nothing about being a fighter pilot or because the Flight Commander Pat Hughes who trained us, he was a bomber pilot. And we were all bomber pilots. We'd just become fighter pilots by accident. So that we had no specific fighter training at all. We just were good at formation and that's all.[28]

It was bad, but not quite that bad. Theilmann and Igglesden had flown Spitfires with 41 Squadron and, shortly after the Spitfires arrived, Pat Hughes had been sent on a week's air fighting course at RAF Northolt. The urgency was increasing as the Germans advanced and the squadron needed to become operational. But despite the increasing war pressures, this was not an automatic sign-off. After six months, and just six weeks on their new machines, the pilots were sent to Church Fenton on 17 April to carry out exercises for passing out as operational. For some reason the decision was delayed pending a further test at Leconfield; something was not quite right. The further test was carried out on 8 May by an officer from 13 Group HQ, who duly pronounced the squadron fit for operation by day. They were now a fighter squadron and a few days later they had their first intercept flights and also began night-flying training.[29]

They were operational just in time, as they were much needed. The Battle for France began in earnest on 10 May; there were ten Hurricane squadrons in France, but Air Marshal Dowding, who was in charge of Fighter Command, held on to his Spitfires 'as a miser clings to gold'.[30] Churchill became Prime Minister on 10 May and five days later the War Cabinet met to consider, among other urgent war items 'the request from M. Reynaud to send more fighter squadrons to France'. It was decided that 'no further fighter squadrons should for the present be sent to France'.[31] But the pressure to release more fighter squadrons continued as the Germans advanced with rapidity through northern Europe. Dowding maintained his resistance with a now famous letter on 16 May to the Air Ministry. In it he reminded the Air Council that 'the last estimate which they made as to force necessary to defend this country was fifty-two squadrons and my strength has now been reduced to the equivalent of thirty-six squadrons'.[32] Dowding knew just how raw some of those defending squadrons were.

616 Squadron, which had been on convoy duty, was at a forward base at Rochford near Southend in Essex and was patrolling over Dunkirk. From 27 May to 4 June they patrolled to cover the evacuation of the British Expeditionary Force.[33] As has been said, 'to the soldier the air support is the support he can see'. Much of the RAF's work was conducted out of sight of the men waiting patiently on the beaches to be evacuated. BEF survivors were antagonistic towards what they felt was the non-appearance of the RAF.[34] While the facts might show otherwise, the attitude was understandable and it was not a good time to admit you were a fighter pilot. 234 Squadron was now on intercept duty and three intercepts were carried out and at least one enemy aircraft was seen in the distance but not engaged. In early June dogfights were practised, with Bob fighting a Hurricane on 9 June in 'his' Spitfire, P9365 (with D for Doe). He was getting to know the abilities of his aircraft and was also thinking independently:

Whilst there a Hurricane squadron came back from France and was based there for while. Our bosses organised individual dog-fights with the Hurricanes technically to give us experience of what war was like. I know I got ticked off for not mixing in with them, but used my superior speed to keep diving on the Hurricane which I thought was the most sensible thing to do.[35]

Paris fell on 4 June, an armistice was requested by the French on the 17th and a second, less well-known evacuation of 144,171 British troops and airmen began on 18 June from the French Atlantic ports.[36] Britain was on her own and needed all her defences. Fighter Command at this stage had 'only 768 fighters in operational squadrons, and of these only 520 were fit for operations',[37] so 234 Squadron was given movement orders on 18 June and was posted to St Eval. The squadron strength was eighteen officers, of which thirteen were reported as effective pilots, six airmen pilots, of which five were effective pilots, 155 other airmen and NCOs.[38] Flights A and B flew down via Filton near Bristol in sixteen Spitfires, one Magister and two Tutors under the command of Squadron Leader Barnett with the rest of the squadron following by train.[39]

St Eval was a newly built airfield in north Cornwall close to the sea. Work began on the airfield in 1938 when nine houses in the small hamlet were demolished. The ancient church, however, was left to remain a solitary monument at the end of the runway. The area was very rural and home to a farming community. The station opened on 2 October 1939 with the arrival of 217 Squadron, which was part of Coastal Command. St Eval could expect to see plenty of action; it was close to France, within easy range of French-occupied airfields, and its area had some major strategic bases. Falmouth, the largest port just before the western approaches, was the last port of call heading out into the Atlantic and the first welcome sight after re-entering the English Channel, while Plymouth was a major naval base. 234 was the only fighter squadron in Cornwall.

The squadron had barely arrived when the next day there was an arrival that underlined that they were indeed now on the very front line of the war. A strange aircraft landed mid-morning. It was a Farman 222 belonging to the French Air Force.[40] The station commander had been alerted by Group that French aircraft might land at St Eval without identification signals. De Gaulle had just made his great rallying cry to his fellow countrymen to join him. But it was not automatically an easy or simple act to respond to that message, with loyalties to family and friends, a split nation and an unclear French political situation. De Gaulle was a comparative unknown and had no constitutional legitimacy, unlike Petain's Vichy government.[41] 'Why did I go to England? Because I felt it was my duty. It was seeing where one's duty lay, not doing it, that had become so difficult.'[42] Vichy France declared them traitors.

Due to the uncertainties and conflicting loyalties, most of the men fleeing to England were very young and unmarried. Approximately fifty French airmen managed to fly to England. Eventually 380 or so airmen would form the Forces Aériennes Françaises Libres (FAFL) and three-quarters of them would die during the war.[43] The French Farman 222 that landed at St Eval was piloted by Capitaine Gounain and contained his first officer, seventeen passengers and Gounain's wife. They had flown from Jean d'Angely near Bordeaux after being shown the way from Lands' End by a Battle aircraft from St Eval.[44] The aircraft was held pending orders and 234's newly arrived intelligence officer, Pilot Officer Krikorian, an Armenian known as Crikey who spoke several languages, was detailed to act as interpreter. The next day it was flown to Boscombe Down near Andover escorted by three aircraft of B Flight, including Bob.[45] A few days later a Potez 540 also landed; its crew was similarly interviewed and then flown to Boscombe Down escorted by two Spitfires of B Flight. Boscombe Down was the base for the Aeroplane and Armament Experimental Establishment, which had previously been at Martlesham Heath.[46]

The French had left everything to get to England and their arrival did not go unnoticed by the local residents, who recalled 'poignant times at St Eval after the fall of France, with the arrival on the airfield of various French Air Force aircraft complete with their air and ground crews, and in addition their families as well'.[47] For the yet-to-be-tested pilots of 234

Squadron, here was an opportunity to get first-hand information from those who had faced the enemy.

Gathering information from those who had experienced combat was as much part of training as any lecture or flying hours and had a more direct impact. Those RAF airmen who had returned from France were keenly interrogated by fellow officers, as one man had discovered. Fenton was based at a fighter operational training unit at Aston Down while waiting to get his first squadron. Several of his fellow instructors were just back from France and Fenton, who was keen to get into action, found that 'the most valuable part for me, was to be able to talk to the gang about tactics and what they had learned in France'.[48] France surrendered on 22 June and the flow continued with a civilian aircraft being escorted from Lisbon on 1 July and a Glen Martin arriving on 6 July. Another Glen Martin arrived on 10 August from Morocco via Gibraltar. On board were Commandant Pigeau, Lieutenant D'Eugasse and two sergeants. The two officers left for London to report to General de Gaulle.[49]

Despite the excitement of the move south and arrival of the French airmen, the pilots of 234 continued the role they had begun in Yorkshire with convoy patrols and intercept flights. Unidentified aircraft were subsequently identified as either friendly or German aircraft testing the defences but no contact was made. Convoy patrols were important, if at times unexciting, duties. Alongside 234 Squadron at St Eval were the aircraft and pilots of the Photographic Reconnaissance Unit (PRU); flying high above enemy territory in unarmed Spitfires taking photographs to be rapidly interpreted. Tensions were high and suspicious activity was questioned, everyone was on the lookout for spies. The station operations book reported an unclassified transmitting station that was being investigated in the neighbourhood of St Wenn, just eight miles from the base.[50]

During these brief few weeks after the fall of France, Dowding and his commanders had a short time to prepare for the battle to come. By 7 July the strength of Fighter Command was fifty-two squadrons – nineteen Spitfire squadrons, twenty-five Hurricane squadrons, two Defiant and six Blenheim squadrons. Manning them were 1,259 pilots ready for duty and 644 operational aircraft. Supporting them were the ground crews, the staff in HQs, sectors and stations, plus those who provided essential repair and salvage of aircraft and not forgetting the Observer Corps and radar.[51] At the heart of this was the Dowding system, controlled from Bentley Priory and utilising the best communications technology and intelligence available. At Bentley sat Dowding, in the 'only room where aircraft attacks over the whole of Britain and the sea approaches were displayed'.[52] From Bentley information was replicated in each Group HQ; in the case of St Eval this was at Rudloe Manor in Corsham, just outside Bath. 10 Group became operational at 12.00 on 8 July.[53] In charge was Air Vice-Marshal Sir Quintin Brand, a South African who had served with great distinction as a fighter pilot in the First World War, where he gained an MC, DSO and DFC. Brand's squadrons covered much of the south west and up to South Wales.[54] A Fighter Sector HQ had been established at St Eval under the command of Wing Commander Harvey and the operations room was created in the educational block. Skeleton operations began on 26 June and it was fully operational by 1 July.[55] Five days later, twelve WAAF air plotters reported for duty and gladdened the eyes of the men on the base.[56]

But direct engagement with the enemy was getting closer. On 7 July Bob recorded the sighting of a Junkers 88 (Ju 88) over St Eval. 'Hun turned up over base but lost him in cloud' and the same day he noted 'Hun dropped six bombs on our convoy. Chased him but lost him in clouds.'[57] In the late afternoon Pilot Officer Dewhurst engaged a Ju 88 over Plymouth and damaged it. The next day the honour of the first squadron kill went to Blue Section under the leadership of Pat Hughes when he, Lawrence and Sgt Bailey shot down a Ju 88 over a convoy.[58]

We saw this Ju 88, it was a cloudy day. Pat recognised it straight away. I was first and shot at it. It still hadn't been shot down and Pat had his go and got in very close and made a proper job of it. It was miles out at sea out of sight of land. After we landed Pat said 'Don't know how you thought you were going to shoot it down at the range you started firing!' I was 19 and to see an enemy bomber with a rear gunner firing at you ... with all the excitement the natural thing is to start firing as soon as you could get a bead on it.[59]

The result was noted with quiet satisfaction by 10 Group HQ, as it had come only hours after the HQ was operational. It was just in time as the British, with their Commonwealth colleagues, were now fully engaged with the German Luftwaffe. It was Dowding's view that the Battle of Britain should be considered to have started on 10 July with convoy attacks designed to lure the fighters out. This was the first big attack by the Germans, with seventy aircraft. It was a somewhat arbitrary date, as Dowding agreed.[60]

There were no massed raids in Cornwall. On the morning of 10 July Bob was alone, attempting to intercept an enemy aircraft over the base. Two days later a solitary Ju 88 dropped bombs on the aerodrome and was immediately engaged by Lawrence and Gordon, who chased it out to sea and damaged it. A few weeks later one section was operating at night, including Bob, who was one of the few qualified for night flying. It was a dangerous role and accidents were frequent. One casualty was Geoffrey Gout, who crashed and died near Porthtowan, cause unknown.

Gout was a gentle, quiet man and a popular member of the squadron. He and Bob had known each other since early training days. Gout scored highly in Bob's estimation as he never let his public school background make any difference to him and he always insisted that the 'sergeants and anyone else always came to any party that we were having'. This was not always popular with senior officers. Gout was also very generous with his dark-green touring sports car, which he happily lent to his friends.[61] Gout was buried four days later in the graveyard of St Eval church. His grave is marked by a large, long white stone with a carved sword, very much in the style of a medieval knight's tomb, and is not the standard war grave headstone that was later used. The squadron adjutant, E. C. Owens, wrote to Gout's mother on 3 August expressing the squadron's sense of loss and describing him as inspiring and cheerful. Gout's car was sent to her and those personal effects she did not want were auctioned off, with the proceeds going to charity.[62] The death of this good friend was also an unexpected minor benefit to the pilots:

> We don't know what happened. He crashed at night. In those days, we had something called flying clothing cards where all the stuff that the Air Force issued to you was entered on this flying clothing card and if you lost it, you were financially responsible for it. When this bloke Geoffrey crashed, we declared that everything we were short of, he had borrowed and the equipment officer at Group sent us a signal asking us what sort of pantechnicon he had been flying![63]

Night flying was dangerous:

> Only 5 of us in the squadron were deemed night operational, who'd done enough night flying and we did night patrols over Plymouth in Spitfires, which was very pointless really. The only way you could see anything was if a search light caught it, the only time a search light caught any bomber when I was up was when I was at about 20,000 feet and the bomber was at about 5,000 and I just never got there in time. They were building a new runway, the first runway, and we didn't have much space to land, between the hedge and the runway, but we coped alright. I bent an aeroplane on one occasion which I was thoroughly told off about. I was too bloody tired to go round again. We were flying day and night.[64]

Bob himself was on the receiving end of his fellow pilots' practicality when he landed overdue from a patrol only to find them already preparing to auction off his belongings.[65] On 31 July Sergeant Thompson crashed into a stone wall on landing after a routine night patrol. He did not fly again.[66]

As August began and the squadrons further east took severe poundings from massed ranks of the Luftwaffe, 234 squadron continued the relentless round of interception scrambles and patrols, including the aptly named Gin A and Gin B over Plymouth. Horton crashed his aircraft on landing but was uninjured.[67] The squadron was meeting the enemy more regularly but usually in single numbers. Harker and Mortimer-Rose claimed the damage of a Ju 88 intercepted off Falmouth and the interception and damage of a Dornier 215 was claimed by Mortimer-Rose, Hardy and Szlagowksi,[68] the latter being one of the two experienced Polish fighter pilots who had just joined the squadron. Polish and Czech fighter pilots brought much-needed fighting experience, but they were unconventional, individualistic and limited by their lack of English.[69] But the routine patrols, convoy duty and interception of single enemy bombers was about to change.

Air Vice-Marshal Keith Park's 11 Group is rightly highlighted in any discussion on the Battle of Britain as it was the main battleground, but Sir Quintin Brand's 10 Group played an essential support role, as did 12 Group. Brand got on well with Park, whose command covered south-east England, and cooperated in providing him with reinforcements at crucial times, an indication of his support for the strategy and tactics of Park and Dowding in confronting raids by the Luftwaffe. His rapid deployment of squadrons in support of Park when there were threats to aircraft factories or aerodromes to the west and south-west of London stemmed from his agreement with Park that it was 'more essential to get a small number of squadrons quickly to the point requested than to delay whilst his squadrons are forming up into wings'.[70] Brand did more than that; he also relieved the operational pressure on 11 Group by taking over one of its bases. As the battle progressed and the geographical pattern emerged, his HQ at Rudloe Manor, outside Bath, took operational control of Middle Wallop at 12.00 on 5 August from Park.[71] Brand now had ten squadrons at his disposal covering England to the south-west of Portsmouth and up to south Wales.[72] Constant pressure from the Luftwaffe, who had been coming in over the south coast in large numbers, was depleting the squadrons at Middle Wallop. 238 Squadron, a Hurricane squadron under the command of Squadron Leader Fenton, had lost both flight commanders, and Fenton himself was wounded and out of action. The decision was taken to move them to St Eval and bring 234 Squadron forward. But there were problems as 234 was not in the best of shape either, although for different reasons.

On 7 August the operational report shows that two pilots were removed from flying duties. Flying Officer Igglesden was taken off flying duties and Flight Lieutenant Theilmann was categorised as non-effective sick and he relinquished command of A flight.[73] The reasons for Igglesden's departure are not clear. He had been one of the few experienced pilots and had joined 234 from 41 Squadron, where he had flown Spitfires with Theilmann. He was apparently not sent to another posting and resigned his commission the next year. He subsequently entered the Royal Navy as an able seaman and gained a commission there in 1943.[74] Theilmann's health problems are slightly better known. He was diagnosed as suffering from asthma, a condition that was not well understood then but which clearly made combat flying impossible. Breathing cold or dry air or exposure to smoke, fumes or pressure breathing can provoke asthma attacks. It had not been picked up in his medical examination but he may have been able to ignore any earlier childhood bronchial problems. Childhood asthma can go into remission but re-emerge at a later age and can be exacerbated by stress and exhaustion.[75] Theilmann has not had a sympathetic press, but perhaps deserves more understanding. Despite his health problems he was a regular in the air leading his section, which included Bob, throughout June and July, performing just as many sorties as the rest of the squadron. Theilmann's last flight was in early August at the early hour of 5 a.m., when he was up for just twenty minutes.[76] After leaving 234 he was gazetted as a squadron leader in 1944 and left the RAF in 1946. Post-war he reappears as the senior pilot of the Experimental Helicopter Test Unit in British European Airways in 1947, demonstrating a Westland Sikorsky S51.[77] Testing early helicopters was not a task for the fainthearted.

The figure most noted by his absence in the air, however, was 234's commanding officer. Barnett was not popular with his pilots; to a young Keith Lawrence he 'was getting on and he was in his 30s, he wasn't a flying Spitfire pilot. He was nominal CO. Don't think he had very good health either.'[78] The ORB records just four occasions in early July when Barnett took to the air and he was always on his own. His last flight was a patrol that took him to Lands' End and Weston-super-Mare on 9 July, which could be said to have been a patrol of 234's area. By comparison Theilmann, despite his breathing challenges, flew regular patrols, convoy duties and scrambles with his flight.

The fact that Barnett never flew with the squadron counted badly against him in the eyes of his young fighter pilots, perhaps even more so given his distinguished record. Fighter leadership in 1940 demanded a man who took the same risks as his men and this was noted with concern at senior levels. Barnett's limitations were apparent to Dowding. Air Vice-Marshal Evill, who was on Dowding's staff, had visited St Eval a few weeks before.[79] Keith Park of 11 Group had already faced a similar situation during the Battle of France a few months previously. In an urgent note to the Air Ministry on 22 May he wrote of a squadron leader who was, in his view, temperamentally unsuitable as a fighter squadron commander. 'Whilst in France he only flew on very few occasions when other squadron commanders were leading their squadrons and this had a bad effect on the other pilots in the squadron.' He recommended a posting to an administrative post 'for which he possesses sound qualifications'.[80] Similarly something had to be done about Barnett, although it seems to have been decided rather late in the day. On 11 August Sir Quintin Brand visited St Eval and spent time with the CO of the Fighter Sector, Wing Commander Harvey. After spending the night in the mess, Brand interviewed Barnett the next morning and Barnett relinquished his command of 234. In Barnett's case, he was a man out of his depth in the new world of air fighting. But there is a sense of sadness that this man, who had done well by the contemporary standards of the 1920s, had to leave in such a way. The RAF must have also thought so, as he was quietly retired in 1943.[81]

The squadron, meanwhile, was on its usual patrols and Bob had a tricky situation that night over Plymouth. He was chasing an enemy aircraft illuminated by searchlights but lost it when the searchlights were doused. He later made a set of terse comments in his logbook that highlights the frustration of these tiring night patrols: 'night patrols, pretty bloody – out of r/t touch – sighted Hun 12,000 below in search light only had one very quick burst'.[82] The next morning, events moved rapidly as they were informed that the squadron, now temporarily under the leadership of the remaining flight commander, Pat Hughes, was ordered to Hampshire. Dowding's 234 'fighter boys' had a job to do at Middle Wallop. If patrolling the Cornish coastline had been dull, life was about to get very much more exciting and very dangerous.

IN THE HEAT OF THE BATTLE AND THE MOVE TO MIDDLE WALLOP

Middle Wallop had been in 10 Group since 5 August and was taking a strong battering from German bombers. Stationed at Middle Wallop alongside 238 was 609 Squadron AuxAF, and 152 Squadron, equipped with Spitfires, was at the satellite base of Warmwell where part of its role was to defend Portland naval base.[1] Sir Quintin Brand moved his squadrons around so there was no break in cover. 238 was in action on 13 August at midday over Portland destroying four Messerschmitt 110s (Me 110s) and one Dornier 17 (Do 17). As 238 Squadron moved out on 13 August, the next day the air party of 234 Squadron arrived to a warm German welcome. Under the temporary command of Pat Hughes, they flew to Middle Wallop and landed in the late summer afternoon on the grass airfield, parking their Spitfires at the far end, well away from the hangars. They then looked around for the officers' mess. At this moment the airfield was severely bombed, the hangars being a particular target.[2]

Joe Roddis, then in 234's ground crew, had been part of the advance party and was in the dining room when the raid began. There had been the usual banter from the other resident squadron airmen, 609 Squadron, as they arrived. 609 were considered the 'big aces' by the newcomers. Just as the men were sitting enjoying

a great big white china mug full of hot sweet tea and as many slices of bread and butter and tins of plum jam as you wanted ... the siren went and the place emptied like mad and we thought 'What have we got here?'. We never used to run when the siren went at St Eval. They'd all gone and disappeared and we sat there talking and the next thing they were dropping everywhere. Lumps of masonry were flying about, cables were erupting, we were right in the middle of it, so we shot outside as quick as we could. Mug of tea in one hand, bread and jam in the other.[3]

The newcomers did not know where the shelters were so they dived into the nearest ditches, still clutching their tea, bread and jam as the raid continued. The raid was carried out by three German bombers and one scored a direct hit on 609's hangar, which blew out the heavy doors just as three of the squadron, a corporal and two aircraftmen, were trying to close it. All three were killed.[4] What Roddis and other squadron members later discovered was that a pilot from 234 Squadron, Sergeant Boddington, was patrolling the base and successfully destroyed one of the three bombers.[5]

The seventeen officers and 199 airmen of 234 Squadron had arrived in the midst of the German campaign to destroy the airfields prior to invasion.[6] The Germans had launched *Adlertag* (Eagle Day) mid-afternoon on 13 August, sending large formations of bombers with the intention of knocking out the airfields across the south of England. Fighters from Middle Wallop, Tangmere, Exeter and Warmwell were scrambled.[7] At 16.30 on that day five bombs were dropped by enemy aircraft on the boundary of the aerodrome, but no damage was done.[8] Along with 238's victories, 609 Squadron at the time claimed a record 'bag' of twelve enemy aircraft, three probables with six damaged.[9] No wonder the newly arrived ground crew of 234 saw them as the aces.

The whole of 234 Squadron was straight into action the next day. It was another heavy day on 15 August, as 'the Luftwaffe flew more sorties than any other day of the Battle of Britain, over two thousand'.[10] Thirteen aircraft from 234 were sent to intercept a big raid approaching Swanage. They were told there were over 200 enemy aircraft and the squadron had to get to 15,000 feet. This was the first big test of the squadron, and each pilot had his own thoughts to consider. Bob was quite clear that this was 'it'; this was when he would be killed. In his own mind, and assisted by poor ratings in training, he believed that he was the worst pilot in the squadron. He felt himself inferior to his fellow officers, who all seemed to have money, background and ability. This was, as he later admitted, largely in his imagination, but he was fully convinced that he would be killed when he first went into action:

Interviewer: Were you scared about that?
Bob: I was petrified but I was more scared of calling myself a coward than if anyone else called me one. There was no way I was going to call myself a coward, so I went.[11]

Pat Hughes was the leader and Bob flew as his number two. Looking back after the event, Bob saw that from the beginning of the scramble they all did everything wrong that was possible to do wrong. They flew off in tight formation, flying nearly five feet from each other. The sections astern were of three aircraft, which meant that there was only one person left to look around, and that person was Bob; everyone else was formatting:

Because you're concentrating so hard on keeping the formation, you haven't got time to scan the skyline. Which is the one thing you should be able to do. We proceeded to patrol up and down. At 15,000 feet which was the same height we were told the enemy were at. Eventually we turned from down sun to up sun to find there were only nine of us left. Did a couple more turns and suddenly found ourselves in the middle of hundreds of planes with black crosses on the sides and how we got there we don't know we were just in the middle of them. Of course, we all exploded like a bomb in every direction. I finished up behind a 110. Realised I had to do something about it so I took careful aim and shot him and he went down into the sea.[12]

In what seems like a variation on Pareto's Principle, a revealing analysis of air combat shows that just 5 per cent of pilots become aces, scoring five or more victories, and that 5 per cent are also responsible for 40 per cent of all victories.[13] Stephen Bungay's analysis of the battle shows a correlation where 3.5 per cent of pilots made 30 per cent of claims.[14] Bungay goes on to explain that there were a small group of hunter-killers, those who were the top scorers, and the majority in the air who were the hunters. 'Then there are the novices who either learn survival fast or simply provided the hunter-killers with targets.'[15]

The novice fighter, Bob, went on to commit more mistakes. In the excitement of realising he had just shot down his first aircraft, and proud that he had not made a fool of himself, he followed the aeroplane down as it went into the sea. He pulled up and another German aircraft, which had been following him and shooting from behind, overshot his Spitfire. Bob turned behind the German and shot him down. Elated with two successes and with the sky now empty of any other aircraft, he flew back to Middle Wallop. As he landed his ground crew saw that he had been in action by the telltale black streaks from the gun muzzles underneath the wing and he was subject to his first interrogation by them.[16] After running the gauntlet of the excited ground crew he then had to see Krikorian, the intelligence officer. Crikey, as he was inevitably known, had to extract the essential information from the pilots. He had to establish the facts, find out about enemy tactics, aircraft markings and the damage inflicted on the enemy. He also had to corroborate claims, which was no easy task in the confusion of aerial battle.

Bob's first combat report was written in those high-adrenalin moments after landing. He reported that he had been twenty-five miles south-west of Swanage at 18.15:

I was Blue 2. patrolling Swanage at 15,000 was led up behind 50 EA. Blue 1 attacked 1 Jaguar then broke away I closed in and followed it down until it hit the water (the rear gunner was firing all the time until at 1,000 ft he baled out) in the dive I gave it a 7 sec burst from 100 yards as the fire from the engines had appeared to stop. I broke away upwards towards a formation of ME 110s which were diving through a thick haze about

4,500. Fired rest of ammunition at nearest aircraft – pieces flew off it – as I broke away I saw Blue 1 engage the same aircraft which caught fire and crashed in the sea.[17]

Pat Hughes, Blue 1, supported Bob's claims and the words extracted by Crikey are simple, crisp and clear. Behind those words, the emotions experienced by Bob on his first operation against a massed raid were quite different. Bob had also witnessed Pat Hughes' actions and was, as ever, deeply impressed.[18] Meanwhile, part of Crikey's job was to discover what happened to the lost men. When the squadron landed they were short of three aircraft; Hardy, Hight and Parker did not return. Cecil Hight was killed but it took some time before further news was heard of the other two. In Bob's combat report he mentioned a thick haze and this features in one of the mysteries of 234's first key engagement. Red Section was led by Mortimer-Rose and comprised himself together with Hardy and Parker. Here is Mortimer-Rose's combat report:

As Red III I was on patrol with the squadron. On sighting the enemy on our port flank 2,000 ft below the S/L gave the order to attack. Red section were somewhat behind at the time and Red 1 and II who were together appeared to lose the enemy in the haze so being well behind I followed the bombers & carried out an attack on one of a pair of 110 in the centre of the formation slightly below. They went in line astern & I followed through a series of turns. I closed to 50 yards and fired all my ammunition. His starboard engine burst into flames, rear gunner ceased fire & before breaking for home I saw him drop away to the left. By then I was in the middle of the formation but noticed no attack & I broke downwards.[19]

The official report from the squadron on casualties dated 19 August puts a slight spin on the event. It refers to both Parker and Hardy and describes them both as 'engaging the enemy approximately twenty five miles South West of Swanage' and that they were 'lost in the haze at sea and not seen again'.[20] Word eventually reached the squadron, some considerable time later, that both men were alive and German prisoners of war. Parker had gone down in the Channel and been picked up by the Germans. At this time there was no effective coordinated rescue service for RAF pilots and the Germans were far better organised. Hardy's fate was more controversial. He landed at a French airfield 'wheels down', as it was later described. He had got lost and was flying towards the French coast and was escorted in by a German pilot, who directed Hardy by means of occasional gunfire. The capturing of Hardy's Spitfire intact was a gift to the Germans and there was even an aircraft kit made out of it. Hardy spent the rest of the war as a prisoner and on return he left the RAF.[21]

For 234 Squadron their first major encounter had been a 'game bag' of two Me 110s (claimed by Mortimer-Rose and Zurakowski plus one shared by Hughes and Bob), one damaged Me 109 (Dewhurst) and two Me 'Jaguars' (Hughes and Bob). They were also now short of three pilots.[22] Cecil Hight had crashed at Bournemouth and later he was buried in the military section of Bournemouth East Cemetery at Boscombe.[23] 234 Squadron would turn up in strength at his funeral to escort the coffin.

But before they could honour their dead, the squadron needed to take stock of their first action and prepare themselves for the next day. Bob headed to bed early and considered his performance. From the outset he had been convinced he was a poor pilot as much emphasis had been placed on aerobatic flying, something at which Bob was not good. He had gone into combat convinced he would be shot down, instead he had been a successful victor against two enemy aircraft. He knew he had been very lucky and he now had to work out what he had to do to stay lucky or, in his own words, to both 'stay alive and shoot things down'. One way of staying alive was to avoid being shot down from behind. His analysis resulted in the following plan:

I decided to go straight down as quickly as I could and that meant going straight down without rolling, because by rolling, I would remain for another second at least in the bullet stream. I had to hit the control column very hard, without thinking about it. And without delay.[24]

This he drummed into his brain every night. He also had to see the enemy before they saw him, so this meant going against the strict formation flying that had been advocated.[25]

The next day twelve aircraft were sent up on an interception scramble at 18.05. It was their second of the day, the first not having produced any results as they had found no enemy aircraft. This time they were in search of a large raid approaching Portsmouth. And this time Bob planned to keep a better lookout. They got to the relevant point at 16,000 feet only to find above them 'a mass of Me 109s at 21,000 ft'. Bob went up to attack as three of the Me 109s dived down. He found himself on the tail of one that had separated from the rest and successfully shot it down into the sea. Circling it, he realised he was being shot at by a Do 18 coming north towards the coast. He closed on it, opened fire at 200 yards and the rear gunner was killed. He shot at both engines and the aircraft landed on the water and began to sink.[26] He had done well; he had shot down two more enemy aircraft and had survived to tell the tale. But any sense of self-congratulation was dashed. 'Pat Hughes came over to see me and confirmed he had seen me shoot the 109 down, but that I had been lucky as he had shot one off my tail.'[27] Chastened, Bob realised his lookout had simply not been good enough. From this moment he changed to a silk scarf instead of the restricting collar and tie and 'planned a more methodical search of the sky'.[28]

Individual pilots were learning the lessons of the new aerial combat the hard way. Bob could see that he had done 'all the things wrong. But I was lucky I survived and I learnt very quickly after that.'[29] As well as luck and an ability to learn fast, successful pilots needed three things: flying ability, good eyesight and situational awareness.[30] Ironically the skill at which Bob was not good, aerobatics, probably saved his life. Those who were good and who had been 'superb aerobatic and formation flyers ... flew into battle as if they were at Hendon air display and never came back'.[31] Brian Kingcombe believed that good pilots were killed because they flew too well and were therefore more predictable. Flying straight and long was not recommended and pilots began to jink across the sky. Good eyesight, especially long-distance vision, was important and Bob also stressed the significance of peripheral vision. Additionally, fighters had to know how to read the sky as distance and speed were difficult to judge in the air. Aircraft could be camouflaged when seen from above flying across towns or countryside. Situational awareness was not analysed until well after the war. It required the ability to be aware of what was going on around them in the different 360-degree world of the air and maintain the knowledge of what was happening as they made the split-second decisions that spelt their fate.[32] Airborne multi-dimensional chess comes to mind, or, for Harry Potter fans, Quidditch.[33] A significant difference is that both of these games have the benefit of rules and umpires.

That day Pat Hughes shot down two Me 109s, Horton shot down one as did Sergeant Klein. Bob shot down one Me 109 plus a Do 18. Dewhurst had baled out from his aircraft over Gosport but landed safely and O'Connor baled out from his machine over the sea but was rescued by a naval launch.[34] Bob was despatched to Portsmouth to collect O'Connor. He had been picked up by a Navy yacht, which was a requisitioned private boat with a well-stocked 'cellar'. As O'Connor was apparently one of the first airmen to be picked up alive, Commander-in-Chief Portsmouth decided to personally welcome him back. Unfortunately, O'Connor was fully the worse for wear on champagne. Bob and the naval lieutenant marched O'Connor to the car and explained to the C-in-C that O'Connor was suffering from severe shock. As Bob put it, 'I'm sure the C-in-C had seen a drunk before and I'm also sure he saw a good reason for it.' Bob's retelling of the story to his colleagues 'caused everyone to fall about in fits of laughter'.[35] Bob takes the laughter for granted in his description but telling a story in an amusing way is not a gift everyone has. It was a skill he developed as a natural raconteur with good timing and pace; perhaps his early drama appearance also helped. He was growing in personal confidence and was no longer the squadron's self-labelled underdog.

A new CO arrived for the squadron. Squadron Leader O'Brien DFC from 92 Squadron took command and, unlike his predecessor, was promptly up with the men the next day over the Isle of Wight. The claims were seven Me 109s destroyed and three damaged. Bob's personal score was one destroyed and one damaged. The squadron returned unscathed.[36] Events in the air were often confused and things changed with great speed. As one veteran described it,

The feel of the bevelled ring on the stick, carefully turned from 'safe' to 'fire'. The enemy is the thing not the man. First a string of tiny silhouettes against a distant cloud. Then suddenly all round you, so close that you note with a sense of shock the rough metal and grey-green paint, with sometimes a vivid yellow nose. You are turning savagely, pressing the gun-button with a fierce exultation as the sight comes to bear. Then – just as suddenly – the utter solitude of the sky. How can you be so alone, when only seconds before was the heart of a battle?[37]

Bob made a very similar comment in an interview:

Bob: Literally you suddenly arrived in the middle of them.
Interviewer: What's that feel like?
Bob: That's a bit startling. You didn't have time to think. You realized you had to do something and I just found myself there … How I got there I don't know. It just happened. Because when you're in a mass of aircraft in the sky there are two weird things about it. Firstly the sky seems absolutely full of aircraft and then half a second later you can't see the aeroplane anywhere. The sky goes absolutely empty.[38]

Over-claiming of victories was a known problem. 'Sometimes the same aircraft would be seen by different pilots at different altitudes and in different stages of disintegration and be identified as different machines.'[39] If matters in the air were confusing, matters on the ground were not much better. The incident at Kings Somborne on 21 August is a useful example of wartime attitudes, witness recollections and propaganda.

In Hampshire, south-east of the village of Kings Somborne, on a footpath and now almost hidden from view, there is a small stone. Just two feet high, it has a simple inscription: 'To 4 unknown airmen Aug 23 1940.' The stone is off the beaten track on the old Roman road and is easily missed but walkers stop to read it. The memorial was placed there post-war and is not on the spot where the plane crashed nor is the date right. The story behind the stone is the human face of war and the details were researched by a determined local historian who wanted to put names to the four German airmen. Her work enabled the later addition of a plaque on the memorial that now gives the names of the four airmen. The pilot was OGefr Gerhard Freude, the observer Oblt Max Birkenstock, the radio operator Uffz. Rudolf Schultze and the gunner Gefr Franz Becker.[40]

They were part of Staffel 1 of Kampfgeschwader 54 in a Ju 88 and they took off on 21 August 1940 to bomb the airfield at Brize Norton. They left Evreux between 12.48 and 14.32. The weather was not good and so they targeted Abingdon instead, apparently, according to German records, 'to good effect'. On their return they were intercepted near Newbury by 234 Squadron. A flight had been scrambled at 13.20. This was their second scramble of the day. Red 1 was Squadron Leader O'Brien, Red 2 was Flight Lieutenant Page and Red 3 Bob. Their combat report shows that they closed in at distances between fifty to thirty yards and the Ju 88 headed for the ground. It crashed north of Kings Somborne near the main road to Stockbridge. Page had not seen the enemy aircraft. O'Brien and Bob touched down at Middle Wallop at 14.20. They reported the Ju 88 on the ground burning at 14.15. O'Brien suggested they went to take a look. Meanwhile, the event had been witnessed by children from the local school; all the boys except one had dashed out to see what had happened. The girls remained in the school with their teacher, Mrs Mathews, who 'burst into tears' and reminded the girls that the men on board were 'somebody's sons'. One of her sons was serving with the RAF.[41]

The day after the crash there was an article in a local newspaper which gives credit to just one unnamed pilot and his 'gunner' and makes two additions; one related to the gunning down of workmen and the second the witnesses from the wedding party.

Workers Machine Gunned

But Nazi raider brought down

A twin-engined Nazi bomber which machine gunned workmen during a raid on a south coast town yesterday was itself machine-gunned by a British fighter, which brought it down.

For several minutes after the raid the fight went on. The British machine firing occasional bursts. Finally, the pilot got into position over the raider and the Nazi's raiding days were done.

With smoke streaking from it the raider plunged down into a field at the side of a main road. As it crashed two of the crew were thrown out and killed. Three other members of the crew were burned to death.

A few minutes after the crash the pilot of the fighter and his gunner arrived having landed nearby and been driven to the scene by a passing motorist.

Villagers who rushed to the spot heard that it was the gunner's sixth Nazi victim. A wedding party from a nearby church were among the onlookers.[42]

Checking for other events on that day, it can only be describing the Kings Somborne crash, with a little embellishment for propaganda purposes.[43]

One eyewitness to the aftermath was an RNVR pilot, W. Blake, stationed at RNAS Worthy Down. Blake and three others decided to take a look, having seen thick black smoke in the distance. His logbook entry read, 'A Ju 88 shot down at Kings Somborne by a single Spitfire from Middle Wallop: viewed wreck no survivors.' His account given in 1982 gives yet another view. In his memory he and three others had seen a pall of black smoke and on hearing it was a German aircraft they decided to investigate. When they arrived the local policeman was keeping onlookers back in case of risk from exploding bombs. The RN group ascertained there was no risk and they all moved forward to examine the wreck. He recalled a party came from Middle Wallop including a squadron leader, a flight lieutenant and the medical officer. The 'victorious squadron leader' apparently walked over to the wreck and the bodies, remarking 'with grim emphasis "That'll larn 'em"'. He then took away as a souvenir the slightly damaged rudder, which had bullet holes. Blake also understood from someone from Middle Wallop that the squadron leader had been up alone testing a Spitfire. 'No others were airborne. He was thus able to engage it.'[44]

The operations record book shows the interception scramble by three aircraft and records the shared victory of a Ju 88 shot down by O'Brien and Doe. Bob's combat report reads,

I was Red 3 I attacked E/A and opened fire at 100 yards closing at 20-30 yards. 2 bursts were fired of 3 seconds each. I broke away down through cloud. Came up again through cloud and found myself underneath. Gave it rest of ammunition from about 5 yards at an angle of 40 degrees astern, went down through cloud and E/A was burning on ground.[45]

His logbook entry is more laconic: 'Met a solitary Hun over Winchester shot him down. Every occupant had at least 5 bullet holes in his helmet.'[46] Here is yet another embellishment, the five bullet holes. This information came from 'some ghoul at the crash'.[47] Bob himself did not inspect this particular, and rather unlikely, evidence and from the various reports he appears to have been a low-key presence at the site.

So there we have it, several different versions of one incident. For some of the onlookers there was a grim sense of satisfaction but for others, notably Bob, it was an uncomfortable clash with reality. Aeroplanes contained human beings and were not simply machines. He preferred not to be reminded, as 'it brought death a little too close for comfort'.[48]

At 16.00 on 26 August the Luftwaffe launched a major daylight raid as fifty-five Heinkels of KG55 and a mass of fighters were sent to target Portsmouth. Bob had already been up once that day at 12.30 on patrol. Now the whole of A flight was scrambled at 16.10. Bob was Red 1, Szlagowski Red 2, Harker Red 3 while Mortimer-Rose was Yellow 1 with Gordon and Horton as Yellow 2 and 3. As can happen, Bob suddenly found himself alone in the air and then saw about fifty 109s. Despite the odds, he decided to attack and to surprise them by climbing above. He then 'dived on the rear of the formation in a perfect bounce'.[49] Bob hit his target but his engine cut out in the slipstream of the enemy aircraft. This was a known weakness of the Merlin engine's carburettor.[50] Bob went into a dive, which restarted the engine and got him away from the rest of the German fighters and then successfully pursued his target. In his logbook he wrote with excitement, 'Intercepted 50 Me 109s over isle of Wight, my engine cut out after hitting a Huns slip stream, chased Huns back to French coast & shot one down over Guernsey with 140 bullets!!!'[51]

In his later memoirs he writes of a second encounter with the human dimension of the battle. He came across a lone Messerschmitt, chased it and fired at it. It was obviously heading down to the sea so he flew alongside and saw the pilot's face as the oxygen mask was removed. He was a 'big man, with fair hair and a round face'. Having seen the human face of the enemy, who was clearly about to ditch in the sea anyway, Bob left him alone and headed for home, being low on fuel. Bob's combat report of 26 August has a reference that might be to this incident:

20 miles n of Cherbourg 20,000 ft. I was Red 1 and chased E/A from 10 miles South of Swanage. Dive from above and behind at angle of 30 degrees. Pilot slumped over controls and a/c went straight down. Saw him hit the water.[52]

It was following Bob's recollection of this incident on *Churchill's Few* that some enthusiastic sleuths decided that the German pilot in this case must be Rolf Pingel.[53] Hauptmann Rolf Pingel was a distinguished German fighter ace with twenty-two British aircraft to his credit and had recalled an incident when he had also seen the face of the enemy as he was shot down.[54] It is a very tempting picture, two heroes of the war meeting in the air, but doubts have been raised over the story as Pingel came down into the sea near Boulogne on 28 September and it is most likely the victor in that case was Ben Bennions of 41 Squadron.[55] That day Bob was in the air but not over Kent. The man Bob saw on 26 August was a different German pilot. Despite the confusion, the telling of the incident reflects Bob's attitude to the fight. Like many he saw himself as fighting the machine not the man. It was also getting more difficult to talk about events unless to make a good story to amuse fellow pilots. 'After all, any description of the fight would include seeing your own chaps shot down and we didn't want to think about that.'[56]

When researching the Battle of Britain for his book *The Most Dangerous Enemy*, Stephen Bungay interviewed Bob extensively and got to know him well. Stephen was impressed with the incident on 26 August, when 'the worst pilot in the squadron had taken on the odds of fifty-to-one and triumphed'.[57] Bob may have thought himself the worst pilot but he was now an ace. Boasting, however, was simply not done:

> Oh when you get it all right you realize – in the First World War you shot five aeroplanes down you become an Ace. I had a private celebration when I shot my first five down, I didn't want to let anyone else know that I was doing – I had a private party – ... Still – I remember Biggles, I used to read the Biggles books. And how important it was if you shot down was to become an Ace, five shot down. I never mentioned it ... but I had a pint of beer on it when it happened.[58]

The attitude of the public towards the RAF had changed since the hard words over Dunkirk. This aerial war was being fought over the countryside in full view of spectators. Following the Kings Somborne incident, which had put a bullet hole through his main spar, Bob flew his Spitfire to the Supermarine works at Hamble to have it repaired. Here he sat idly, for once a bystander watching other pilots, including those from his squadron, above him on interceptions. The foreman invited him for a meal while his aeroplane was being repaired. His wife was effusive about the actions of the RAF pilots and Bob found it embarrassing. Until then it had not occurred to him that they were 'doing something that ordinary people could see and admire'.[59] There were also VIP visits. HRH the Duke of Kent had visited on 23 August, and a week later Viscount Trenchard arrived.[60] He came across to Bob as 'a wonderful man ... He was most impressive and had the ability to talk to each one of us. I could understand how he had achieved the creation of the Royal Air Force.'[61] On another occasion, on a rare outing to a local pub, after a few pints the local farming community persuaded the pilots to expand a little on their moments in the sky. The landlord sped them on their way with the words, 'Thanks for coming – we have no doubts we'll win!'[62] Such was the mood of optimism in 1940. Bob and his fellow pilots continued to fly and to attack, knowing the personal risks but determined to carry on the fight no matter what. It was personal; the enemy was at the gate and heading for his mother's back yard.[63]

After the aeroplane repair it was back to work. There were occasional days of inaction, such as 28 and 29 August, when nothing arrived to interrupt their day. The enemy was changing tactics and London was now the main target. The first extensive bombing raid on London was on 22 and 23 August, before the British bombing of Berlin.[64] 234 Squadron was ordered further into 11 Group's territory, starting with security patrols by A Flight over Guildford and B flight over Northolt. Northolt and Biggin Hill had fighter sector rooms essential to the Dowding system. While the pilots from 10 and 12 Group protected their bases, the men of 11 Group fought the raiding aircraft.[65]

Days settled into an exhausting routine. He was woken by a batman with strong, sweet tea an hour before dawn. This was followed by breakfast in the mess and then, still before dawn, out to dispersal in a truck. In the Nissen hut they took what relaxation they could on camp beds and drank more tea. After various trials they found the best way to get fully kitted for the aircraft in a scramble. The parachute was particularly bulky and the eventual solution was to leave it in the aircraft. Bob abandoned flying boots and preferred to use his shoes. By now take-off was less formal. It was a grass airfield so there was no concrete runway and they simply took straight off and sorted themselves out once in the air as they already knew which sections they were in. Strict formation flying was a thing of the past.

'Having got airborne, I started to spread out from the leader and from listening to the directions he received, decided where to position myself.'[66]

Lunch and dinner was back at the mess, sergeants to their mess and the officers to theirs. Middle Wallop officers' mess is the classic Lutyens design of a simple two floor building with large spacious rooms. Bob recalls a large dining room, ante room and bar, but the term bar is misleading. Bars were discouraged and instead the officers rang a bell for service and drinks were brought into the room. This formality extended to strong views on the correct attire for the mess by the resident 'penguins' (officers who 'flapped but did not fly').[67] The arrival of tired and hungry pilots dressed still in their flying gear did not initially find favour, but one hour for lunch was simply not long enough to get back to the mess to eat, look at the newspaper and return to flying duties.[68] These were yet another set of pre-war attitudes that needed to change in order to recognise the realities. Some meals were brought round to dispersal by van, usually sandwiches, and a NAAFI van brought a welcome change of rock cakes or sticky buns. Sticky buns and the inevitable tea featured highly on return from a sortie after the inevitable debriefing. If there was time in the evening there might be some chat in the mess, but nowhere is there any reference to organised games for this squadron and usually for Bob it was an early evening to plan his tactics. He was never a regular night owl.

As the switch of German tactics from airfields to major bombing attacks on London was now seen as a more permanent change the fighters from 11 Group were moved from defensive base patrols to direct contact with the German aircraft. On 4 September twelve aircraft scrambled to meet sixty-five Me 110s near Haslemere. It was to be a record-breaking encounter. Fourteen Me 110s and one Do 17 were destroyed and seven Me 110s were damaged. The highest scorers of the day were Bob and Pat Hughes with three apiece and Sergeant Boddington with two to his name.[69] This record 'game bag' made 234 one of the highest-scoring squadrons in one day.

The Me 110s had adopted the tactic of circling to protect each other. Pat Hughes had dealt with this by attacking the leader head-on while Bob attacked the circle at right angles and shot down two aircraft. By then they were ten miles out at sea and as Bob returned to base he came across a third Me 110 near Littlehampton and successfully claimed his third victim of the day. Short of fuel, he had to land at Kenley.[70]

On 5 September the squadron engaged a large formation of enemy aircraft over Kent. The squadron aces were the same names again: Hughes and Boddington two each, Zurakowski and Bob one each. The composite squadron combat report written a few days later describes how the squadron were ordered to patrol Kenley. When over Kenley they sighted ack-ack fire in the direction of Gravesend and went to investigate. What later became clear was that they arrived in the region of the Thames Estuary as the enemy raid was returning. Bob witnessed the raid on the docks and watched them erupt into smoke and flames, then 'having to turn like a demon because four 109s seemed to be shooting at me all at the same time'.[71] Bob's flying skills are fully evident in the squadron report of the incident. Bob was Red 2:

He dived down and fired at the first e/a but missed him. He then saw his bullets enter the second me 109, soon afterwards the third Me 109 burst into flames and blew up. Red 2 went right between the rest. He was then attacked by the remainder who left the Hurricanes. He did tight turns with three e/a shooting at him; three above him came down in their turn. He half rolled down around the edge of the balloons went through a pall of smoke above burning oil tanks and returned at full boost at sea level weaving up the river and landed at Kenley.[72]

The next day in the early morning the squadron was over Beachy Head in Kent engaging a large formation of enemy fighters and bombers. Eight Me 109s were destroyed with two probables and three Dorniers damaged. The success was led by O'Brien, Bob, Hughes, Harker, Zurakowski and Boddington. They returned to base and, after the inevitable wait as the Spitfires were counted in, they discovered that 'Scotty' Gordon was missing (later known to be killed) and Hornby had crashed (his Spitfire exploded and he was severely injured). In the second interception scramble of the day Horton was shot down, baled out over the sea and was rescued comparatively unhurt by a naval launch from Weymouth. News eventually came in that 'Scotty' Gordon had been killed; he had been involved in a dogfight over the Sussex Downs and his Spitfire came down near Hailsham in East Sussex. Gordon was from Dufftown in Scotland. He was aged twenty and a Cranwell officer who had joined 234 Squadron at the same time as Bob. Bob remembered him as a 'delightful man. He was quite a small chap, but a very handsome man.'[73]

In this combat Bob's name is linked with 'Budge' Harker. Sergeant Harker and Bob teamed up to provide support to one another. It is not clear exactly when – it may have been before this date – but they had worked out a system that gave them freedom of manoeuvre but also support. 'At dispersal, no one saluted anyone ... but everything got done.'[74] In this informal setting, with pilots on the same level as each other outside their different messes, conversations could develop. Bob and Budge agreed to fly abreast about a couple of hundred yards apart to give each other cover. Bob claimed one Me 109 and damage to three Do17s. He was in Red Section, led by O'Brien as Red 1 and Budge as Red 3:

I was Red 2 when I saw Red 1 attacked. 2 me 109s got on his tail. I attacked rear one and eventually shot it down. Just NE of Dover and it crashed on land. I pulled up and at 5,000 ft I found 14 Do 17s in sections of 3, 5, 3 and 3 astern. Attacked each aircraft of the rear section from above and behind. Each case saw my tracer go in and rear fire encountered and ceased in each case after fired. Broke away between A/C downwards – and out of ammunition and came home full boost.[75]

The squadron was very successful; the ground crew could boast of the aces in its midst and they celebrated by painting the scores on the pilots' favourite aircraft. But the reckoning was due. 'On 5 September a German order was intercepted ordering an attack of 300 bombers on London docks for the afternoon of 7 September.'[76] The 7 September was to be the squadron's hardest day. Daytime fighting meant large formations of German fighters, some of which were fighter bombers. The Me 109s were now flying well above 20,000 feet, where they had an advantage.[77]

Twelve aircraft took off on an interception scramble chasing large formations of enemy fighters and bombers. What they were witnessing was the first massive daylight raid on London as the Germans switched their focus from the airfields and other targets. The squadron was ordered to patrol Kenley and Biggin Hill at Angels 10. The squadron again climbed to Angels 20 and arriving over the patrol position they saw heavier than normal numbers of enemy bombers and fighter formations going south and south-east.[78] Bob recalls climbing like mad 'in an attempt to avoid the trauma of the two previous raids where I had been at a disadvantage from the very start and managed to reach London at reasonable altitude where I could have a go at the bombers on my terms'.[79]

In the melee five enemy aircraft were destroyed and one probable with two damaged. Bob shot down a He III, Harker two Me 109s and one damaged, Klein had a probable Me 109 and Keith Lawrence shot down one Me 109 and damaged a Do17. Pat Hughes destroyed a Do17. But the tragedy for the squadron was the deaths of O'Brien and Pat Hughes, both of whom were shot down.

The squadron's combined combat report gives the following detail. Red Section, which included Pat, Bob and Budge Harker were attacked by a formation of Me 109s that was escorting about 150 bombers. Red 1 (Pat) was shot down in a 'manner not ascertained'. Red 2 (Bob) dived on a rear Heinkel of the bomber formation and gave the port engine a one-second burst. The engines burst into flames at the same moment three Me 109s attacked him. Bob dived, pulled up underneath the enemy bomber and gave the starboard engine a one-second burst. This also caught fire and one person baled out of the rear cockpit. The three Me 109s were still firing at him and he avoided them in the region of Dover and joined up with Red 3 (Harker). When the Heinkel was last seen, both engines were well on fire. Red 3 had meanwhile attacked a Me 109 over south London and gave him a three-second burst that set fire to the port wing of the enemy aircraft, which went down in a vertical dive.[80]

Bob's report and his recollections show his confidence in picking off the aircraft he wanted to attack while avoiding being the victim of another. 'The same 3 Me 109s were still firing at me so I went down over Dover and there met Red 3 and with him attacked 7 109s in line abreast. I got the right-hand one but did not have time to notice the result as 1 Me 109 with white spinner and engine was on my tail.'[81] He was indeed a successful hunter-killer. But there were other risks in the sky, and not just from enemy aircraft.

When chasing a/c in the distance I found it to be a Hurricane. I dived past it and looped. He followed me round firing all the time (confirmed by Red 2) the Hurricane had red white and blue roundlets.[82]

Harker confirmed what he saw:

I saw what I thought was a Me 109 attack a Spitfire. As I was about to attack I recognised it as a Hurricane, he was definitely firing. He broke away and disappeared before I could get his markings.[83]

On being attacked by friendly fire, Bob's final words in his combat report on the incident were 'Please note I don't like it'. One can only guess from what earthier words this was translated. Meanwhile, somewhere in another squadron there was a very scared and probably shocked Hurricane pilot. It happens in all wars, but the consequences can be hard to deal with, as in the controversial 'Battle of Barking Creek', which was early in the Battle of Britain and involved the famous ace 'Sailor' Malan, when lives were lost.

Bob and Budge Harker had not directly witnessed the loss of Pat Hughes. The cause of Pat's death is still uncertain and there are several theories, the most plausible being that his plane was hit by debris as he got in close to finish a Dornier.[84] Pat had been the de facto leader of the squadron. A highly respected and gifted leader, he knew when to encourage and when to offer advice. He was a good-looking, warm and friendly Aussie who, despite being a part of the RAF, insisted on wearing his dark-blue Australian uniform. He left a very big gap in the squadron and Bob deeply missed him, seeing Pat as his mentor. There were some similarities in their social backgrounds, although Pat had had rather more scholastic success. Relaxed and unstuffy, he had not been impressed on arriving in England by the Yorkshire social scene. Local families he declared were either 'terribly county or else strict church goers'. Pat, too, had been destined for bombers but had successfully appealed.[85] In Bob's view, Pat 'has fully qualified for the history hall of fame as an Australian who came to help us when we needed him'.[86] Many years later, at a simple service dedicating a plaque in the place where Pat was killed, Bob, then in his eighties, found it hard to say the words to convey what Pat had meant to him and the men of 234.[87]

Back at Middle Wallop, Flight Lieutenant Page was appointed the temporary squadron leader and following the disastrous day for the squadron, Brand took swift action to move 234 out to St Eval and bring a rested and refreshed 238 back again to Middle Wallop. 234 Squadron returned to St Eval on 11 September, it is said, with just four pilots.[88] This is a slightly puzzling statement as the facts do not fully support it. The squadron had certainly taken some severe punishment and in four weeks they had had lost five pilots killed in action. Additionally Hornby had been severely injured, Olenski, Lawrence and Bailey were posted to other front-line squadrons and two pilots were prisoners of war. Of the founding members who joined in October 1939, still with 234 Squadron were Bob, Horton, Mortimer-Rose, Dewhurst and sergeants Boddington and Harker. There were also those who had joined the squadron in July 1940: Flight Lieutenant Page, Pilot Officer Zurakowski and three sergeant pilots, Sharpley, Szlagowski and Klein.[89]

While they did return with more than just four pilots, what is important is that psychologically they felt totally depleted as a squadron. 234 returned to St Eval, as they had left, without a commanding officer and with just one flight commander. Page was temporarily CO and Mortimer-Rose and Dewhurst acted as officer commanding A and B flights respectively. In the mess, many familiar faces were missing.

The men who returned to St Eval were only one month older but emotionally and mentally they were several years older. They were also exhausted, living off their nerves with adrenalin almost constant. When he slept, Bob slept deeply – so deeply on one occasion that a bomb burst blew out the windows of his room and he slept on through the raid.[90] The pilots had lost valued colleagues and friends and had been tested in the heat of the battle. The disappearance of Parker and Hardy in that first major combat was still a mystery, and, while it might not have been discussed openly, Hardy in particular had been a propaganda gift to the Germans. That must have stung and so it was not surprising that the squadron who had headed almost leaderless into battle might have condemned without question and jumped to the conclusions they did. Hardy, of course, was not there to defend himself and the true circumstances may never be known. But, rightly or wrongly, their contemporaries did judge. In a war of attrition they could not afford weak links and there was a very real fear of contagion. The friendly-fire incident involving Bob and witnessed by Harker was another example of the strains of war.

'Waverers' were discussed at the Air Ministry in 1940. A memo on 9 July 1940 considered the disposal of waverers. These were described as men who had lost the confidence of their COs in their resolution and courage in operational flying.[91] The difficulty was how to differentiate between those who were 'genuinely medical cases where there is definite nervous or mental disease' from those cases of 'loss of courage and resolution'.[92] The latter cases were not to be invalided since there was awareness that 'financial benefits for invalided personnel are often better than those for ordinary exit'.[93] But trying to distinguish what was termed as a genuine medical case was not easy. It was from this debate that the term Lack of Moral Fibre (LMF) was created. Unique to the RAF at the time, it would continue to be a controversial and contentious issue.

By 7 October 1940 Keith Park of 11 Group was using the term, and he was of the firm view that there should be speedy handling of cases in aircrew. 'It is essential that any such cases be removed immediately from the precincts of the squadron or station as experience has shown that a great deal of damage can be done if cases of this nature remain at the station pending lengthy disposal.'[94] LMF became a term to be dreaded and one that was used indiscriminately in informal settings but with great caution by medical officers.[95]

Meanwhile, as an exhausted 234 recovered in St Eval, the challenge for each Group HQ was to rebuild squadrons speedily with a mix of effective, battle-hardened pilots and inexperienced pilots. Some 234 men had already gone to other front-line squadrons, Olenski and Zurakowski to 609 at Middle Wallop and Lawrence and Bailey to 603 at Hornchurch. New pilots arrived at 234 to be welcomed by the old guard. Among those arriving at St Eval were two men who would become good friends with Bob, 'Bertie' Wootton and Terry Kane. It is through Terry Kane's eyes that we get a glimpse of the man he met in September 1940 at St Eval.

> I had known him before 234 Squadron. When I arrived at St Eval Bob was the first one I recognised. Him, I liked from the word go. He was extraordinarily friendly, cheerful, joking sort of chap and very open and very approachable. He was quick thinking and was obviously a bright chap, but he never thought he was.[96]

On 22 September Squadron Leader 'Minnie' Blake assumed command of the squadron and it was also Bob's last day with the squadron. He was flying with his partner Budge Harker that morning on his last flight with 234. Later that day, Harker went up with Kane and they shared in a Ju 88 victory.[97] As for Bob, the man who had feared he would let himself and others down had emerged, in the words of the officer commanding Fighter Sector St Eval, as

> a courageous and dashing type of officer, who has shot down 9 enemy aircraft (confirmed) and has been recommended for the DFC. He is

however a little irresponsible but is only 20 years of age but with experience he will be able to accept more responsibility.[98]

This young man was to be tested in more ways as the Battle of Britain continued.

5

THE BATTLE CONTINUES WITH A NEW SQUADRON AND A NEW AIRCRAFT

In his logbook for 28 September Bob noted 'posted to 238 and given my flight'.[1] The promotion was a big step for him; he was now in charge of a flight and expected to lead his men, guiding, advising and training them. If he needed a role model he had a good one in the late Pat Hughes. Bob's new squadron was in almost every way different to 234 Squadron. The style of a squadron is defined by several factors: its role, its history (which gives it battle honours and traditions), the cohort of men with their differing personalities and, importantly, the character and style of the commanding officer. The role of 238 was, of course, the same since it was a fighter squadron and its RAF history was very similar to 234 as it had also been a seaplane squadron in First World War and then disbanded in 1920. 238 was reformed in May 1940 with Spitfires, but these were changed to Hurricanes and the squadron became operational on 2 July.

If 234 had suffered major leadership losses, 238 had been fortunate to retain the same CO for much of the time, even though he was away for most of August due to injury. Squadron Leader H. Fenton was born in Argentina and had graduated from Trinity College Dublin and joined the RAF in 1928. He saw service with 5 (Army Cooperation) Squadron in India. At the end of his short service commission he continued flying, becoming a civilian flying instructor at Hamble where he trained RAFVR entrants. On rejoining the RAF, he spent some time in bomber training, but he wanted to be a fighter. Eventually he persuaded the RAF that he should command a fighter squadron and was posted to 238 Squadron at Middle Wallop in July 1940. In contrast to Barnett, he led very much from the front.[2] He ditched in the Channel on 3 August and was not back with the squadron until 13 September.[3] During his absence one of his flight commanders, Flight Lieutenant 'Minnie' Blake, had held the squadron for him.

The squadron Bob joined now comprised fourteen operational pilots in addition to Fenton. There were eight officer pilots: Considine, Covington, Davis, Kings, Rozycki (Polish), Simmonds, Urwin-Mann and Wigglesworth. Added to these there were four sergeant pilots, Batt, Jeka (Polish), Kucera (Czech), McLaughlin and Sibley. This list of names hides a set of appalling losses for the squadron. When they were pulled out of Middle Wallop to St Eval on 13 August, eight pilots had been killed in action, two of whom had been in the squadron barely a week. Sergeant Seabourne was badly injured and was to spend seven months having plastic surgery. When the squadron returned to Middle Wallop from St Eval in September the losses continued. Two others had been shot down but were badly injured. Hughes, Duszynski and Pidd were killed, and Towers Perkins was badly burned; he would later become a founder member of the Guinea Pig Club.[4]

On his first day Bob had two hours' practice on his new machine. He found the Hurricane to be an effective gun platform, sturdy and very manoeuvrable, a good fighting machine despite lacking the finesse of the Spitfire. John Ellacombe flew Hurricanes with 151 Squadron at the same time and provides a good description:

It was a stable aeroplane. Quite easy to land once you got the sort of feel for it. You had to land in your semi-stall position otherwise you would start bouncing, but once you learnt all that, it was a delightful aeroplane to fly, stable, and you could pull a very tight turn, and we were taught all that, and we were told that we could out-turn the Messerschmitt 109, as long as you saw him coming. The good thing about the Hurricane, it had a big mirror above the cockpit, so if you looked at that when you were looking around you would, with luck, not get somebody on your tail.[5]

The mirror did not impress Bob. As a section leader he found it useful for checking if his number two was in place but deadly if relied on to see the enemy due to the difficulty of judging distance in the air. In Bob's view, if the enemy appeared in the mirror it was probably too late.[6] He was operational with the squadron on 30 September, but even as he practised there were further losses. 238 Squadron would continue to have losses, earning the dubious honour of having one of the highest casualty rates of all the squadrons. It was surpassed only by 264 Squadron, which flew Boulton Paul Defiants, and 501 Squadron, equipped with Hurricanes.

Such numbers do not testify to the individual losses. Losses were felt by the colleagues, even if the situation, mental and physical exhaustion and the sheer number of losses numbed the senses. Each name is linked to a life and another story. In his own way the compiler of the Form 540 for 238 did his best to remember the lost men. Squadron operations record books are surprisingly different in style and tone from one squadron to the next and those written in wartime can be very distinct. Each write-up portrays a certain style and attitude and reflects the author's priorities. They were authorised and signed by the CO, who might influence some details. Forms 540 and 541 together constitute the record books. Form 541 should show names of aircrew, initials and rank, plus details of sorties. 540 is the narrative, usually in diary form, but it was mostly written after the event:

> The important thing to realise about Forms 540 and 541, and especially the latter, is that they were being compiled on airfields which could be in the thick of the fighting, including being bombed, and their compilers had other things on their minds than the convenience of future historians.[7]

In the case of 238 Squadron, the compiler was Flying Officer Noel David, the adjutant. His words are fluent and reflect the values of the squadron. Each loss of a pilot generated a small paragraph to give a glimpse of a lost personality, even if they had been with the squadron for a few days. So on 29 September, while Bob was discovering how to fly his Hurricane, the squadron was meeting twenty-five Me 110s accompanied by Me 109s over the Isle of Wight. This is Flying Officer David's later description of the operation, in which Pilot Officer Rozycki destroyed one Me 110:

Sgt Bann baled out and was killed because his parachute did not work. P/O Harrison and Sgt Little have not returned. P/O V G Simmonds landed at Andover and crashed taking off as he could get no fuel and his tanks had been deployed below take off level. Sgt Bann, S E was one of the 'foundation' members of this squadron and was held in high esteem by all members of the squadron. He was an able and reliable pilot and was very popular. He took particular interest in the Polish pilots.

P/O D S Harrison had been with squadron only since 12 September. He was a VR who had graduated through the rank of ST pilot. His quiet, equable temperament gave promise of a sound and useful performance to come and his loss is to be greatly deplored.

Sgt R Little was also a foundation member of this squadron. He was an able and reliable pilot who was highly esteemed by his fellow pilots.[8]

David's final sentence sums up the day: 'This was a very bad day for the squadron.' The day was remembered among the many days of losses by Squadron Leader Fenton in his memoirs, written years later. He used the same simple phrase to describe it.[9] In total, four pilots were lost on one day, including Sgt Horsky, a Czech, who did not return. The pilots fighting the battle were increasingly international. Bob had served with Australians and New Zealanders, and now there were more Poles and Czechs. Urwin-Mann remembered it as 'one of the most cosmopolitan squadrons ... and we all cooperated together with extraordinary ease'.[10] Noel David's words on Horsky reveal some of the challenges of the international squadron.

Sgt Horsky was the first Czech pilot to be lost from this squadron; he had been with the squadron a fortnight, and was the first Czech to join us. He had but little time to get to know us, and, as in the case of his compatriots and of their Polish friends, diversity of language had set a hedge about him through which converse was not easy. It may be placed on record that the dash and bravery of these men is the more striking when it is remembered that they must pass many hours of loneliness in a strange country even when surrounded with pilots of their squadron.[11]

From the CO's perspective, the arrival of the Poles and Czechs was like

manna in the wilderness. What they lacked in English, they more than made up in with experience and spirit. It is amazing how quickly we all became firm friends. The only snag was that after an engagement and, not being much good with radio transmissions due to their lack of English, they were liable to land at various other airfields in southern England so I could never be sure what casualties I had until it had been sorted out. Most of them were regulars in their own Services and more experienced than our own crowd.[12]

If the adjutant endeavoured to record the passing of colleagues by entering a paragraph to reflect each lost personality, the intelligence officer had his own way of keeping up morale. Flying Officer Wills was clearly an accountant at heart and he attempted to sum up the squadron's successes in monetary terms. He created an accounting table with a credit of ten Me 109s at £5,000 each, twenty-three and a half Me 110s at £10,000, one Ju 87 also at £10,000 and one He 113 at the same price. Three and a half Ju 88s were rated at £15,000 each, while four Do 17s and eighteen He 111s were the most expensive at £25,000 each. The total was £865,883. Against this was put the loss of just twenty Hurricanes valued at £5,000 each. The credit balance in favour of the squadron was £765,833, a small fortune in contemporary values.[13]

Another morale-raising tradition in this squadron was the appointment of an officer to the role of *Magister Ludorum*. In Ancient Rome, the honour of *Magister Ludorum* was conferred on the greatest gladiator at the Games, or at least the last man standing. So one member of the officers' mess was given the title and led entertainment that might include music and energetic mess games, which all helped to bind the team. However the use of such terms was yet another difference. While those with a Classics education would have understood the allusion automatically, others such as Bob would not. Fitting in to a very different style of squadron was not going to be automatic. It might not have been helped either by the arrival on the same day of Flight Lieutenant Robinson, the son of Lord Robinson. Michael Lister Robinson was posted from 601 'millionaires' Squadron, and brought with him his private aeroplanes including a powered glider, which were soon well known over the local countryside. However, there was one familiar face – Sergeant Batt had trained at the same FTS as Bob. Batt found 238 Squadron egalitarian, with little or no distinction between officer and sergeant pilots, although he had come across an example in Middle Wallop in a Nissen hut of a blanket separating the two groups, a practice of which he did not approve.[14]

What mattered most was performance in the air, and Bob was up with the squadron on 30 September on four occasions. They patrolled Kenley and Biggin Hill without incident and then Bournemouth, where two pilots, Kings and Simmonds, collided, but both baled out safely. Losing aircraft was very expensive but despite the various claims of aircraft shortage Fenton, as CO, was full of praise for the supply of replacements. Pilot Officer Covington landed in a field next to Kings, returning safely to base, and Sergeant Sibley lost his way and landed at Weston-Super-Mare to refuel, returning without damage to his aircraft or himself. After sorties, each squadron assessed the damage to men and aircraft and waited in many cases for men to arrive back from other parts of the country. Tom Neil, who was in 249 Squadron, provides an image of pilots clutching their parachutes and heading in a variety of directions on any transport they could find across southern England in order to get back to base, where an aeroplane would be waiting for them to fly again.[15]

In the late afternoon those left in the squadron were in the air again, and this time they engaged 100 enemy aircraft south of Portland. Robson,

Kucera, Doe and Jeka destroyed four enemy aircraft and damaged two. They all returned safely to Chilbolton, which was the new base of the squadron. David summed up the heavy fighting in September. Seven pilots and fourteen aircraft were lost by enemy action and five aircraft were damaged beyond squadron repair. He reflected that the losses made sad reading, but 'add another page of excellent accomplishment to that of August'. He was less than happy about the move to the squadron's new home. 'It appears to have been regarded as mobile, but its mobility is small in contrast to an RFC squadron of the last war. Hired transport as in former moves had to be used.'[16]

In this way, the 238 Squadron of the line entered the depths of the Hampshire countryside, to a common, where, in the bright early autumn weather, they renewed their guard and saw the thorns and trees changing colour, as to bring to mind the lines

> Royal the Pageant closes
> Lit by the last of the sun
> Opal, and ash of roses
> Cinnamon, amber and dun.[17]

The verse is a quote from Rudyard Kipling's poem 'Bridge Guard in the Karoo', which was written in 1901 about the Boer War. Other lines in the rest of the poem refer to the few, the lost and the lonely and reflect the feelings of a small group of men manning a lonely outpost. It had indeed been a tough month.

On 1 October Bob's flight was ordered to Middle Wallop to meet 609 Squadron and intercept an enemy raid heading south over Poole. Park ordered squadrons to operate in pairs, with Spitfires high to engage German fighters and Hurricanes low to break up bomber formations.[18] 'As usual when the Controller gave us the enemy's height, I added another five thousand feet for luck and the added advantage it gave us.'[19] With him were Covington, Sibley, Batt, Rozycki and Wigglesworth.[20] They found the enemy formation of 200 bombers. As on the previous day, the German fighters formed a defensive circle. To Bob the 'raid seemed more like a swarm of bees'. In a swift decision, Bob led his team down through the hole in the centre of the swarm to attack the bombers, relying on the Spitfires to attack the fighters above and with the knowledge that the Germans would hesitate to shoot with the risk of shooting one of their own. After his section had turned over into the dive, Bob saw the 'Spitfire squadron turning away'.[21] Committed to the dive, A flight carried on and downed three Me 110s and damaged one Me 109.

A flight returned without Sibley. 'Of stocky build and solid character, Sgt Sibley was lost before he had found opportunity to show his mettle.'[22] Bob had successfully led his flight but lost one man and he was also furious with 609 Squadron. He headed straight for his CO to make a complaint. 'I made a complaint against the Spitfire squadron, because I was sure that we could have done a lot more damage with our six, now five, planes.'[23] What had happened to the other squadron? 238's record states clearly the gathering of the flights from each squadron but 609's narrative makes no mention of any activity by the squadron on that day, although the accompanying Form 541 lists Flight Lieutenant Howell leading a section of pilots on a patrol. No other details are given.[24]

It is possible that the flight from 609 did not see the same scene in the air as seen by 238 and therefore made a different decision, but the complete omission of any mention of the enemy formation in 609's narrative is puzzling. All the more so when, many years later, Bob met 'the leader of that squadron' and asked why he had not attacked at the same moment. The reply was that 'he was giving top cover'.[25] The challenge for the COs of both squadrons was how to handle the situation. 609 Squadron was a very successful squadron and both the young fighter leaders, Bob and Howell, were effective fighters. Howell would be awarded his DFC on 25 October. The lack of narrative in 609 suggests a general smoothing over of the event and a carefully worded description in 238's narrative. Perhaps by coincidence, a few days later 609 had a new CO; Flight Lieutenant Robinson left 238 to take over as their new commander.[26]

The next few days allowed the incident to settle. The sunny days of the summer were now changing to cloud and rain which gave visibility problems. Heading north over Middle Wallop on 5 October, the squadron was surprised by an attack by fifteen Me 109s from astern. Ten of the squadron landed successfully at base but one, Rozycki, had to land at Fareham to refuel and Sergeant McLaughlin baled out. He was admitted to Shaftesbury hospital suffering from multiple burns and his aircraft was lost. 'But has subsequently been reported as holding his own.'[27] Burns were a big fear for pilots, with the Hurricane in particular being a serious danger to the men, who risked life-changing non-fatal injuries through fire. Dowding, in his later despatch, noted the serious risk to Hurricane pilots.[28] Bob was well aware of the danger:

I think the only thing I was scared of was fire in the sky because in both Spitfire and the Hurricane you were sitting on 85 gallons of petrol, about twelve ... from your face. The tank was right in front of the cockpit between the engine and the cockpit. And if anything happened to that you were in trouble. In fact I learnt very quickly about petrol. For example I was not aware until I started asking questions that a petrol tank does not blow up if it's full. It only blows up below half full. The reason I know that is because when I was shot down eventually, I saw something, must have been a tracer bullet, and how I saw it I don't know but I became aware of something going over my shoulder into the dashboard and behind the dashboard was the petrol tank. But it must have been very nearly full 'cause I'd only just taken off and climbed up so it didn't explode. I started asking questions when I ... discovered that.

Interviewer: But fire that was the thing was it?

R. Doe: Fire was the thing I was more scared of than anything else. 'Cause if you'd seen people been burnt. They're a horrendous fright and remain that horrendous fright for the rest of their lives.[29]

That same day the squadron was up again with eleven aircraft and saw fifty enemy aircraft five miles out to sea between Southampton and Portland Bill.

'No attack was made by our aircraft although other friendly squadrons were in vicinity as a trap was suspected. The e/a made no attempt to offer battle.' Meanwhile the news was received that Bob had been awarded a DFC. The squadron noted with satisfaction that Bob had 'downed 12 skyrats'.[30] In the recommendation Bob was described by his air officer commanding as 'a fighting pilot of outstanding qualities'. His station commander commended his 'outstanding dash and eagerness to fight the enemy at close quarters. His courage and marksmanship are of a very high order. The majority of his successes were obtained in combats using deflection at very close ranges and so penetrating the armour of his opponents.'[31]

On 7 October the full squadron, now back up to strength with twelve aeroplanes, was involved in another skirmish with a large raid of 100 aircraft heading for Bristol. It comprised Ju 88s, Me 110s and 109s. 238 had been patrolling at 20,000 feet and the day was sunny with wisps of cloud, but before the bombers could be reached the enemy launched a surprise attack with Me 109s diving out of the sun. In view of their tactical disadvantage, the end result was a surprising success for the squadron. They lost one Hurricane, Covington baling out with slight injuries, and claimed four enemy aircraft. Bob, Jackie Urwin-Mann and Sergeant Jeka each destroyed a Ju 88 and Squadron Leader Fenton claimed one Me 110.[32] Fenton now needed to get more Hurricanes:

Arrived back at Wallop at 9pm and found, that through casualties in the engagement, we could only muster five serviceable aeroplanes. I decided to cut corners and rang direct to Fighter Command and spoke to Wing Commander Rich, the Chief Supply Officer, and told him my problem. He said 'Promise you have sent your signals?' I replied 'cross my heart' and he said 'I will do my best for you.' By lunchtime the next day, no less than eight Hurricanes had been delivered to us. To this day I think this was quite remarkable at the very height of the battle.[33]

In the Ju 88 shot down by Bob were four crew: Oberleutnant Hey, Leutnant Bein, Oberfeldwebel Konig and Oberfeldwebel Rell. The aircraft crashed and burned out at Sidling St Nicholas, Dorset. The crew were captured unhurt, which provides a view from the German perspective. The pilot, Sigurd Hey, had volunteered for this flight (normally he was a night flyer). He and his crew set off from Orly.

We arrived over Cherbourg where the Bf 109s had already been waiting for us for half an hour. They escorted us to the British coast and had to return because they were all low on fuel. Thus our only fighter escort from now on was made up from Bf 110s – no protection against thirty or forty Spitfires and Hurricanes now coming from all directions. I was hit in the radiator on my starboard engine. Although I dropped my 500 kilogram bomb immediately and I feathered the damaged engine, I could not hold my position in the formation and began to lag behind. I therefore turned southwards, diving a few thousand feet and tried to reach the French coast on only one engine. Then three spitfires came, attacking from all angles. At first a hit on the controls forced me to hold the aircraft straight and level just by using the trim wheel. Next, the fuselage tank was hit and the aircraft caught fire. It was then I gave the order to bale out but I received no reply because the three of them had already left because of the dense smoke. When the aircraft went into a flat spin I was lucky to get out and landed safely by parachute where I was quickly taken prisoner by two old men with shotguns.[34]

Bob's combat report shows that he was 20,000 feet over Warmwell when they met the raid. He dived straight for the lower bombers,

which were straggling considerably and attacked a Ju 88 from astern, opening fire at 300 yards. The first burst stopped the starboard engine. Overtaking speed was very high so I half rolled upwards and attacked the enemy aircraft from above with a short burst at 100 yards, I broke away and carried out a beam attack from the port side from 300 yards. Enemy aircraft turned away and started diving. As it dived, a burst of fire appeared in front of the tail which flew off. Three people baled out and the enemy aircraft crashed in flames 6 miles north of Maiden Newton.[35]

In 1985, parts of the crashed Ju 88 were recovered and a small piece was sent to Sigurd Hey, the pilot. In his reply, Hey recalled the significance of that day in his life because being shot down ensured his survival. While he went to a British prison camp, many of his colleagues were later transferred to the Russian front and very few came back. Hey's wife also expressed her gratitude to Bob, although the outcome could well have been a more final one for Hey.[36] He had just been lucky. As indeed had Bob since his Hurricane was found to have eleven bullet holes including one in the engine.[37]

Fatigue was becoming a major problem and was probably a factor in the earlier crash between Kings and Simmonds. But overconfidence was also a problem and Bob believed this was to blame for the shooting down of his Hurricane. On 10 October the full squadron scrambled at midday for Portland Bill, where twenty-five enemy aircraft were flying. As the squadron flew upwards they entered cumulus cloud and were split up, so that only five aircraft engaged the enemy. As his aeroplane was emerging from the clouds, Bob was hit: 'A loud explosion under my bottom, a knock on my left hand and a thump as from a hammer, on the left hand side of my body.'[38] His self-imposed training for such an eventuality went into action instantly as he hit the stick to go straight back down through the cloud.

Being shot down was a profound shock. He had felt himself invincible:

I fell out and all I can tell you is that falling through the sky without a parachute was the most wonderful feeling I've ever known. It was a lovely feeling. Anyway, I realised that I ought to do something about this and so I looked around and I gave a mighty tug and the parachute came out. I was very grateful especially as when I looked up and saw that the parachute was actually a colander! This cannon shell had exploded onto the parachute I'd been sitting on and had sent bits through all sorts of places. Anyway I came down through cloud and came out of the cloud at about 4,000 feet over the most beautiful blue lagoon it really was the most wonderful sight! This was Poole Harbour and I was going towards this island which was Brownsea Island. In those days all the drains of the isles went into a sort of quagmire and where did I land? In that quagmire! I was minus one leg, minus one arm and was knocked out. I came to with an Irishman standing over me saying 'Who are you?' And so I told him in no mean fashion who I was and he was brilliant. He carried me all the way to the jetty where the Navy said they would pick me up and took me to hospital in Poole where they sewed everything up.[39]

One of his first thoughts when he was hit was regret that he would miss his planned wedding on 7 December, but instead his fiancée was given the news that he had survived. He was in one piece but was wounded in the arm and leg.

He had gunshot wounds in his left hand, his shoulder and right foot and was given twenty-eight days' sick leave. While on sick leave, Bob heard the news that he had been awarded a second DFC. The citation commended his initiative and success on engaging the enemy and particular mention was made of his vertical dive through the hostile aircraft.[40] The award reflected success on his new squadron. The squadron recorded it as sixteen confirmed victories (this would be slightly modified later). Urwin-Mann was also awarded a DFC and this was of 'particular satisfaction' as he had been a foundation member of the squadron and therefore 238 could claim all of them while Bob, it was noted, 'had most of his victories with 234 before joining this squadron'.[41] Team spirit in the squadron meant a scorecard was kept of each pilot's individual score while serving with 238.

Meanwhile, as Bob recovered his wedding plans could still go ahead. His bride-to-be was Sheila Ferguson, the daughter of a dentist. When and how they met is not clear but it was in Cornwall and it is possible that she had been a WAAF at St Eval. She was eighteen to his twenty and such a marriage then required the consent of both sets of parents as they were under the legal age. He also needed his CO's agreement. He and Sheila were married in Newquay on 7 December, witnessed by 'Bertie' Wootton.[42] After a fortnight's wedding leave Bob returned to 238 on 21 December, settling his new bride into quarters in the local village at Chilbolton. Things were very different. The air war was now in a new phase, and 31 October would later be defined as the end of the Battle of Britain. Operations slowed down and more off-duty time could be taken. This was not to everyone's satisfaction, and four pilots volunteered for service in the Mediterranean, where they might see more action. The sad news came in that one of the missing pilots from the squadron in August had been found. Word had got through from France that Pilot Officer Cawse's body was washed ashore at Cayeux-sur-Mer and was buried among the English graves there.[43]

In his absence the squadron had been experiencing problems. The Chilbolton site was still being built and progress was far too slow. Just two days before Bob's return, Air Vice-Marshal Sir Quintin Brand arrived by air to inspect and 'spoke in very acid terms' to Major Adams of the Office of Works.[44] Maintaining discipline was not easy. From time to time a pilot would beat up the airfield but the trick was not to get caught in any way and usually resulted in a ticking off. A promising young pilot officer, Wigglesworth, with two and half kills to his name, was an issue. He damaged property in a particularly low bit of flying. He hit the hedge between the pilots' huts and orderly room – the top of the hedges were cut off 'as with a hedging hook' – and broke the operations telephone line. Amazingly he did not crash. On landing he was placed under open arrest and a Committee of Enquiry was held at Middle Wallop. He was tried by court martial, found guilty and fined £10.[45] On 26 December he left the squadron for 67 Squadron. He was killed on 6 February 1942 with 67 Squadron operating Buffalos from Toungoo in Burma. He was twenty-one years old and was buried in Rangoon war cemetery.[46]

There were other reported problems too. An aircraftman used threatening language to a sergeant pilot and was awarded twenty-eight days' detention. He managed to run away and had not yet been found. Another aircraftman had been awarded fourteen days' detention for falsely wearing an air gunner's badge, but he too deserted. When he was found in Bath he was wearing civilian clothing but also had with him items of flying clothing, which he had stolen from the pilots' hut. Theft was an occasional problem both on the camp and in the village and it was noted as 'most disquieting'. Perhaps not so severely looked on was the occasional poaching of fish from the nearby river.[47]

The new base was the recipient of gifts. For the officers' mess came a small billiard table and several sets of chess from Mr Lewis of Leckford. John Spedan Lewis was a very wealthy man who was the chairman and founder of the John Lewis Partnership. It was he who had the idea of creating the partnership, a very advanced idea for its time. Squadron Leader Fenton was fortunate enough to be a frequent guest at Lewis's home at Leckford, where Lewis also maintained his office.[48] The chess sets encouraged a 'nascent passion for chess, which had been steadily growing for some time', and there was also a passion among the pilots for making model aeroplanes. Bob retained a strong enjoyment for chess but model making was never of interest to him. The officers' mess was now at last a wooden hut (it had formerly been a tent), and was nicknamed Fenton's Folly. A top for the bar was donated and was erected in the mess just before Christmas at mess expense. The base of the bar was painted blue and decorated with figures of Hurricanes in gold applied by stencil cut by Sergeant Pearson. Other gifts included chocolates for the pilots sent by Mrs Baines, who was the wife of a previous CO of 238, while warm woollies were also received from a Miss Robertson of the Drywock, Wendover and the Paignton knitting circle. The airmen had dances and cinema shows in the village hall and the village maintained 'their care of the men in the usual generous way'. Christmas dinner was kept in 'warm and cheerful style' by those officers not on leave. All were present, among them Bob.[49] It was, it seems, as good a Christmas as they could make it, not knowing what might come next.

6

A NEW FACE AND A NEW REALITY

Dorset in January 1941 was very cold, with snow on the ground, and there was little happening. The operations record for Warmwell station uses the phrase 'nothing of interest' on both 1 and 2 January. There was an incident on the third day, but it did not cause much concern: 'A Hurricane plane from Wallop crashed on the 'drome late in the afternoon. The pilot injured but it is not thought seriously and was taken to Sick Quarters.'[1] There was apparently nothing more to report, but the accident was rather more serious than the reporter indicated and the station itself was partly to blame for the crash. The pilot was Bob and the injuries were life-changing.

Warmwell was the forward station for Middle Wallop, situated near the coast. Squadrons from Wallop took turns to base themselves there for a couple of days during operations. 609 Squadron regularly had to use Warmwell and their diarist wrote that it possessed 'in rather irregular proportions, the two chief characteristics of a forward station – action and discomfort'.[2]

Every third day at mid-day the pilots would set off from Wallop in squadron formation, their cockpits bulging optimistically with sponge bags, pyjamas and other articles of toilet which they got very little opportunity of using. Sleeping accommodation was provided for visiting squadrons in the Sergeants quarters, but after some experience the pilots preferred to accommodate themselves as best they could in the Dispersal tent which was furnished with beds, dirty blankets and an assortment of unreliable telephones.[3]

Meals at Warmwell were a particular bone of contention between the station authorities and the airmen. The Central Gunnery School was based at Warmwell and had meals at fixed times. The visitor pilots on operational duties rarely had fixed times and Warmwell, even at the height of the battle in August 1940, failed to see the visitors' point of view. Wing Commander Howard DFC, the station commander at Warmwell, was quoted as remarking, 'I commanded a Fighter Squadron myself some years ago and we always had our meals at regular times.' As 609 reported with a dry sense of humour, 'All our efforts to get the Luftwaffe to respect the Central Gunnery School meal times having failed, dead-lock occurred.' The pilots and their crews resorted to bacon and eggs on a primus stove in the tent.[4] Warmwell seemed incapable of understanding the needs of a first-line fighter squadron.

Five months after 609 had highlighted the attitude problems at Warmwell, 238 Squadron had a serious need for facilities at the station. 238 had been at readiness over Christmas and on 3 January 10 Group asked for volunteers as they wanted to put day fighters up at night on a clear, moonlit night. Fenton was absent and Bob, as acting CO, would lead them. Jacky Urwin-Mann, the other flight commander, also volunteered. Bob was still suffering from a severed Achilles tendon so needed a couple of crew to help him into his Hurricane. Once in the air at 15,000 feet, they could see a thin layer of cloud below but the brilliant moonlight shone through it, showing the countryside underneath. It was exceptionally cold and Bob realised there was a problem when his instrument readings failed to make sense. The temperature gauge was unchanged but the pressure was dropping. He called up Middle Wallop on the VHF. The more reliable VHF had only been installed in 238 Squadron since 13 October and was much appreciated by all the pilots for its clarity of speech and lack of interference from other stations, such as the BBC's Overseas Service.[5] Wallop, realising the seriousness of the situation, recalled Bob and gave him a course for Warmwell where they would instruct the duty officer to fire rockets to show him where it was. Bob was advised to try to get back before the engine stopped.

At 10,000 feet the engine did what it had been threatening and stopped and Bob was gliding down on that moonlit night with plenty of time to think about his situation. The course given by Middle Wallop was 'brilliant', in Bob's words, and he came through the cloud right over Warmwell, which could not have been better. Bob had been to Warmwell before and knew it had a long runway, with hangars at one end and a wood at the other. Bob chose to come in over the hangars and was secure in the knowledge that a Hurricane could land at speed with its wheels up and he could walk away. Sergeant Batt of 238 Squadron had done just that in August in his Hurricane. However, unknown to Bob, the airfield had been bombed since his last visit and several tons of large rocks had been brought in to fill the craters. He landed and his aeroplane went straight into the rocks. For many years after he thought he had gone into an unmarked crater but was told later that it was the rocks into which his plane had slammed.[6]

I sat in the harness with a broken arm and my face was knocked off on the gun sight but I wasn't knocked out. I remember looking up at the sky and then it suddenly went dark, so I put my good hand up to my head and found my nose on top of my head, which didn't seem quite right somehow! About that time, a couple of blokes turned up to try to get me out. My feet were tangled up in the rudder bars and I remember getting very cross with them because they tore my trousers pulling me out and they were my only decent pair of trousers![7]

The following month another airman from 238 Squadron had a similar problem with an iced-up plane; he lost control in a thunderstorm and was killed. Accidents happened and men were shot down; Fenton, the CO of 238, was fatalistic: 'In the earlier part of the battle there was little time to get to know people. Sometimes I would say hello to a new arrival, tell him he could fly with me that day, a day or two later he would be gone.'[8] Bob was later told, although there is no evidence, that the duty officer, having seen no action for a few days, was in the pub. This could also explain the hopeful assumption in the station records that the pilot had not been seriously injured. He did note a great deal of enemy bombing activity during the night and an 'explosion not very far away about mid-night'.[9] The station's sick bay nursing sister was more aware of the seriousness of the crash.

After a night spent on the base, where Bob could clearly recall even many years later the soothing and warm voice of the nursing sister, he was transferred to the local cottage hospital. This hospital had an operating theatre but no resident doctors as the local Army division supplied their needs. The Army surgeon was called in to stitch up Bob's damaged face and he was able to replace his dislodged right eye and secure his nose.

They used to have VAD's which were trainee nurses, usually young girls. They left one of these young girls and I came round perfectly well and she chatted away to keep up my spirits but the only thing she could talk about was the large lady who'd died in this bed! Which didn't really make me very happy![10]

He was then transferred to the nearby military hospital at Bovington Camp, Dorset. The cheering news there was that he was on the ward where Lawrence of Arabia had died in 1935.[11]

The trauma of such a crash and the resultant injuries were life-threatening. In 1940, reliable methods of controlling bacterial infections were limited – penicillin was not in medical use at this stage of the war – so relatively small injuries could quickly develop into life-threatening situations, especially if the injury involved contamination with dirt.[12] Bob was young and very fit, which helped his survival, but as his body recovered it was clear he needed specialist plastic surgery for his facial injuries. He was moved again, this time to Park Prewett hospital in Hampshire, where he was treated by Harold Gillies, a New Zealand surgeon of considerable repute. To most people, a combination of plastic surgery and the RAF in the Second World War instantly conjures up Archibald McIndoe and the famous Guinea Pig Club. But the wards at East Grinstead were not the only specialist treatment places for badly injured servicemen, nor was McIndoe the only plastic surgeon.[13]

In 1939, specialist maxillofacial units were established by the Ministry of Health in consultation with two eminent surgeons, William Kelsey Fry and Harold Gillies. Both men had developed considerable expertise on serious facial injuries during the First World War, Fry gaining an MC for his very considerable courage in tending men while under heavy fire in 1915. Pioneering techniques, processes and attitudes in plastic surgery were developed during and after the First World War and astonishing strides were made in helping to rehabilitate men whose facial injuries were deeply distressing. The Queens Hospital at Sidcup in Kent was to become known as the birthplace of modern plastic surgery and leading this was Harold Gillies. In 1936, Gillies earned the lasting gratitude of a young Cranwell cadet. Brian Kingcombe had just arrived at RAF Cranwell and shortly after his arrival suffered a serious car crash. His nose, cheeks and jaw were crushed and his left eye had dropped down, giving him double vision. The RAF surgeons could do little but his tenacious mother tracked down Harold Gillies, who restored his face and his eye and enabled Kingcombe to complete his training at Cranwell. Kingcombe would later earn DSO, DFC and Bar. Assisting on that operation was a young cousin of Gillies, Archibald McIndoe. McIndoe's career had been considerably assisted by Gillies and Archibald was to make his reputation in the Second World War.[14]

McIndoe based himself at East Grinstead. At the outbreak of war he was thirty-nine and he and his Guinea Pigs would become famous, assisted by his effective use of publicity and his 'courage and belief in the proper course of action for treating the injured'. He was assisted by his 'well-developed irreverence for rank and officialdom', which was a quality much appreciated by his RAF patients.[15] East Grinstead may have been the best-publicised unit, but it was not the only one. Other RAF specialist centres for burns and maxillofacial injuries were at Ely, Cosford, Halton and Wroughton.

Gillies selected Park Prewett, a psychiatric hospital outside Basingstoke, for his use. Rooksdown was the private wing of the large mental hospital and in 1939 it was in use as temporary quarters for nurses. Fry and Gillies arrived to take a look and one young nurse exclaimed, 'Ye gods … a man at last!' Gillies turned to Fry and remarked, 'Obviously this is the place for us.'[16] So it became a 200-bed maxillofacial unit, the biggest unit in the country. The largest room, despite opening straight into a busy corridor, became the operating theatre, complete with the original plaster ceiling and dust-laden cornices. That Basingstoke was also not far from some excellent fishing rivers may also have influenced Gillies, who was a highly skilled fly fisherman.[17]

The RAF was the only service to have centres for its own men. Casualties of the Army and Navy were treated at regional units. Gillies was consultant plastic surgeon to the RAF, consulting advisor to the Ministry of Health, civil consultant to Admiralty and chief plastic surgeon to London County Council. Rooksdown had Marine, Army and Navy personnel from the campaign in France and, with the Blitz, an increasing number of civilians with injuries due to flying glass. Many of the cases of burns at Rooksdown were more severe than at East Grinstead. Gillies personally supervised the largest plastic surgery unit at Park Prewett. 'No British surgeon can have spent more time in the operating theatre in the care of the Army, Navy and civilian air raid casualties than Gillies at Basingstoke.'[18]

Gillies described the scene: 'On the front lawn could be found burned pilots and soldiers, cleft lip and palate babies, bombed housewives, half a dozen Army gunshot wounds to the face, and several German prisoners of war.'[19] Plus at least one pilot from 238 Squadron was there, Sergeant McLaughlin. This was the environment to which Bob was admitted, being looked after in a hospital where he sat side by side with those civilians from London and other places whom he had been trying to protect. The surgery he required was extensive and would result in no less than twenty operations. Gillies had a cheerful and relaxed bedside manner, visiting Bob with a bottle of whisky and a choice of noses.[20]

10 March 1941 was Bob's twenty-first birthday. This was a major milestone then since it was the legal age of majority. It was normally a date

to be celebrated; he could now sign legal documents and vote, although there were no elections in wartime. He was officially an ace, with two DFCs to prove it, but he did not know if he would fly again. He had been married for three months, but his accident was a major shock to his young wife. He was a very different man in many ways and the most obvious change was the physical one to his face. 'I suffered every time I looked in the mirror and was sure that I had been quite handsome. But now, to me, I was unrecognisable. I had found that to some extent, your face creates your character and your character creates your face. Either way I had changed, and I did not know what I was.'[21] While the strain on the men so affected is obvious, the strain on the wives is less clear. They knew they were the lucky ones; their men were still alive. However, this had come at a cost and dealing with the aftermath of the crash and life-changing surgery fell on the shoulders of a nineteen-year-old bride who was simply not equipped to deal with a husband who had changed so much. Bob, to some extent, blamed himself and felt he, just one and half years older, should have done more to assist the young Sheila, who 'could not understand my temper or the trauma'. It was not just his face that had changed but also his personality as he endeavoured to come to terms with the trauma of the situation and an uncertain future.

The effect of this crash and my previous wounds had left me very bad tempered. I had it explained to me that my nerves had been working overtime for some months and my body had suddenly stopped, but the nerves carried on for a while, and everything had to give. How correct this was I don't know. But it made sense to me.[22]

Today we have a slightly better understanding of such trauma and in Gillies he had a surgeon who had a long history of dealing with the psychological effects of facial mutilation. Gillies' biographer quotes Thomas Hardy in this regard: 'More life may trickle out of man through thought than through a gaping wound.'[23] It would not be until 1942, with the publication of the memoirs of a young pilot, that the public at large began to understand the impact of facial disfigurement. Bob kept a copy of Hillary's book *The Last Enemy*. He at least had not been burned, but he could relate to Hillary's experience.

Brian Kingcombe, whose facial injuries pre-dated the war, was later admitted to the Guinea Pig Club by McIndoe in the post-war years, as was Bob. Kingcombe felt like an outsider and uncomfortable among the rest of the club's members as his injuries had not occurred in combat. He observed,

> Whenever those who have had a shared common horrendous experience gather together, they have a special bond, an intimacy, an invisible but almost intangible barrier that outsiders can never penetrate, however warmly they may be welcomed.[24]

Gillies did not leave any record of his views on disfigurement, but his cousin and protégé McIndoe's views were:

> The impact of disfiguring injuries on the young adult is unusually severe. The majority have been strong and healthy, and have given no consideration to illness and injury, or to its possible effects. They are usually unprepared mentally for the blow, so for a period they may be physically lost, depressed, morose, pessimistic, and thoroughly out of tune with their surroundings.[25]

Both Gillies and McIndoe knew that rehabilitation was important for the young men they treated and group therapy was an essential way of maintaining morale. Apart from their facial and other injuries these men were in their early twenties, and were otherwise 'fit and healthy, exuberant and above all intelligent – a *sine qua non* for being accepted and trained by the RAF in the first place'. They may have been wounded but they weren't sick.[26] McIndoe encouraged his famous Guinea Pig Club. Park Prewett also had a club, the Rooksdown Club, and since Gillies, unlike McIndoe, avoided the press, the role of 'Rooksdown House and the Rooksdown

Club with rehabilitant injured servicemen and civilians during the war remains virtually unknown'.[27] It was, like the Guinea Pig Club, a way of patients keeping in touch with each other, establishing a support network and educating the public. Its more diverse membership meant that close relationships, as with the Guinea Pigs, were less likely to be formed.[28]

While fellow sufferers may assist in many essential ways, it was the attitudes of the public that were the key to full rehabilitation. McIndoe encouraged his men to visit public houses in East Grinstead, and similarly Gillies' patients, Bob included, went into Basingstoke. Bob, together with other likeminded patients, would pile into a car and head into town, in just the same way they had done in previous times. Only now the situation was very different and it took courage to face the public. The Red Lion still exists today and was an old-fashioned coaching inn. Walking into the pub in numbers helped, but, as they arrived, the sight of their badly damaged faces, disfigured by burns and with no eyelids or noses in some cases, caused those in the pub to shrink away. As the regulars flinched from the horrifying sights, the big blonde barmaid took the opposite approach. She came out from behind the bar and threw her arms around each man, warmly welcoming them, blithely ignoring their injuries and treating them as the young men they were. It was balm to their damaged souls and in Bob's words 'she deserved a medal', even if they did think she was on Gillies' payroll.[29]

Outings such as this assisted rehabilitation, but all they really wanted was get back into the air and be a normal pilot again. The official policy was tough and there was a ninety-day rule. If after this time the man in question was not fit for active service he was invalided out and passed into civilian hospitals. He 'arrived back in civilian life without hope, broken in spirit, bitter and disillusioned'.[30] McIndoe and others fought hard over this, proposing that the men be actively employed during convalescence as ferry pilots or in control towers.[31] This ninety-day rule seems to have been relaxed in some cases as Bob was back on strength in May, even if he still required some friendly medical assistance.

Grateful for not having been burned and with a new face and a new nose, albeit not what it should have been owing to an accident with a door shortly after that operation, in Bob's mind there was only one way forward: 'My overriding love of flying was the banner I followed.'[32] The trouble was that his eyesight was affected by the smash to his face. His right eye was lower than the other by about a quarter of an inch. Looking straight ahead was fine, but when looking up it resulted in double vision (diplopia). However, he managed to conceal this fact, knowing that eye examinations were conducted at eye level. 'So I went back with a fairly phoney medical review.'[33] He was going to fly again.

On 15 May 1941, Bob was posted to 66 Squadron at Perranporth, on the northern coast of Cornwall. Two days later he was back in a Spitfire for the first time since his accident. He spent thirty-five minutes in flying practice and then did a thirty-five-minute sector recce.[34] It was essential practice as the next day he had an important appointment in London at Buckingham Palace for the investiture of his DFC and Bar. In his exuberance and the excitement of flying again, he headed off without a map; after all, he knew southern England very well by now from the air. But he lost his way on the flight to Kenley and had to land at Lympne to refuel, where some friendly directions finally led him straight to Kenley. He attended Buckingham Palace accompanied by his wife and his mother to receive his DFC and Bar from King George VI, followed by a celebratory meal at the well-known Lyons Corner House.[35] This was not a champagne family.

After this excitement it was back to work at Perranporth and the routine of convoy patrols. Perranporth was a very new airfield, built as a satellite base to Portreath. It had several disadvantages as it was – quite literally – on the cliff edge. Just a few yards from the runway the cliffs fell two hundred feet to the sea, and the airfield was exposed to fierce storms. There were no hangars so the salt corroded both the aircraft and the cars. There were also old mine workings close by. There was no aircraft control tower or any means of radio communication between aeroplane and ground, which was challenging.[36] Taxiing accidents and landing accidents were frequent. There was one advantage: as summer approached, the nearby beach proved popular.[37] It was, after all, a holiday destination in normal times.

66 Squadron had been based at Exeter and was moved to Perranporth in late April 1941. Accommodation was very difficult. The officers were given rooms in the nearby Droskyn Castle Hotel, which remained open to guests. Sergeants were billeted at 'Tregundy' and St George's farm at Perranporth. Airmen were billeted to a point of extreme overcrowding in Atlantic View Hotel and Fair View Hotel, sleeping side by side on the floor of hotels with no lights or hot water. Shortly the airmen of the flights moved out into billets on the camp.[38]

The CO of 66 Squadron was Atholl Forbes, who was finding administration very difficult owing to the lack of offices and communications. Bob was posted to 66 to take command of B Flight. Commanding A Flight was 'Dizzy' Allen, who was described as being 'anything but conventional. He was twenty-one, resourceful, unpredictable and one hell of a fighter pilot.'[39] But Bob's record as a fighter pilot did not go unnoticed by the squadron and it was recorded in the operations record book: 'It is noted that F/Lt Doe has 14½ confirmed victories to his credit, plus 4 probables.'[40] What was not fully known until well after the war, when the dust had settled and overclaiming had been checked, was the considerable success by Bob in the Battle of Britain. He was confirmed with fifteen victories, most of which can be verified from German records, making him one of the highest-scoring aces of the battle, just behind Frantisek, Ginger Lacey, Eric Lock and Brian Carbury.[41] This, it should be noted, was achieved in just six weeks' operational flying, with two different aircraft; four weeks with 234 Squadron at Middle Wallop and less than two weeks operational flying with 238 Squadron.

Bob returned not to the full, adrenalin-charged action of the battle but to the routine patrols he had found so boring. The typical routine was mainly flying in pairs on interception patrols. 'We started doing convoy patrols which is flying round and round a lot of ships, nothing happening. Grey skies, rain falling, miserable, no action, no fun, nothing! We were bored to tears.'[42] Occasional sightings of an enemy aircraft relieved the boredom. On 2 June Bob was the leader on such a patrol with Sergeant Stevens. At 14,000 feet about fifty miles off Lands' End an order came through on the radio which Bob could not fully hear but Stevens could. It was an order to intercept an enemy raid over the Isles of Scilly. With the fully working radio Bob signalled to Stevens to take the lead, and as he passed under Stevens Bob saw an enemy aircraft, a Ju 88. Before it was totally obscured by thick cloud and haze he managed to get in a two-second burst at 400 yards which entered the fuselage behind its engines.[43] This was a rare moment of excitement. Other duties might include escorting damaged bombers safely back to land, as when he escorted a Wellington in from the sea on 19 June.[44]

He was certainly not alone in feeling frustrated at the inability to get to grips with the enemy. With him in 66 Squadron was a young pilot officer, 'Laddie' Lucas, who referred to the operations from Perranporth as humdrum.[45] Also joining 66 on 14 July was William Raoul Daddo-Longlois, aged nineteen. He was, wrote Lucas, exactly the 'calibre of young officer whom the RAF wished to attract. Public school educated, intellectual sharp, above average at games, smart, personable and determined.'[46] He was a superb flyer but he was 'restless and impatient, easily bored and possessed of an undisguised urge to engage the enemy'.[47]

Keeping a young group of action-oriented fighter pilots motivated and keen was not an easy task. Something was happening, however, as their Spitfires were gradually removed to have extra fuel tanks added under one wing. Spitfires were designed as short-range fighters and the modifications enabled the Spitfire IIa to escort the bombers further into enemy territory. The changes were not popular; the modified Spitfires were heavy, very slow and the polite phrase was that they flew like a 'brick-built shed'. Taking off on the clifftop was bad enough but these made it harder. After his first practice in the new aircraft, Bob's description was succinct: 'bloody dangerous aeroplanes'.[48]

The regular shipping patrols were now interspersed with occasional daylight sorties with Bomber Command across 120 miles of English Channel to France's Brittany peninsula. The key target was Brest, where Hitler's prized warships *Scharnhorst*, *Prinz Eugen* and *Geisenau* had been based since 31 March.[49] On 24 July the squadron acted as close escort wing, together with 152 Squadron and Bob's old squadron, 234, on a heavy and highly successful daylight raid on Brest.[50] Bob counted the aircraft: thirty-six long-range Spitfires escorting three Flying Fortresses, eighteen Hampdens, seventy-eight Wellingtons, fifteen Stirlings and fifteen Halifaxes.[51] He was in the air for two hours and escorted a damaged Hampden back. The escort was as much for reassurance as anything else, so that someone would know if they went down and where. He was in the air for another two hours later that same day, escorting a Sunderland looking for men in the sea at 1,000 feet five miles off French coast.[52]

These daylight raids took a heavy toll on the bombers. A witness recalled the return of the bombers, many badly damaged, many with dead crew on board and several 'belly landing' with bombs still hanging from their racks. 'We were kept busy with tractors and heavy lorries pulling the aircraft wrecks away from the landing area to make it safe for subsequent aircraft to land.'[53]

During August there were two more long-range sorties. On 16 August twelve Spitfires of the squadron together with 152 Squadron carried out a daylight offensive sweep over Brest. It was led by the CO, Atholl Forbes, and included 'Dizzy' Allen, Bob, Daddo-Longlois and 'Laddie' Lucas. The next day there was a disconcerting reminder of Bob's injuries when during a fighter sweep over Cherbourg he had to turn back after thirty minutes: 'Had to return & land with one eye didn't like it at all.'[54]

Meanwhile there was other, more personal news from home. His father's employer, Sir Emsley Carr, died on 31 July.[55] On 5 August, his widow, Lady Carr, wrote to Winston Churchill thanking the Prime Minister for his kind enquiries during Carr's short illness and described Sir Emsley's death as beautiful: 'Just 5 minutes before the end, a flight of 12 planes flew over our house towards the setting sun to herald his arrival at the Portal.'[56] Of more practical consideration was the impact on Bob's parents in their tied cottage, but Lady Carr, although not in the best of health herself, remained at Wonford.

On 18 August, Bob was posted to 130 Squadron Portreath as B Flight Commander. 130 was a newly minted fighter squadron and Bob's task, with his fellow officers, was to create team spirit in this newly operational squadron.[57] Despite the eyesight scare – and Bob had kept any eyesight concerns strictly to himself – his previous CO, Athol Forbes, assessed him as an above-average fighter pilot.[58] Bob's stay with 130 was short, but there were two memorable moments.

Predannack was another new airfield created in 1941. Situated on the tip of the Lizard peninsula on the south coast of Cornwall, it was well placed as a forward base. 130 Squadron was sent there on 31 August to join three other squadrons on a mission to escort six Blenheims to bomb Lannion aerodrome in France. 66 Squadron was close escort, with 263, 313 and 130 Squadrons taking off ten minutes later on fighter sweeps at different altitudes. 130 Squadron flew on patrol twenty-five miles from French coast at 25,000 feet. They saw two Me 109s but these did not come into range. The squadron returned to Portreath at 18.30.[59] 'Dizzy' Allen recalls it slightly differently in his bullish memoirs. In his recollections, published in 1982, he writes of his squadron, 66, attacking Lannion airfield on an opportunistic basis and claims full credit for the successful attack. Unless there was a separate, completely unrecorded incident, 66 Squadron was not alone and Lannion was an official target.[60]

Like many others, 130 Squadron was becoming more international, with Canadian, Free French and other pilots of various nationalities. Despite the occasional cross-Channel sortie, the convoy patrols were hard work and occasionally high spirits overcame caution. A Canadian sergeant pilot, A. E. Mokanyk, indulging in some aerobatics over the airfield, failed to pull out of a dive and crashed into the dispersal hut. He was killed almost instantly.[61]

By October 1941 Bob had been back on operational flying duties for five months – three with 66 Squadron and just two with 130 Squadron – when he was posted, on 22 October, to a training unit. 10 Group was taking stock in 1941 of the state of their fighter pilots. Since April, squadrons had been asked to send quarterly returns to HQ listing operational dates, separating out war operational duties, the number of operational flights, number of times a pilot had baled out, and the number of times he had been wounded or injured. This was to be collated in order to determine when a pilot 'should be considered for period of rest for six months or more off operational flying'.[62]

In Fighter Command in 1940, due to the high demand for pilots, there were insufficient Operational Training Units (OTUs). This meant that, in effect, over one-third of all squadrons became training organisations as Command tried to manage the clash between 'immediate operational requirements and the long-term needs of training'. Too many young pilots were lost due to having been sent straight from flying Harts in SFTS to an operational squadron. One instance is quoted of a pilot who had only flown a Tiger Moth. The view was that the OTU syllabus had been makeshift and unstandardised, so in December 1940 Fighter Command drew up a standard syllabus.[63]

With difficulties in the OTU and longer courses, the output from the fighter OTUs in winter 1940/41 was small. Demand was still high; new squadrons were being formed because of this. The fighting may have died down, but invasion was still a strong possibility and a renewal of the fighter and bomber daytime attacks was still probable. Night attacks by the Germans continued. With the expansion of the number of OTU courses, over 100 experienced pilots, including Bob, were taken out of the front-line squadrons to become instructors.[64] The first-line squadrons were requesting improvements in fighter tactics and gunnery. Target towing was introduced and by the end of 1941 masters had been added to the flights so that dual instruction in air-to-air firing could be carried out.[65] By autumn 1941 there were eleven fighter OTUs. A day OTU had sixty-eight operational aircraft and around ninety pupil pilots on six-week courses. There was expansion overseas also, with an OTU in Canada, two further OTUs in the Middle East and one in India.[66]

Bob was posted to 57 OTU Hawarden, Cheshire, on 22 October 1941 to command C Flight and his rank as flight lieutenant was confirmed on 6 November. His relieved comment was, 'Rather glad of a rest'.[67] 57 OTU was established in 1940. Unlike the rather more primitive conditions on his previous bases in Cornwall, Hawarden had the well-equipped gym and theatre at Hawarden County School, placed at the disposal of officers and airmen for physical training and recreation. The officers' mess was Hawarden Castle, once the home of W. E. Gladstone, an impressive building still privately owned today by the Gladstone family.[68]

By January 1942 Hawarden had become the recognised beacon among the OTUs. As a result, all day-fighter OTUs were reorganised on the Hawarden model, which was seen as an efficient and successful system. The peak year was 1942, when training effort was at its maximum and 4,353 pilots were trained.[69] It had a creative attitude to training and had developed a synthetic trainer. This was a mock-up of an aircraft with situations that the trainer, sitting at a desk behind, could change for the pupil. During February 1941, the Hawarden trainer became well established under the direction of Pilot Officer N. Hutchison and all OTUs were ordered to inspect it.[70] In March 1942, Hawarden had three concurrent courses beginning their training. There were eight flights led by well-decorated and operationally experienced officers. A Flight was led by a New Zealander, Flight Lieutenant G. H. Francis, DFC, while B Flight was Flying Officer Tony Gaze, DFC. Gaze, an Australian, was to gain three DFCs during the war and later became a racing driver.[71] There was also Flight Lieutenant Rose, DFC, who would remain with 57 OTU as long as Bob, and Flight Lieutenant McMullen, DFC and two Bars.[72]

The flying training was intensive but the emphasis had changed from aerobatics to effective air fighting. 'It was constantly being drilled into us that air fighting was our role and that flying ability was only part of it. We were allowed almost limitless clay pidgeon [sic] shooting to get us used to allowing the all-important deflection to bring down our opponents.'[73] There were inevitable accidents and, occasionally, a death in training and the instructors had to rescue aeroplanes from strange places. Bob went to Sealand, a short distance from Hawarden, where he had to fly a Spitfire out of a small field where it had force landed.[74]

The students were well aware of the distinguished men in their midst. Even if they were of much the same age, these experienced and well-decorated men were objects of awe. One excited pilot wrote to his parents, 'These Spits are wizard kites and I enjoy being here and being among the chaps who have done the work in the famous tussles.' The same writer also observed that some of the instructors resented being on training when they would rather have been operational and that some were still recovering from flying accidents.[75] Indeed, working as a training instructor was not to everyone's taste. The Flying Training Research Committee was aware of the challenges this posed for some. There were criticisms of the policy of relief employment at OTUs between operational tours.

The duration of stay at OTUs is too long, namely 6 months. Personnel tend to lose the offensive spirit. The atmosphere at OTUs lacks the freedom, excitement and spirit of adventure of the Operational Station, so that when personnel return to operational work they are not properly attuned, at least until they have done several sorties.

Instructional duties at OTUs are the reverse of a rest for at least 50 per cent of personnel. Unless a man likes teaching the job is harder work for him than operational flying. The long hours of duty at ITUs tend to produce fatigue and staleness.[76]

Bob, however, was one of those who enjoyed instructing. He remained with the OTU for two tours of duty and his success earned him a promotion in May 1942 to acting squadron leader.[77] Tony Pickering, a fellow Battle of Britain pilot, was also based there and recalls his boss with great affection. Bob was a hard taskmaster but never asked his men to do things that he personally would not do.[78]

For all his enjoyment of training, there was a family problem. Lady Carr, the widow of Sir Emsley Carr, did not survive her husband for very long and died in May 1942.[79] This posed a challenge as Bob's parents now needed to move since they lived in a tied cottage. They moved to a small thatched cottage on the corner of Police Station Lane in the village of Droxford, in Hampshire. Just across the road was the old White Horse pub. Bob occasionally worked in there on his visits, pulling pints behind the bar.[80]

Meanwhile in July 1942 he was selected to attend a pilot gunnery instructors' course at Sutton Bridge, home to the Central Gunnery School. Here he was reunited with his friend Budge Harker, with whom he had formed such a successful team during the Battle of Britain. Harker now was commissioned.[81] The man in charge of CGS was 'Sailor' Malan, the South African war ace. On 12 July Bob piloted a Magister III with Sailor Malan and by the end of the instructors' course Malan's assessment of Bob's marksmanship air to ground on drogue was 'average' and as a marksman in combat he was rated 'good average'. This is not bad for a man with double vision. But as an instructor Bob was rated 'above average'.[82]

After the course it was a return to Hawarden, where his wife Sheila was now expecting their first child. But the RAF in wartime did not make things easy as 57 OTU was ordered to move to Eshott, Morpeth, in Northumberland in November just when Sheila was due. This distance at such a crucial time would have been a major difficulty for someone in any other service but he was a pilot and he had access to aircraft. Bob flew to Eshott on 6 November and then back to Hawarden as a passenger the next day; this was repeated on 7 November as he delivered three more Spitfires. He remained with the unit at Morpeth and flew with them until 19 November when he headed back to Cheshire. Lynne, his daughter, was born the next day and he entered the notable event in his logbook.[83]

It was to Eshott that the irrepressible Eddie Sparkes was sent after having completed his basic flying training in Canada. He wrote home,

Have just arrived in Eshott, north of Morpeth Northumberland. Am even further off the map than when I was at Watton. There is a lot of Bull here, everyone is on their toes to salute and we get periodical parades. I do not think much of that side of it. Being new I am without friends as yet but am in no hurry until I can see the lie of the land. We are four to a nissen hut with a stove in the centre which is lighted about 4 pm. They are certainly going to keep us busy. We work literally from dawn to dusk and for the first three weeks there is not one hour free. Beyond that I have no idea as the orders have not been posted. The food here is truly excellent. A very unusual mess in that respect.[84]

Also posted to Eshott, but as an instructor, was a former colleague of Bob's. Keith Lawrence, with whom he had served in 234 Squadron, now arrived to take over as flight commander of 10 Flight. Bob was now the chief flying instructor (CFI) and, in Keith's view, Bob had not changed. He was 'still Bob. He had his own aeroplane. He decided to make his Spitfire distinctive. So if you saw LZ 33 you knew it was the CFI lurking about in the sky.'[85] The work was intense as there were large numbers of flights to take on the training of the many pilots trained in the Commonwealth. The men came from training camps in Australia, Canada and Rhodesia straight to OTUs where they were trained to become ready for squadron operations. As CFI, Bob was busy managing the vagaries of flying conditions with mixed weather and the challenge to keep up the flying training hours, constantly being chivvied along to finish the syllabus. While there he was involved in training many pilots and two exceptional pilots stood out in Bob's memory: Screwball Buerling, a Canadian, and Dominic Salvatore Gentile, an American. Both went on to very distinguished flying careers, each becoming an ace.[86]

In Keith's view Bob was a natural leader, but he had rather less of a warm recall of the Wing Commander in charge. Wing Commander Palmer was 'a bit of an old B'. He was married to a Frazer Nash heiress. Frazer Nash were expensive and very upper-class cars. 'Palmer spent a lot of time off station looking after his heiress wife.' Much of the load was on the shoulders of his CFI, Bob, and the chief ground instructor.[87]

Eddie Sparkes had a particular memory of Wing Commander Palmer:

Met the CO for the first time in the mess. He was short and tubby but as taut as a set mousetrap. Little black eyes, never at rest, flamed from a putty coloured face. Sitting in his chair, his feet twisted round the back of the chair legs as though he was controlling a fractious animal, he was a fascinating study of restrained violence, punching the air with a stubby forefinger to emphasize every word. I had just met another new pilot at the bar and we started talking to one another in self defense. He was, if anything, a little too smartly turned out with a languid air that I opined could be infuriating. We took our beers to the fireplace. We had hardly turned around when the CO ignored me and came straight to the point with the chap I was talking to. 'So you are married!' 'Yes Sir.' 'Well you should not be flying fighters – and – by the way what is that stuff you've put on your hair. If I went home smelling like that my wife would think that I had been in a brothel!' Instead of quailing before the out-thrust chin the intended victim looked at him calmly and said 'My wife does not know what a brothel smells like sir.' He turned to me and said 'I shall not be in for dinner tonight' and walked out of the mess. The CO also left. I did not see the young officer again. Dinner was a strained affair. I had made a bad start.[88]

Eddie Sparkes was a man destined to continue to fall foul of authority. Sparkes, by his own admission, was not well cut out for service discipline. He disliked taking orders, could not take authority or rank seriously and his standard response to a ticking off, dating back to his schooldays, was to take it in silence and then carry on as if nothing had happened. In a wartime RAF this attitude was not going to go down well and it threatened overall discipline. As he later admitted, 'It must have been difficult for them as well.' It certainly was. Sparkes was already unpopular with the CO and also with the chief flying instructor, Bob, whom Sparkes, who was physically short, described as a tall, thin, bemedalled officer. Another problem with Sparkes was that his sheer joy of flying made him oblivious to any other objectives and he frequently indulged in low flying. Eventually, in exasperation, the CO had him posted to an RAF disciplinary centre.[89]

Sparkes' summing up of the CO at Eshott was not complimentary and was, as seen, reflected by Keith Lawrence, who also served under Palmer. Wing Commander Palmer's assessment of Bob, on whose shoulders he had left so much, was that, while Bob was a good instructor who got results, his temperament was erratic. He summed him up as 'a good worker with a bad temper'.[90] Bob was still coming to terms psychologically with his new situation and he had a very short fuse. As a large man with an exceptionally deep voice, an explosion from Bob was notable. Despite this, Bob's RAF career continued to move upwards even if some of his superiors, such as Palmer, did not always find him easy. Bob was recommended for the newly established Fighter Leaders School.

The Fighter Leaders School was a pet project of Air Marshal Trafford Leigh Mallory. There were twenty pilots only to each course and all were to be carefully selected squadron leaders and wing leaders in embryo. They were all operationally experienced and the three-week course was to provide practical training in the art of formation leadership and tactics. It aimed to give the future leaders experience in leading 'under conditions as nearly representative of active operations as possible', and also to give them some idea of the administration and training of a squadron under field service conditions.[91] Leigh Mallory wrote to the Air Ministry Under-secretary of State after four courses had been held that

the pilots themselves have shown the greatest keenness on these courses and are unanimous in their appreciation of the benefit they have received. Particular attention has been paid to practice in the interpretation of operational instructions and pre-operational briefing. Tuition has also been given in the wider aspects of fighter operations in support of the Army and in Combined operations. Instruction in the elements of squadron administration and discipline is also included.[92]

The flying exercises included sector recce, formation-leading practice, formation attacking and evasive tactics, formation-rendezvous practice and close escort for bombers. The Bristol Channel stood in for the English Channel and much of the day was taken up with flying when practical. Lectures were from 17.30 to 19.00 with a lengthy list of subjects and speakers. These included Air Commodore Basil Embry on escape (he escaped from occupied France in 1940), the lessons of the Dieppe operation, fighter aspects, deflection shooting, Bomber Command from the bomber pilot's view, a fighter reconnaissance squadron's work, tactics over France and an Army officer on Army support. The manufacturer of the latest RAF aeroplane, the Typhoon, came to speak on its performance and further development. The emphasis was mainly tactical but, included under administration – hardly the most exciting subject for fighter pilots – was a brief mention of the airmen in the form of a small booklet entitled 'The Airmen's Welfare'.[93] One aspect not normally found on courses was that these pilots all had the opportunity to fly on operations at the end of the course.

Brian Kingcombe had been sent to the early Fighter Leaders School as 'observer-cum-advisor', but due to the new CO's illness Kingcombe took over the job of establishing the school. It was a task he enjoyed, assisted by, among others, Laddie Lucas. The school moved to Charmy Down in Somerset; obligingly close to Bath and its pubs. He recalls a 'relaxed and enjoyable life if not a health hazard'.[94] The Fighter Leaders School record certainly gives the impression of regular celebrations, and this free and easy style brought it in for criticism.[95] Criticisms included slack systems and lack of detailed briefing and debriefing on operational exercises, and it was recommended that all those on the course start the day with twenty minutes' physical training at 7.30 and that half a day a week set should be aside for organised games. This was presumably with the aim of combating the hangovers.

The official response by Air Commodore Stevens, MC to Group Captain Oliver, DSO, DFC, at HQ Fighter Command referred to Oliver's several pages of 'helpful' suggestions and concluded,

To summarise, I think there is room for detailed improvements in some respects, but one must not lose sight of the fact that this is a Fighter Leaders School wherein the higher principles of leadership and tactics are to be imparted to pilots who are already experienced in operational work. ... We are endeavouring to run the OTU [the OTU was run on the same site] on the lines of a university, the Fighter Leaders School should be run on the lines of a postgraduate course, without regimentation. I think it is fair to say that this course is easily the most popular in the Command, not because of the free and easy atmosphere, but, I believe, because the pilots who attend it feel that they have learned something useful and if they can both learn and like it, then I do not think there is much wrong with the system.[96]

The emphasis on fighter leadership was fully on tactical leadership in the air. Training of the leadership of men was not a well-studied subject by any service at that time and learning came on the job. Most leadership models came post-war, John Adair's action-centred leadership being one of the best-known and most influential.[97] It was not until 1948 that the RAF produced a small booklet, *Leadership: Some Notes for the Guidance of Royal Air Force Officers*, which was given to newly commissioned officers. The power to lead, it states, is achieved through 'force of character'. While some were born as natural leaders, others, it suggested, could hone essential key qualities which it divided into efficiency, energy, sympathy, resolution, courage, tenacity and personality. While admitting the last one was the most mysterious, it emphasised personal integrity as an essential element.[98]

During the war, the Flying Personnel Research Committee touched on elements of leadership while investigating combat stress. It agreed after discussing the matter with ten general duty and eight medical officers that good leadership was a very important factor in enabling men to carry the load. It therefore followed that selection of leaders was most important. One station commander believed that boldness was essential and preferred a young and relatively inexperienced wing leader who was bold to an older and more experienced man who had lost some of his boldness. In addition to having the essential personality a leader also needed to be a first-rate pilot, but one wing leader remarked that the combination of first-rate flying ability and leadership in the same man was rare. All agreed on the importance of squadron commanders flying operationally. The morale of a squadron depended heavily on the quality of leadership rather than on the amount of stress. Medical officers who had the opportunity of observing the fortunes of a squadron over long periods confirmed this. The influence of a leader of outstanding quality, they agreed, might be felt in a squadron long after he had gone.[99]

Success, team building and the recognition of effort were also significant factors. Among day-fighter pilots, the majority considered that individual success mattered far less than the success of the squadron or wing. 'It is the success of the wing that counts. Team spirit is the essence of the game, individualism is hopeless.' And 'so long as the squadron does all right all is well'. Confidence in the aircraft and its maintenance was crucial and many senior officers felt that married men whose wives lived nearby were under more stress.[100]

These lessons were being learnt by the leaders on the job, by watching others and by their own experience of being led and of leading men. Bob had been made an acting squadron leader but had as yet not led an operational squadron and he was keen to get back to a first line role. With his current tour of duty coming to an end, Bob applied for service overseas. Immediately after passing out of FLS and pending his next main posting he joined 118 Squadron at Coltishall in Norfolk on 3 July 1943 as a supernumerary. This squadron was escorting bombers targeting industrial areas across Belgium and Holland. Their CO was Squadron Leader Freeborne, DFC, who had served with Malan in the infamous Battle of Barking Creek. His views on Malan were not positive. Also in 118 Squadron was Cyril Talalla, the Malaysian ace.[101]

Bob was there but a short time and did not fly operationally with them. He was then attached on 15 August to 613 Squadron, based at Snailwell in Cambridgeshire. By chance this was close to his father's birthplace. 613 Squadron had been flying Mustangs since April 1942 and was a tactical reconnaissance unit operating within the short-lived RAF Army Cooperation Command. It was largely long-distance work over the North Sea flying 'Jim Crows' – coastal patrols to intercept enemy aircraft crossing the British coastline, originally intended to warn of invasion in 1940. Flying so far over the sea had its own dangers, of which Bob was well aware: '150 miles out to sea and no dinghy (fool).' (Pilots had to rely solely on their 'Mae Wests' for survival during the battle, but by now most were supplied with inflatable dinghies.[102] These were of most use, of course, when taken with them.)

Events were changing on the Continent as the Germans increased their grip on occupied countries. This shows up in the squadron records:

31 August. After photographic recce F/Lt Doe and F/O J F Overton searched for 1 and half hours for Danish refugees who were escaping from Denmark after the German Declaration of Martial law there. The Danes were in a fleet of small boats which had already been bombed by the Germans but had been sighted and escorted on the previous day by our own aircraft. The little boats disappeared during the night and this attempt to locate them was also unsuccessful.[103]

This event is too early for the famous rescue in October and November 1943, when around 7,000 Danish Jews safely escaped to Sweden on fishing boats all organised by the Danish people. The declaration of martial law led on 29 August to German military forces attacking, disarming and disbanding what was left of the Danish armed forces. Some managed to evade German internment and escaped. Many of these tried to get to Sweden by boat, often with the intention of joining the British armed forces. The view is that these fishing boats were a part of this escape, which would explain the use of costly resources to locate the 'refugees'.[104] Interesting as this new squadron may have been, what Bob was really waiting for was his overseas posting and on 19 October 1943 he left for India with hopes of a less restricting role and more freedom to act.

Right: 1. Bob's mother, Linda Coster, in September 1916.

Below left: 2. Linda Doe with her baby son in 1920.

Below right: 3. The sturdy toddler, aged two years and eleven months.

4. Broadfield House, Reigate, where Bob was born and lived until 1927.

5. Toddler Bob with toy horse and cart.

6. James and Linda
Doe with Bob.

7. Bob in the
countryside.

8. Wonford.

9. James Doe, front right, with his team after building the rockery at Wonford.

10. Bob sitting on the rockery at Wonford.

11. The successful athlete Bob, front right, at Leatherhead Central School, aged thirteen.

12. Bob as a schoolboy with his mother on a church outing to the seaside.

13. Sir Emsley Carr.

14. Bob in 1939.

15. Scotty Gordon of 234 Squadron standing by a 616 Spitfire 'digging for victory' at Leconfield.

Another photo of 234 Squadron pilots taken at
Leconfield in 1939.
Left to right -:
Ken Dewhurst, Cec Hight, P/O Redman,
Pat Horton, Pat Igglesden, Geoff Gout,
Hugh Sharpley, Morty Mortimer-Rose, Bob Doe.
Plus two Station Bods (One with brevy might
be Roy Macey)

16. 234 Pilots at Leconfield.

Right: 17. Squadron Leader Barnett MBE.

Below: 18. 234 Pilots, March 1940. Note: this has to be March 1940 as this was when they got Spitfires.

Some of No: 234 Squadron pilots at Leconfield in December, 1939
Left to right:
Cecil Hight, Hugh Sharpley, Budge Harker, Morty Moetimer-Rose, Pat Gordon, Dick Hardy.
Budge Harker was wounded, Dick Hardy was taken P.O.W., and the others were killed.

19. A relaxed Pat Hughes.

20. 234 Squadron in August 1940. Squadron Leader Barnett flanked by his flight lieutenants Pat Hughes and Theilmann. Hemingway is in civilian clothes and the others are Connor, Owens, Horton, Hight, Hardy, Mortimer-Rose, Dewhurst, Hornby, Bailey, Harker, Boddington, Klein and Szlagowski. Note: dated as Klein and Szlagowski joined 3 August 1940.

21. 234's essential ground crew.

22. Middle Wallop bomb crater.

23. Middle Wallop hangars after the bombing.

24. Middle Wallop bomb damage.

25. Hardy's captured Spitfire in Cherbourg with 234 markings.

26. Hardy's Spitfire repainted in German markings.

Above: 27. The crash at Kings Somborne with the RAF party just leaving the scene.

Left: 28. The memorial to four unknown airmen from the Kings Somborne crash.

29. The funeral of Cecil Hight. Bob is on the left.

30. Members of 234 Squadron on standby in the dispersal hut. The swastika came from an aircraft shot down by Mortimer-Rose.

31. Pat Horton in his Spitfire with A Flight insignia.

Left: 32. 'Minnie' Blake of 238 and 234 Squadron.

Right: 33. Sgt Sibley, 238 Squadron, 'of stocky build and solid character', shot down 1 October 1940.

34. Gordon Batt of 238 Squadron with his Hurricane.

35. Oberleutnant Sigurd Hey, shot down by Bob on 7 October 1940.

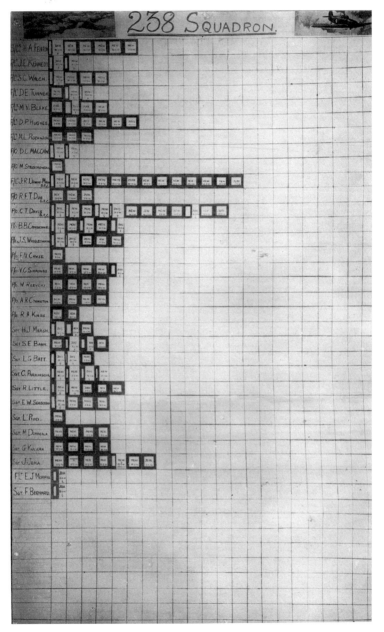

36. The 238 Squadron scorecard.

COMBAT REPORT.

Sector Serial No.	(A)	457
Serial No. of Order detailing Flight or Squadron to Patrol	(B)	
Date	(C)	15.8.40
Flight, Squadron	(D)	Flight: B Sqdn.: 234
Number of Enemy Aircraft	(E)	APPROX 50
Type of Enemy Aircraft	(F)	JAGUARS ME109A + ME110s
Time Attack was delivered	(G)	1815
Place Attack was delivered	(H)	25~S.W. SWANAGE
Height of Enemy	(J)	11,000
Enemy Casualties	(K)	1 JAGUAR + 1 110DE
Our Casualties Aircraft	(L)	NIL
Personnel	(M)	

GENERAL REPORT.   (R)

Jar Blue 2. Patrolling Swanage at 15,000' we
led up behind 50 E.A. BLUE 1 attacked 1 JAGUAR
- then broke away I closed in and followed it down
until it hit the water (the rear gunner was firing all
the time until at 1000' he bailed out) in the dive
I gave it a 7sec burst from 100yds as the
fire from the engine had appeared to stop
I broke away upwards towards a formation of ME110's (3)
which were diving through a thick haze at about
4,500' FIRED rest of ammunition at nearest aircraft -
Pieces flew off it - as I broke away I saw Blue 1 engage
the same A/c which caught fire + crashed in the sea

Signature Robert Doe

O.C.   Section BLUE
        Flight B
        Squadron 234 Squadron No.

Rounds fired 2720

(2557—1611) WL 27388—2553 850 Pads 9/39 T.S. 700 FORM 1181

37. Bob Doe combat report, 15 August 1940.

SECRET. FORM F

COMBAT REPORT.

Sector Serial No. _____ (A) 62

Serial No. of Order detailing Flight or Squadron to
Patrol _____ (B)

Date _____ (C) 16.8.40

Flight, Squadron _____ (D) Flight: B Sqdn.: 234

Number of Enemy Aircraft _____ (E) 40

Type of Enemy Aircraft _____ (F) Me 109.

Time Attack was delivered _____ (G) 18.25

Place Attack was delivered _____ (H) 85 miles S of Isle of Wight

Height of Enemy _____ (J) 21,000

Enemy Casualties _____ (K) 1 Me. 109. 1 Do.18

Our Casualties _____ Aircraft _____ (L) —

_____ Personnel ____ (M) —

GENERAL REPORT _____ (R)

I was Blue 3. When over interception point, at 16,000 I
saw a mass of Me.109's at 21,000 & went up to attack. 3
Me 109's dived down behind us. I climbed up to 21,000
& came across 7 in line astern going S. out to sea. I looked
behind & found 3 on each side diving to attack me. I turned
away & found myself on the tail of an Me.109. I gave 4
bursts of 2 secs. each. Smoke came from engine. It turned on
his back & dived straight down to sea level. I followed it
& landed on water & went straight in.

I went over it & a mile away, I saw a Do.18
coming N. towards coast. I closed my throttle & put
my flaps down. A 740 to 160 m.p.h. I dived & fired at 200
yards & gave it a burst of 4 secs. the rear gunner so as
killed. The rear engine stopped dead. It turned to the right
& I gave it the rest of my ammunition & the front engine
stopped. It landed on water & tipped up before going down
by the rear.

Robert Doe
Blue 3,
B. Flight,
234 Squadron

Signature _____ Blue 3
Section _____ B Flight
Flight ____ Squadron ____ Squadron No. 234

(3567—1511) Wt. 27585—2556 850 Pads 9/29 T.S. 700 FORM 1151

38. Bob Doe combat report, 16 August 1940.

FORM "F"

COMBAT REPORT.

90

Sector Serial No ....(A).................................

Serial No. of Order detailing Flight or
Squadron to patrol.........................(B) 56.

Date...(C) 30/9/40.

Flight, Squadron.............................(D) Flight A. Sqdn. 238.

Number of Enemy Aircraft...............(E) 100+

Type of Enemy Aircraft....................(F) HE 111's + ME 110's

Time Attack was delivered...............(G) 1630

Place Attack was delivered..............(H) 20 miles S of Portland

Height of Enemy..............................(J) 15000 ft.

Enemy Casualties.............................(K) 1 HE 111 destroyed

Our Casualties, Aircraft.................(L) NIL.

Personnel...............(K) NIL.

Searchlights....................................(N) N/A

A.A..(N2)

Range at which fire was opened and estimated
length of burst.............................(P)   1 sec 300 yds
                                                              2 sec 150 yds
                                                              1 sec 200 yds also 3 sec + 5 sec

GENERAL REPORT................................(R) 6 sec 50 yds.

I was Yellow 1. and I attacked with Squadron firing at HE 111 from 2900
300 yds shot 1 sec. burst from front + above. Broke away to port and Rou.
came up underneath and gave 2 sec. burst from below behind
at 150 yds. Starboard engine caught fire + undercarriage dropped.
He broke away from main formation jettisoning bombs. I let him get
away from protecting fighters & turned S. I then attacked front beam Starboard
firing 1 sec burst at 200 yds + a 3 sec burst from astern 5 sec
burst point just quarter sport engine caught fire. He dived down
towards clouds turning back to English coast just above clouds.
Both engines then on fire but rear gunner still firing.
I got to 50 yds range above behind + fired rest of ammunition.
E/A then dived + crashed into sea 15 miles S of Portland Bill. There
were no survivors. Returned base and landed 1700 . No cine camera
gun carried. No of rounds fired 2900.
Confirmed Green 3

Signatures,

Robert Doe

(Section YELLOW
O.C. (Flight A
       (Squadron.   Squadron no. 238

F/o R F T DOE

39. Bob Doe combat report, 30 September 1940.

40. Bob Doe marries Sheila Ferguson in Newquay on 7 December 1940.

41. Harold Gillies at Rooksdown, Park Prewett, with wounded RAF pilots.

42. 130 Squadron pilots. From left to right: Unknown, Sgt Buzz Ogilvie, F/S Mace, P/O Lloyd, unknown.

43. 66 Squadron pilots at Perranporth. From left to right: Sgt Stevens, Sgt Green, Sgt Thomson, F/S 'Duggy' Hunt.

44. Spitfire IIa with a long-range tank.

45. Bob and his flight at 130 Squadron, Portreath, in September 1941.

Officers and N.C.O.s of a Fighter Squadron Somewhere in England

Front row : Fly. Off. L. W. Collingridge, Flt. Lieut. R. F. T. Doe, D.F.C., Sq. Ldr. A. S. Forbes, D.F.C., Fly. Offs. J. H. Pickering, A. L. Clow, E. J. Partridge. Back row : Sergt. N. Reid, Plt. Off. W. R. L. Daddo-Langlois, Sergts. C. G. Green, R. Thompson, Plt. Offs. J. E. Hogg, W. M. Whitamore, P. Olver, Fly. Offs. F. N. Beaufort-Palmer, C. Cookson, Plt. Off. N. J. Durrant, Fly. Off. K. M. Willis

Above: 46. 66 Squadron at Perranporth in 1941.

Right: 47. Tony 'Pick' Pickering in a Master with Bob at Eshott.

48. Local men inspecting a crashed plane in India.

49. 118 Squadron, Coltishall, July 1943. Cyril Tallala, Malaysian ace, is on the aeroplane, Bob is second from right, and third from right is Sgt Joseph Hollingworth.

50. 10 Squadron IAF on the move again.

51. 'Synchronise watches'; Bob and his pilots get ready to set off.

52. Aircraftmen of 10 Squadron IAF.

53. Nawab of Bhopal and pilots of 10 Squadron IAF. From left to right: Eddy (AC), Jonny Milne, L. S. Grewall, Jaspal Singh, R. B. Davis (Adj.), Les Smith, unknown, A. S. Picken, Bob, HH the Nawab of Bhopal, unknown, unknown, unknown, unknown, Ron Jones, Roshan Suri, R. Sujir, unknown, Latimour (?), Ned Sparkes, Chrishna.

Above: 54. Living accommodation; bamboo basha of 10 Squadron IAF.

Right: 55. 224 Group order of battle, showing 10 Squadron at the front.

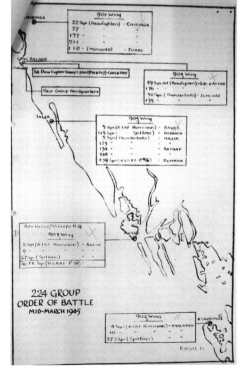

Above: 56. Accident to a 10 Squadron Hurri-bomber.

Left: 57. 32 Squadron Vampires in Egypt.

Below left: 58. 32 Squadron travelling Ops Wagon at Deversoir. From left to right: Pinky Stark, Trevor Copleston, George Smith (at the back), W/C Courtney and Bunny Harvey, with Bob carrying the chair. On the right, Dickie Dicken and Willy Billings.

59. Bob in his 32 Squadron jet.

60. Bob, Gee, Susan and Helen in Egypt.

61. A favourite occupation, Liar Dice.

62. Another winning game of cricket in Egypt; 32 Squadron cricket team.

7

INDIA AND SQUADRON LEADERSHIP

Bob arrived in India in 28 November 1943 at Bombay and headed straight for the transit camp at Worli north of Bombay, remaining there until 15 December. It had not been a comfortable journey out. He had boarded the *Strathmore* at Liverpool together with twenty-five other badly needed aircrew, all of whom were going to India. The ship then went north to the Clyde, where it joined a fast convoy, which headed south for the Mediterranean. This was the first convoy to risk heading through the Mediterranean. The alternative route via Cape of Good Hope was relatively safer but considerably longer. Bob, whose one and only experience at sea had been his boyhood cruise to Scandinavia, sighted the coast of Morocco and then the ship headed into Gibraltar, where no one was allowed onshore. The convoy then proceeded along the north coast of Africa to Bizerta, the most northern point of Africa (in Tunisia). Although the Allies were now in control of the northern coast of Africa, shipping was still at risk and the convoy was attacked at night by both torpedoes and bombs. To the pilots on board, more used to attacking than being sitting ducks, it was a restricting, frustrating and frightening situation. Their naval escort managed to bring down two bombers, one of which damaged another ship as it crashed. The convoy then sailed on to Sicily, sighting Mount Etna and Italy, and then to Benghazi, Alexandria, Port Said and through the Suez Canal, stopping overnight at Ismailia.[1]

Tim Elkington was also on board and he was part of the group which formed itself around Bob. They were all great company, he recalls, and certainly the most vital group on board. Tim makes an interesting observation: 'Although only my age, Bob had already lived more than most and was a keystone of the group.' There was an additional major disadvantage to being on board; with the entry of the US into the war, it was agreed that all troopships would no longer carry alcohol. This was, not surprisingly, an unpopular measure and a plot was hatched. Bob faked a serious toothache and eventually it was agreed that he could go ashore to have it seen to. When they stopped at Tawfik port, at the southernmost end of the Suez Canal, Bob headed ashore with the funds he had collected from his fellow officers and aircrew. After a successful shopping expedition he had some difficulty in getting it delivered back to the jetty. He finally arrived there, only to watch the last tender leave for the ship. By good fortune, a few minutes later a naval commodore arrived at the jetty. With him were four naval ratings carrying a crate that was heard to 'clink' when it was put down.[2] The tale has all of Bob's hallmarks as a raconteur.

> I stood smartly to attention, saluted him, and asked if I could thumb a lift with him back to the ship, and he asked if my crate 'clinked' when I put it down also? I admitted that it did and he became most reasonable. He then arranged for the military police to carry my case to my cabin. Apparently there was no offense against alcohol in the cabins at that time. We sailed from Suez in a golden haze.[3]

Once on shore in India, Bob, as so many before him, took in the sights and sounds. Few men of his background did much international travel unless they were in the services. Travel abroad for the majority of British people was an unknown and Bob's school trip to Scandinavia had been exceptional. Holidays were taken at home and England was far from a multicultural society, with the exception of the major ports such as London or Liverpool, where crewmen from Asia were a more common sight. For most, their knowledge of other parts of the vast British Empire came from books and newsreels, with the attendant Anglo-centric perspective.

Militarily the situation in India was difficult to say the least. Allied forces were building up in India in order to fight the Japanese on several fronts: protecting India, supporting the Chinese military in southern China and recapturing Burma. The Japanese advance in 1942 had been rapid and the Allied forces in Burma, then a British territory, were overrun by a fast-moving Japanese attack. The poorly equipped British forces in Burma were overwhelmed and on 8 March 1942 Rangoon fell. 'Within three weeks of the loss of Rangoon the Allied air force in Burma had been wiped out.' By May, Mandalay, the northern airfields and Akyab on the western coast were also occupied.[4] The Allies retreated to India and considered the situation. China, seen as a key ally by the Americans, had been forced back by the Japanese along their coast. Previously the Chinese had been supplied via the road though northern Burma, but this was cut off by the Japanese.

The Japanese now had an eye on India, opening an offensive against the RAF airfields in Bengal in October 1942 after the monsoon season. The air defence force in India consisted of twelve squadrons by the end of 1942 and they were equipped with old aircraft, mainly Hurricanes, described as 'clapped-out rubbish from the desert war'.[5] In December 1942 General Sir Archibald Wavell launched an attack to capture Akyab on the Burmese coast, known as the first Arakan campaign. This 'led to bitter fighting with heavy losses for the Army' and it ended unsuccessfully in May 1943 with withdrawal of troops. Lessons were learnt about the problems of land communications in that difficult terrain and the essential need for air transport.[6] One campaign that was seen as a success, more from a morale point of view than any significant strategic success, was the first Chindit campaign, led by Orde Wingate. His men demonstrated that it was possible to fight and beat the Japanese in the jungle and that a lightly equipped group of men could operate well into enemy territory with air support, assisted by embedded RAF officers who liaised over air supply drops. Much was learnt, often the hard way. But it was a success in an otherwise deeply gloomy picture and was celebrated as such.[7] It proved that it was feasible to maintain a force behind enemy lines by air alone.

In 1943 the Allies increased their forces in India and new airfields were built. With this build-up came a major command change. South East Asia Command (SEAC) was formed at the Quebec conference in August 1943, which was attended by Roosevelt and Churchill and hosted by the Canadian Prime Minister, Mackenzie King. Admiral Lord Louis Mountbatten was appointed Supreme Commander, with the American General Stilwell as his deputy. Stilwell also retained an independent military role with China.[8] Air Chief Marshal Sir Richard Peirse, previously Air Officer Commander-in-Chief RAF India, was made Allied Air Commander-in-Chief South-East Asia, bringing all air units under one command. The decision to integrate all air units was made in the face of considerable opposition but was achieved in January 1944. Peirse now had to oversee the expansion of the air force in India to defend India and to go on the offensive. The need to supply the Chinese led to an 'aerial lifeline' across one of the most difficult air routes in the world, across uncharted country and the mountains of northern Burma in 'piston-engined unpressurised aircraft'. This notorious route was known as the 'Hump'.[9] The USAAF supplied the aircrew and heavy aircraft for strategic bombing and transport, while the RAF, including RCAF and IAF, had the tactical role and were equipped with fighter aeroplanes and light bombers.

Bob arrived as part of the build-up of experienced airmen. On 15 December he was posted from Worli with orders to proceed to Air Head Quarters at Delhi. There, Bob was interviewed and assessed and he was asked if he would like to form and command a new IAF squadron. Bob leapt at the opportunity and headed for Risalpur to take up his post, arriving on 21 December 1943. Based at Risalpur was an officer training unit which would supply many of the men for the new squadron. Establishing a new squadron from scratch took time and the newly appointed CO and his adjutant had plenty to occupy them in acquiring the necessary pilots, airmen, ground equipment and aircraft and the inevitable administration. There was, however, always time for a bit of light relief and they found an old aircraft in one of the hangars. This they fell upon and, probably in the guise of training, got it repaired and refitted and then flew it around the area. It was a Vickers Valentia, a biplane first introduced in 1934 for use as a transport aircraft. In Bob's logbook he notes that on 26 January 1944 he flew it with ten passengers on board. His co-pilot was Group Captain Darley DSO, the CO of the OTU.[10] The pilots sat in an exposed cockpit and Bob felt like an early aviator, just requiring a peaked cap worn back to front to complete the picture.

On 20 February 1944 the squadron was officially formed at Lahore and remained there until 10 May. In planning the formation of his new command, Bob could draw on his previous experience such as his short stint as a flight commander at Perranporth with the newly formed 130 Squadron. He could also reflect on his experience of 234 Squadron and the leadership gap he witnessed. While all of this, together with his time as chief flying instructor, would be useful, he was in a new country with new cultures. It was a challenging environment from almost every aspect, including the geography, climate and the political scene. British officers of IAF squadrons needed considerable flexibility and understanding if they were to succeed.

Before the war the total air force in India consisted of eight RAF squadrons and one IAF. The latter had mainly British senior officers. Three more IAF squadrons were established at the outbreak of war. The plan was that the IAF would act solely as a tactical air force. It was trained and equipped only for reconnaissance and Army cooperation work. In the view of the official Indian Air Force historian this meant that the more 'spectacular work of the air force which lends glamour to the achievements of the air crew was outside the scope of the Indian Air Force'. This, it was said, affected the morale of the pilots and there was a sense that as far as equipment was concerned 'the IAF had for long to be satisfied with the scrapings of the RAF'.[11] But this was not just the case in the IAF; the same problem affected the whole of the RAF in India, and the other services. The priority for the Allies was Europe, and not until success on the Continent was assured did equipment flow better into India.[12]

By the beginning of 1943, the decision was made to increase the IAF to ten squadrons. But it was not a simple matter. In equipment, as a largely agrarian economy, India was wholly dependent on the US and UK for aircraft and aeronautical stores and was 'low in the order of priority for deliveries'. The shortage in equipment also induced a grave shortage of men to maintain, service and repair the aircraft, and instructional staff. As for recruiting aircrew and airmen, there was no lack of material but the 'numbers possessing the necessary educational qualifications and technical ability and who are suitable in other respects are not very large'.[13] While the ideal was that the IAF would be solely manned and maintained by Indian nationals, it was not feasible in 1943. A general plea requesting officers and other British military personnel for the military forces, plus managers and foremen for ordnance factories, was made by the Secretary of State for India, Leo Amory.[14]

Amory was a supporter of reform. In 1942 he had successfully challenged an anomalous situation whereby Indian officers who had commissions in the Indian forces were excluded from powers of punishment of British personnel. The Indian Army had, by tradition, a majority of British officers and the Army as a whole in India did not wish to change matters, citing planned civil disobedience campaigns. The RAF and IAF were different. Twenty per cent of RAF personnel in India were Indians and were on the same pay scale as British ranks while the IAF, as seen, was majority Indian. The planned expansion of the IAF and shortage of skills meant that inevitably there would be a mix of Indian and other nationalities.[15] Amory agreed the rule had to go and he was supported by the Viceroy and the Commander-in-Chief, who both felt it was the right time to make the change. But one interesting phrase used by the Viceroy's office was that such a change would have 'no adverse affect on the white man in the East'.[16] Attitudes in general in the government of India were still pre-war. The AOC-in-Chief, Peirse, was frustrated by the 'obstructive effect on all his plans of the ponderous, cumbersome and antipathetic Government of India machine'.[17]

For those who needed a fast response to build up a new fighting force against the credible Japanese threat to invade India, the staff attitudes were hard to believe. Paul Richey was an experienced fighter pilot who was posted to India just before Bob and he was asked to write a report on Fighter Command in India. His words were scathing about the use of Hurricanes in fighting the Japanese Zeros and he called for the supply of Spitfires. He was particularly unimpressed with the staff functions in India:

Visits by staff officers, and especially Commanders, to forward stations and units are very rare. When they did occur, their object appears to be sight-seeing and nothing results beyond a shrinkage of the unit's slender stock of refreshments.[18]

Richey observed two classes of officer who existed in large and 'equally undesirable quantities' in India: the old deadbeat, who is 'ignorant, inefficient, out of date and out of sympathy with the young element'; and the 'deadbeat, old or young, who has been sent to India because he is not wanted elsewhere'.[19] Such men, he considered, had dug themselves in and constituted a serious block which the 'newer, younger, more up-to-date and more energetic arrivals find impossible to move in any direction and unwise to try to disturb'.[20] Bob, keen, energetic and aged just twenty-three, was in for many challenges in a very different country and a different air force. Indeed Mountbatten, disliking the attitude prevalent in India, based his headquarters in Ceylon rather than at India HQ Delhi.[21]

RAF commanders in charge of IAF squadrons were not an automatic choice since it was a deliberate policy to have Indian commanders where possible, unlike the Indian Army where there was a very long tradition of British officers. However, a shortage of IAF pilots and a rapidly expanding air force required a change in policy and it was agreed with the government of India that an RAF element would be introduced into Nos 4, 7, 8, 9, 10 and 12 Squadrons (in the event, 12 was not formed until post-war). If necessary the RAF element would comprise the officer commanding the squadron, one or two flight commanders and one flight of crews.[22]

Bob's task was to create an efficient and effective fighting force from a multinational group of men. His previous experience was all coming to the fore, but before he could get the training fully organised there were other problems for the new CO. An RAF booklet on leadership issued in 1948 suggested that during the war, with the emphasis on operations, there was a tendency to fully delegate the welfare of the men to one junior officer. Bob was not of that frame of mind. 'An officer's first duty is to satisfy himself that his men have shelter and food.'[23] In India, in his brand-new squadron Bob believed that this was not simply something to be delegated and then forgotten and both shelter and food became an immediate challenge.

An Indian squadron comprised a large number of men of many different religions with different catering needs. An external contractor was used to supply the food for the enrolled followers, the large number of Indians who made up many of the other ranks. There were complaints and on investigation it was found that the person in charge was swindling and so the men were moved to the hutted camp area and provision made to feed the men as part of the whole squadron. Bob appointed one of his Indian officers, Flying Officer Roy, as the messing officer for all the Indian other ranks.[24] Sorting out the food was just one part of a CO's task in order to achieve the right standards to get and keep a squadron operational. In addition to training his pilots, he had to ensure they had the necessary equipment and that the engineers kept the elderly aircraft serviced and flying. Morale, discipline, living conditions and hygiene were all matters that came across his desk. In Lahore the heat was extreme and the men were suffering in temperatures in excess of 105 F. Heat exhaustion was just one of the many illnesses that affected men in India.

India and Burma were unhealthy places for Europeans. In 1944, a survey on health in the RAF and IAF concluded that the danger from disease remained considerably greater than the danger from actual warfare. The risk came from malaria, dysentery, heat effects, venereal disease and jaundice, with malaria being the biggest problem. Education, preventative measures such as mepacrim tablets and improved hospital facilities assisted in driving the rates down but dysentery was a continuing challenge. But illness did not just affect Europeans. A comparison between the RAF and the IAF showed that malaria had a higher incidence rate in the latter, mainly due to a fatalistic acceptance of what was, for many in India, a habitual problem. While the CO had a medical officer reporting to him, the two needed to work together on these issues. COs were instructed to ensure that all men took their tablets on a daily basis.[25] Recommendations had been made for better buildings at RAF bases more suited to the climate and health needs and improving working conditions. But providing shade where possible for ground crew servicing aircraft was not always possible, particularly in the forward areas. Bob pressed for a change of location while starting dusk flying to allow for the cooler evenings.

As a newly formed squadron, a close eye was kept on progress and in April Commodore Proud arrived to inspect. At AHQ, Proud had been appointed the previous year as the Inspector General for the IAF and he continued that role under SEAC. Proud had visited the seven existing IAF squadrons at the end of the previous year and reported on them. He gave advice on personnel problems and all matters of IAF administration at squadron, group and headquarters levels. Shortage of equipment was an ongoing challenge, as was the lack of spares, all matters that needed action at staff level. Proud also turned his attention to conditions and terms of service such as recommending the same kit and clothing for IAF airmen as for RAF airmen. He had also submitted a detailed plan for the building up of IAF maintenance, training and administration units appropriate to the first line strength to Air HQ for approval.[26]

In his previous inspections Proud had approved of the training and discipline in most of the IAF squadrons, although one commanded by a British officer had severe problems:

The squadron returned from detachment about 1st July. It did not appear to have settled in at its new station and the equipment section particularly was in a most disorganised condition. The airmen were reasonably accommodated but the kitchen and recreation arrangements are not up to standard. The Commanding Officer was not in happy state of mind and admitted that he was baffled by the many problems of his unit. The officers were sullen and lacked spirit and altogether a most unhappy impression of the conditions in the unit were received by the inspecting party.

The flying training, notwithstanding the bad state of discipline and administration, was proceeding satisfactorily.[27]

It probably did not help that it was the first command for the new CO of 2 Squadron IAF and he had previously served in the Indian Army, which had a very different ethos to the new IAF and a more colonial attitude. He was in command for just a few months and was posted away shortly after the inspection.[28] But now it was 10 Squadron's turn to be under the microscope, and the squadron passed with due note taken of the living conditions and a promise of a word at AHQ. Bob personally flew the air commodore to Lyallpur in the Harvard with, no doubt, time for a private, informal discussion between them.[29]

Training continued and Bob was keen to get the pilots flying well in formation, which required strict discipline and adherence to orders. The squadron was equipped with Hurricanes and there was soon an opportunity to show off the work of the squadron with the chance for some exhibition flying. The War Services Exhibition unit travelled around India setting up exhibitions, putting on demonstrations and flypasts at various sites in order to raise the profile of the war and to help with recruitment. It was a travelling circus of tents, cookhouses and equipment. They had exhibition stands and static aircraft to encourage the public to learn more about the Indian Air Force. When the IAF Exhibition unit reached Lahore, its air force display was improved by new equipment obtained from AHQ India. This included a Hurricane permanently allotted to this unit and a Hoppity. The latter was described as a 'training aircraft not aerodynamic' and had been obtained from No. 2 CMU (Civil Maintenance Unit). It was felt by the unit that the two aircraft would 'greatly improve the Air Force display' together with aerial displays by the local air force squadrons.[30]

There was another underlying agenda in showing off the work of an Indian Hurricane squadron to the public. The OTU based at Risalpur had experienced difficulties in the training of Hurricane pilots and had expressed a concern at the number of pilots who had been turned down because they 'could not, or did not, want to fly Hurricanes'.[31] Air

Commodore Hunter, the AOC of 223 Group, was concerned and thought that many of the cases had wrongly been labelled as 'moral fibre' and he was of the opinion that 'somebody had been spreading rumours against Hurricane aircraft at SFTS. He considered this was the reason why a number of IAF pilots try to avoid completing OTU training and prefer to go to safer appointments.'[32]

Flypasts of aircraft from the RAF, including 10 Squadron IAF, were duly arranged for the exhibition. The Hurricanes would fly past in formation and also do dummy attacks during the 'tank battle' arranged by the Army section. The Chinese Air Force also participated in flypasts during the exhibition days.[33] It was a major event held from 10 to 21 April in Minto Park in Lahore. After a press preview day it was opened to the public, with an official opening address by the Governor of Punjab. Over the next few days the crowds visited all the war exhibition stands and the Air Force stand remained popular. On the final day of the exhibition there was a flypast of nine Hurricanes in formation and demonstrating dummy attacks during a mock tank battle. 10 Squadron flew on most days, including a low flypast over the Mall in Lahore. Bob personally flew on most days of the exhibition, both in formation and in some exhibition aerobatics, the latter seeming a bit of a surprise for a pilot who had disliked aerobatics. The date 17 April was a dedicated Indian Air Force day and Air Vice-Marshal Thomas, Air-Officer Commanding Air Forces of India, visited the exhibition and gave a speech in the hall. He also inspected the squadron and the hutted camp at Lahore and was made fully aware of the unpleasant living conditions due to the terrific heat.[34]

Getting the message through to senior officers about the living conditions was one thing; another key task was to organise the men in the squadron. Men appeared to have been posted to the squadron to make up numbers and not by trades, leading to an imbalance of skills. Experienced fliers were needed, so these were posted in to assist. One officer was posted in from Ferry Command and he was well known to Bob. It was Eddie Sparkes, last seen by Bob heading for a disciplinary centre. Bob put the past firmly behind him and welcomed Eddie warmly to the squadron and promptly put him in charge of communications. Not surprisingly, the idiosyncratic Sparkes came with a poor report in which a medical officer from Bombay hospital had judged him mentally unbalanced and it was also deemed that his flying was highly dangerous. Bob kept an open mind and asked one of his flight commanders and the squadron medical officer to keep an eye on Eddie and to report back. After two weeks came the reports and Bob called in Eddie to discuss the situation. 'The Flight Officer had said that if they had any other pilots who flew as dangerously he would be glad to have them and the Medical Officer had found me perfectly sane.' [35] Eddie was just one part of the new group of men Bob needed to blend into an effective team as soon as possible. The squadron was majority Indian, and the two flight commanders were Flight Lieutenant Davies (RAF) and Flight Lieutenant Pattinson (RCAF). There were twenty Indian pilots, three British and two Australian. There were 1,400 other ranks, twenty of whom were British.[36] The chief engineer was a British warrant officer and it was his job to ensure that the squadron's sixteen Hurricanes were serviceable at all times.

There was a challenge of low morale among the Indian other ranks, few of whom had any experience of what it was to be part of an air force squadron as many had come straight from training. Bob called a conference of all the officers to consider the problem and invited ideas. As a result, all the men were divided into groups with one officer responsible for the well-being of all the men in that group. The officer was to visit them as often as possible in their spare time and deal with their complaints so that the men would feel an active interest was being taken in them. A sports officer was established and an inter-station football competition started. Finally Bob agreed to give a talk to the men on what was happening in the squadron and give a sense of the objects of a fighter squadron. The talk was a great success – Bob was a natural speaker – and he was kept a further hour answering their questions.[37]

Gradually the various sections were observed to settle down to squadron life, but it was 'hard work in view of the lack of experience of most of the men'. The IAF badly needed more pilots and three IAF officers interviewed twelve other ranks who had applied for aircrew. The applicants were all seen afterwards for a personal interview with Bob. Many men had never been in an aircraft before, so Bob had previously taken two men, aircraftmen Hamilton and Khan, on a 'joy ride' in the Harvard.[38]

It was with considerable relief that the squadron heard that it was to move from the plains of Lahore to Risalpur, where it was cooler. An advance party was sent off and, in view of previous catering problems, it included the messing officer, who took with him the Indian cooks to arrange messing in preparation for the squadron's arrival. Food was a complex matter in an IAF squadron, with a wide range of religions and backgrounds. Food was an important part of life for Bob and he came to deeply appreciate the Indian food, although the Indian cooks were not so good at the English type of breakfasts.[39]

Moving 1,500 men, sixteen aircraft, assorted equipment and ground transport was not easy even for the relatively short distance from Lahore to Risalpur, and it would be the first of many such moves. The air party was the simplest and it took off under Bob's command. Then came the rail party in the charge of Flight Lieutenant Davies, accompanied by ten armed men. The third group was the road party, with Warrant Officer Heathcote in charge assisted by Flight Sergeant Noor Khan. The transport included two Chevrolet fifteen-hundredweight trucks, a three-ton Ford, the essential Bedford petrol bowser, a Chevrolet station wagon, a Humber station wagon and finally a Matchless motor bike.[40] An air force unit required plenty of ground transport.

Risalpur was very different to the poor and basic conditions at Lahore. It was an old and well-established RAF station with large rooms, two tennis courts and a swimming pool. The surrounding countryside was green, with snow-capped mountains. Eddie Sparkes was suitably impressed by the officers' mess.

The billiard, ante room and dining rooms are huge and are panelled with wood that looks to be at least 2 inches thick. The ante room is long with two huge fireplaces and decorated with carved wooden crests or previous squadrons. Above the panelling are mounted animal heads and at about twelve feet from the floor are the windows. The dimensions of the dining room are similar and in proportion to the dining table that is of heavy polished wood and eight feet wide by fifty feet long. Our poor little squadron is quite lost as there is ample room between each chair for another. Most of the table service is of heavy silver.[41]

Fighter training continued in the better conditions of the mountains, with practice attacks and dogfights, although on one day work ceased early due to a dust storm and all personnel were called out to secure the aircraft. Other compensations were occasional variety shows. All of this helped, but Bob still kept a close eye on morale. He called a conference of the section commanders, who reported a few general complaints from the Indian other ranks that the British other ranks were not treating them properly, but there was nothing definite and most of the men agreed that they were happier at Risalpur than they had ever been before. It was agreed that the situation had to be watched closely.[42]

The squadron was still short of various items, and Bob and one of his flight commanders arranged for the Harvard to be flown to Peshawar to collect radios, a gramophone and various games. Servicing provided its own challenges, with aircraft engines becoming unavailable through petty defects, but at least the Hurricanes were well understood by the ground crew. The American Harvard was a trickier matter. This two-seater aeroplane was the essential runabout, and in addition to two aircrew it could also carry supplies. But it needed specialist American tools to service and repair, and the Harvard instruments caused 'a spot of bother' as the squadron's solitary repairer had no knowledge of American instruments.[43]

Bob concentrated on accurate formation and obedience to orders, which seemed 'the only way I could deliver an effective punch with the material at my command.' His pilots he assessed as a mixed bunch; some were brilliant but the average was low.[44] In his assessment he was looking only at skill levels. He saw no national differences between fighter pilots: 'There's no difference between German pilots and British pilots I don't think. Some of them are better than others ... as I found out when I commanded an Indian squadron.'[45]

Eddie Sparkes noted the squadron becoming a cohesive unit; its reputation was good, and this is reflected in the words of the squadron's diarist, who recorded the first squadron formation from Risalpur. 'Both flights in 3 sections of three were used and when the formation flew over base in excellent line abreast there was a considerable expression of pride and enthusiasm among the ground personnel.'[46]

The CO, Bob, pleased with progress, arranged a sightseeing trip for nine officers and fifty men to visit the famous Khyber Pass. Under his command the party consisted of one station wagon and two three-tonners with an officer in charge of each one. At Peshawar the lead was taken by a station wagon from 223 Group and their vehicles made up the convoy. All went well until four of the party strayed over the border by accident. One of them walked a little further than the others and was captured at gun point by some angry Afghan soldiers. The captured pilot was Eddie, who was marched off to the frontier post while the rest of the party looked on helplessly. The frontier guards had no English and so they waited for the Kabul bus that was due, on board which might be a potential interpreter. Luckily there was a young Afghan pilot, Lieutenant Mohammed Akshbar Khan. He was accompanied by a British officer, Squadron Leader King, who was on secondment to the Afghan Air Force. By the type of coincidence that could only happen to Eddie Sparkes, King had been his previous CO in England. Once Sparkes was recognised and vouched for, the Afghan pilot used his influence – his uncle was the officer in charge of the whole frontier – and he persuaded the guards to release Eddie.[47]

After a predictable telling-off by Bob, Eddie had to appear before an inquiry held at Group HQ with Bob and others there as witnesses:

Things were pretty sensitive at that time. Technically, I had led a party of four men in uniform across a frontier; this, under international law, constituted an 'invasion'. Churchill was informed and I was to be court martialled. Before this could take place there had to be a Court of Inquiry.

This was convened and I was marched to a chair facing a panel of officers the leader of which was a young F/Lt a year or two older than I was.[48]

Eddie was not court martialled, as it was agreed that the frontier markings were not clear. Meanwhile, leisure pursuits continued for the men. A squadron magazine was started and was able to report on the various sports activities among other things. Football was popular and the ground crew continued to give the 'pilots a sound drubbing at football'. Cricket bats and balls were obtained – Bob as ever was a keen cricketer – but the days were now heating up quickly and the game was abandoned once the heat became discomfiting. The swimming pool in the officers' mess was put to good use and Bob organised a dinghy drill.[49] Getting into a dinghy once an aircraft had ditched was not an easy matter. It was also a time for some fun:

After leaving from the water those who were attempting to demonstrate that dinghies were superfluous, F/Sgt Evans, our Australian stoic, clambered onto the high diving board complete with seat pack, mae west and bush hat. He held his nose, jumped and everything disappeared but his hat. After surfacing it took about 5 minutes to complete the drill, the trouble only being found in locating the release valve.[50]

Leave was something to look forward to and in June Bob managed to get away from it all, with four days in the cool of the hills. Bob heard the news of the Allied invasion of Europe while sitting on the lawn of the Cecil Hotel, Murree, up in the hills above Rawalpindi. He was 'drinking iced Golden Ribbon lager and thinking what a pleasant war it was!'[51] The squadron diarist also noted the opening of the second front and reported that 'the entire squadron expressed regret at not being there'.[52] The squadron was beginning to feel frustrated by their lack of action. Meanwhile, there were new problems to manage with the aircraft and the political environment in India.

In May, Bob had experienced an unpleasant situation when returning from an exercise, a practice attack on an aerodrome. The squadron had performed well but Bob suddenly found the sky going black around him and realised he was about to pass out. He speedily returned to the aerodrome, landed and was violently sick. Subsequent inquiries found there were problems with the glycol coolant, which showed an acid reaction and caused the cooling systems on the aircraft to deteriorate. Eleven aircraft were grounded as a result until the problem was resolved.[53]

Sabotage was a real threat in India. The country was pressing for independence and Gandhi was undertaking high-profile fasts to draw attention to the campaign. He had also begun civil disobedience strikes. There were others who took more direct action, such as Subhas Chandra Bose, who had fled to Germany in 1940 and met with Hitler. Both Germany and Japan assisted him in establishing the Indian National Army, which was fighting alongside the Japanese in Burma. Stories of spies were in abundance and it was a real possibility that the glycol problem was part of the sabotage. Bob put Eddie Sparkes in charge of the investigation. A typical Eddie comment on this was that his CO used him as a general 'trouble shooter' if something unusual occurred. 'Whether this was because he wanted to give me the opportunity to make a complete hash of things or just to keep my energies fully employed I never discovered.'[54] More likely it was the latter. The coolant used was glycol from RAF stores which was mixed with distilled water from a local supplier. Eddie obtained samples from the supplier and sent those with samples from the squadron to the government laboratories for testing. The supplier's distilled water was found to be the issue and a new source was used.[55]

It was in June that the squadron experienced a first obvious sabotage incident. When the hangar was opened one evening to wheel out the aircraft for test flights, five aircraft were found with oiled chock-rope fixed to the tail units and lit. Luckily, all but one had gone out. The hangar was closed and a guard put in place while Group Headquarters ACSEA were notified. 'The reaction of the great majority of the squadron was one of anger and indignation and the incident frightened no one.' This put the aircraft out of use yet again for several days while the whole event was investigated. This involved a wing commander who interrogated the airmen and also talked to the Indian other ranks, where he received and dealt with some complaints. No culprit was identified and the incident was an isolated one.[56] It was, however, a timely reminder of the political situation in India. Pillaging was a routine event and equipment and belongings had to be guarded with care. If an aeroplane had an accident it was quickly brought in under cover as there would be little left of it once the local inhabitants in the region had access.

Security was an issue on the minds of all commanders, but it could also be taken too far. Eddie referred to stories of 'spies abounding' and in the rapid expansion of the IAF it was recognised that some less sympathetic men might get recruited. In AHQ they had received a report by the CID with concerns regarding men who were potential recruits and some who were already serving in the IAF. Sir Guy Garrod was robust in his review of the information:

It is necessary to make a distinction between terrorist activity or subversive activities of any kind on the one hand and political activities on the other. A man who has been an active member of some political society, especially at university, is probably intellectually alert and providing his activities are not anti-social may be just the type of man we want in the IAF ... Similarly a man should not be refused enlistment without question because some relative of his has committed a political crime or misdemeanour some years ago.[57]

Garrod decided 'not to slavishly accept the opinion of the CID and Civil Police'.[58]

At the end of June the squadron was given the good news that they were to attend an air firing course. This was a matter of some pride as Bob was told they would be the first Indian squadron to go through there.[59] The base was the other side of India at Armada Road. The train party would take five days, while the air party under Bob's command flew to Delhi, Cawnpore, Allahabad and Goa. They took the journey in short hops but even so one pilot, Pilot Officer Sujir, had to force land at Lucknow with heat exhaustion.[60] Bob was determined to show what the squadron could do and they arrived over the training camp in 'impeccable formation' and landed so that the last aircraft was on the ground before their CO had turned off the end of the runway.[61] It was a stylish and effective arrival.

The officer in charge of the training was another Battle of Britain veteran, Wing Commander Carey. He had fought in France and in Burma. He put his considerable experience to good use in creating ways of countering enemy tactics. Seen as the 'backroom boy' of the eventual Burma victory in air supremacy, his school near Calcutta 'produced some of the most ingenious fighter pilots of the war'.[62] As Bob had done when he was CFI, Carey had his own distinctive Spitfire which boasted a red marking on each side of its fuselage so that his students could spot him in the air.[63]

As Carey was so highly rated for his training courses, there were several reasons why Bob was keen that his pilots made a good impression. He had, of course, been a chief flying instructor specialising in air gunnery, he was naturally highly competitive and he was not going to see his men shown up in any way.

We were there a month, doing air to air and air to ground gunnery and did not shame the Indian Air Force. The comment at the end of the course was that 'this squadron has attained a very high standard of efficiency'. I was proud of that, when you consider the bias that existed against the Indians at the time.[64]

What Bob omitted to add was that Wing Commander Carey was highly complimentary about their CO. Carey's exact words in his report were, 'This officer took the squadron through the course and by his energy and leadership enabled them to attain a very high standard of efficiency.'[65] Bob's comment about the bias against Indians was accurate. Old colonial attitudes still prevailed in many places while South Africa, Rhodesia and the USA were segregated societies. While some changes had to be made to appease American sensitivities within the USA, the Indian situation was a little more complex. Official propaganda was keen to promote Indian flyers for publicity purposes to counter German and Japanese attempts to exploit anti-British and anti-Imperial sentiments in India.[66] That may have been official policy, but there were many who did not see it in the same way. Bob's view was liberal for the time.

After the successful course at Armada Road, the squadron moved on 23 July to a new base at Chharra and remained there for four months. Here they were co-located with another Indian squadron, No. 7. Their CO was the newly promoted Squadron Leader P. C. Lal. No. 7 was operational and had flown light bomber sorties in the battles of Imphal and Kohima.[67] Bob was the senior officer and so he became station commander.[68]

The only thing that sticks in my memory for that period was when P. C. Lal, who was the Indian squadron commander, got married. I attended his wedding and ate foods I didn't know existed. It was wonderful.[69]

Bob selected his two best pilots, Sparkes and Suri, and sent them on an Air Fighting Instructors Course. It was identical to the Fighter Leaders Course in Britain and it was something of an honour to be selected.[70] During their time at Chharra the two flights within 10 Squadron were split. One remained at Chharra (close to New Delhi), carrying out the normal flying exercises such as formation flying, low-level cross-country flights and quarter attacks. The other flight was based at Salboni, and then Dhubalia (close to Calcutta), and it carried out affiliation exercises with a Liberator squadron stationed there. Besides formation flying, this included low-level cross-country and ground attacks.[71] Keeping an eye on both flights involved constant flying by the CO between the two locations.

On the anniversary of the Battle of Britain the squadron had a parade of all British personnel and the salute was taken by Flight Lieutenant Davies as Bob was in Calcutta. Bob was there broadcasting in a programme celebrating the Battle on All India Radio. The work of the squadron continued, with practice including dogfights, targeting bombers and air-to-ground firing. There were constant problems with aircraft as the fabric on the Hurricanes had a tendency to rot in damp conditions. Sport was still an essential part of life and a cricket match was arranged between the British and the Indian members of the squadron. The British won on this occasion. Other entertainment included ENSA shows which were always much appreciated. These were touring groups of British artists who performed for British troops overseas. Bob, however, was attentive to the predominately non-British men in his squadron and on 27 September the squadron records note that the CO gave the squadron the morning off 'owing to last night's Puja ceremony'.[72] Diwali is the most important ceremony of the year in India and it brings together Hindus, Jains and Sikhs. Puja ceremonies are held to bless a house and to encourage the victory of light over darkness, knowledge over ignorance, good over evil and hope over despair. It was also a good excuse for a party involving most of the squadron.

The squadron was getting closer to the moment when it would be operational and training was increased in survival techniques. The pilots would be operating into Burma with its inhospitable terrain and an enemy known for its cruelty to prisoners. The men had already had lectures on V Force. This was the arm of the Special Operations Executive (SOE) that operated well into enemy territory and which was tasked with rescuing those 'unfortunate enough to land in Burma or occupied territory'.[73] Additionally, all pilots were given practical training in getting back to base. They were taken out by lorry some twenty-five miles. They had no food and only ten rupees and their instructions were to find their way back to the aerodrome without the use of roads or railway lines. They all managed to return the next day. More detailed specialist training was held at the jungle training camp and Pilot Officers Roy and Katrak were sent to this.[74]

It was not just the risk of getting shot down; aircraft could malfunction and pilots could get lost, as did Flying Officer Thandi on 6 October. When he realised he was lost he managed to find a small airstrip at Ram Pur Hat. It had no telephone, so, after leaving his aircraft in charge of the Army captain who was responsible for the strip, he walked to the nearest railway station. Here the station master telephoned the USAAF at Gushkara who promised to send him petrol and to inform his unit. Meanwhile his CO, Bob, and Picken flew to Dhubalia to investigate and to try to find him. He was eventually successfully refuelled by a DC3 and managed to find his way back to base.[75]

The squadron was beginning to wonder if they would ever become operational. Air Vice-Marshal Thomas from Air HQ arrived to inspect and delivered a lecture to the aircrew. A combined sports meeting was subsequently held, with every member of the squadron taking part in one event or another. It was a great success and built on the team spirit that Bob had encouraged. The aircrew, to their delight, 'took the cup from HQ by a large margin'.[76] Then, at last, came the news for which they had been waiting – but it was not what they had expected to hear.

On 3 November, a signal arrived bearing 'most unexpected news'; after months of fighter training, the squadron's role was changed to fighter bombing. For Bob it was ironically almost the reverse of his situation in 1939. The squadron was somewhat stunned.

On the one hand the blow that we are not to be fighters is heavy, on the other we are beside ourselves with the idea of early operations. Everyone went even further round the bend and spontaneous roughhousing broke out everywhere. It was fated that there was fruit in the officers' mess for dessert.[77]

Eddie Sparkes was detailed to take the news to the other flight at Dhubalia and, being Eddie, in his excitement he could not resist beating up the aerodrome. As the diarist quaintly put it, 'A certain officer was torn off a terrific strip.'[78]

Disappointed as they may have been in their change of role from fighters to fighter bombers, 10 Squadron IAF was part of an essential rethinking of battle tactics. By July 1944 Kohima and Imphal battles were over. The Japanese attack had been thwarted and the close support provided by the RAF to the 14th Army was recognised: 'The measure and quality of ground support provided by fighter-bombers and dive bombers in peculiarly difficult terrain of Burma proved of inestimable value.'[79] Ian Lyall Grant fought with 17th Division and his praise was high: 'Never has an army been so dependent on air support and ... credit due to RAF and USAAF for their remarkable achievement in one of the most hostile flying climates in the world.'[80] Between January and July of 1944 it was the Hurricanes that took the brunt of the losses, with ninety-seven aircraft lost through enemy action or crashes. Of the other Allied aircraft the loss figures were thirty-eight Beaufighters, fifteen Vengeances and thirty-four Spitfires. The Battle of the Admin Box was hailed as one of the decisive points in the Second World War – a 'Japanese army defeated on level terms in the jungle'.[81] Before the monsoon season in mid-1944 stopped campaigns, essential territory had been held, an invasion of India had been halted and air superiority had been gained.

Important lessons had been learned. The effectiveness of dive-bombing by 8 Squadron IAF and No. 82 Vengeance Squadron had been disappointing. Due to the deeply hidden Japanese bunkers, Mountbatten recognised that heavy bombers were not suitable to the terrain. It was agreed that the need was for pilots of light and fighter-bombers who 'knew the country and the enemy tactics and could achieve the necessary accuracy'.[82] Lessons on reading the jungle had been learned by pilots involved in supply dropping and essential casualty evacuation. The Hurricanes of 6 Squadron IAF were employed in tactical reconnaissance – 'operating usually in pairs they flew at about 50ft in open country and 100 to 150 feet over the jungle, heights at which they could achieve surprise and actually see something: as the pilots gained experience they learned to look into the jungle rather than at it'.[83] All of this would need to be absorbed by the new fighter-bomber squadrons.

10 Squadron was informed they would move to Ranchi. While waiting for the departure date, some of their aircraft were fitted with bomb racks and they were inspected with great interest by the squadron.[84] There was sense of keen anticipation and the night before the squadron was due to leave for their bombing training prior to operations, the two squadrons, 7 and 10 IAF, held an unusual concert. The two commanding officers,

P. C. Lal and Bob, presided over what was described as an 'interesting experiment'. The concert combined Indian and European entertainment and was much appreciated by everyone in the two squadrons.[85]

Before they could finally move out, there was a VIP visit. Air Commodore His Highness the Nawab of Bhopal and his retinue arrived in a Dakota. After visiting the Indian other ranks in their quarters and chatting to them, he then watched Bob brief his pilots for the move to Ranchi. Dealing with the arrival and interest of VIPs was part of the job and Bob knew the significance of the Nawab's visit. The Nawab of Bhopal was the hereditary ruler of a large part of central India that was the second-largest state in pre-independence India. The Nawab was a Muslim ruler and was close to Jinnah, who would become founder of Pakistan. The hereditary rulers were at the time an important force within India as the country agitated for independence from British rule. Conscious of this, Air Marshal Peirse, the Allied Air Commander-in-Chief, appointed the Nawab and the Maharaja of Jodpur to his personal staff as honorary air commodores.[86] The visit to 10 Squadron IAF was part of the Nawab's tour of Indian Air Force squadrons that November. Relations with such VIPs needed tactful handling. Peirse had previously been involved in a delicate matter; the request by the Nawab that he should be permitted to wear flying wings on his uniform. Peirse had written to the Air Ministry for support over the issue. He was wholly averse to any 'deviation from rule' but needed chapter and verse to assist him. The Nawab had quoted precedents of wings being worn by the Prime Minister, Winston Churchill, and by the ruler of Iraq. The request was turned down. While the ruler of Iraq had made his own decision to wear RAF wings, Winston Churchill, who never did succeed in going solo in the air, was a wholly different exception. The Nawab backed down gracefully; he had no wish to ruffle too many feathers since he was keen to make Bhopal a centre for RAF training.[87]

At last, after the obligatory VIP photographs, the squadron took off led by Bob and they performed an immaculate stream landing at Ranchi. Here they were on three weeks of a course on short bombing and strafing as part of their conversion to light bombing. There was the usual combination of lectures and practice. The squadron was highly commended for its 'remarkably good flying discipline and shooting'.[88] There was some experimentation as this method of bombing had not been used by Hurricanes on the Burma front. They found that higher-level dive-bombing was more accurate and the diarist wrote, 'We think we have hit the nail on the head now ... Who knows but it may shake the Japs a trifle.'[89] High-level dive-bombing was extensively practised and the results were deemed 'very good indeed'. There was one sad incident when Flying Officer Chackerbutty was killed while strafing. It was the squadron's first casualty.[90]

By 21 November they were practising with 250 lb live bombs. High-level dive-bombing – diving from 6,000 feet and releasing bombs at 4,000 feet – was found to be more accurate than low-level bombing. The pilots 'went in a gharri to have a look at the target, which is a pretty useless looking hill, still, it's a target'. Bob went first, taking off with Pilot Officer Milne; both Hurricanes were armed with two 250 lb general-purpose bombs each. They both scored direct hits on a big rock at the top of the hill. Even in practice there were dangers and Bob reported that he had received shrapnel through his tailplane.[91]

By the end of November the squadron was ready for action in its new role, and they were now part of a new wing and in a new group. Bob had melded his new squadron into an effective fighting force but it had yet to be tested. His achievement was recognised. His new wing commander, Baldwin, had only known him for two weeks but already Bob had impressed him very favourably. Air Vice-Marshal Thomas knew him better and he gave Bob a ringing endorsement as the squadron headed into battle.

S/Ldr Doe has served with his IAF squadron in three groups of ACSEA and is about to serve in the fourth group since leaving my command over 7 months ago. I have, however, inspected his unit on 3 occasions. He formed No. 10 IAF Squadron and has trained it to a high standard of efficiency. An enthusiastic and able leader who sets a fine example in the air and on the ground. I consider him to be the best RAF sqn commander in the Indian Air Force.[92]

8

THE BATTLE OVER THE BURMESE JUNGLE

Much to their excitement, the squadron was operational at last and they could put their training into action. They were to be part of the new Arakan offensive beginning in December 1944. Since June the Allies had gained complete air superiority over much of Burma and now the land war began in earnest.[1] Geographically Burma was the same size as Germany and the war front during the campaigns in Burma was 700 miles long, the longest front in the Second World War after Russia. Burma was two-thirds mountains with the rivers and the mountain ranges running north and south. The jungle was exceptionally thick and almost impossible to see through.[2] The original plan had been for a series of amphibious landings along the coast of Burma. This would entail vast numbers of landing craft, but the European campaign took priority over the available craft.

In India the scene was set for Operation CAPITAL, the offensive into central Burma in the attempt to destroy the main Japanese Army and to clear the way to Rangoon. Essential for its success was the seizure of the coastal bases and airfields in the Arakan. This would be the task of Christison's XV corps, together with 224 Group RAF and Force W, the substantial naval force that had recently been built up in the Bay of Bengal and was commanded by Admiral Martin.[3] The role of the RAF and IAF in the Arakan was to sweep the air clear of Japanese fighters, support ground troops, supply forward troops and strangle Japanese communication lines.

224 Group was led by the Earl of Bandon, popularly known as

the Abandoned Earl, a larger-than-life character whose exploits were numerous and usually outrageous. He was an officer who was often viewed with some misgivings by his seniors, who were (rightly) slightly wary of his practical jokes, but adored by those he led. Bandon had arrived in July 1944, taking over from Air Commodore Gray, who was described as 'respected but reserved'.[4] Mountbatten was impressed by Bandon's leadership and noted that Bandon was always the most popular man in any mess. Mountbatten's support was well rewarded when Bandon and General Christison developed a close working relationship, setting up joint headquarters at Cox's Bazar. From here the true value of the land–air cooperation was developed in this difficult war. Bandon understood and highly valued the Army's work and provided unstinting support.

> I must just mention here, that this was done to help the West African troops who put up such a wonderful performance – they walked right the way through the jungle from the top of the Arakan to the bottom – supplied only by air for everything – ammunition, food and any amenities we could give them. Due to the frightful country in which they were operating they could carry no artillery, and the whole of their support which should have been done by mortars or artillery was carried out by close support aircraft.[5]

The Arakan campaign was one continuous series of combined operations. The Navy and Air Force cooperated with the Army all through this offensive, which started in mid-December in the Mayu and the Kaladan valleys and virtually ended with the capture of Taungup in the third week of April. This theatre saw the strongest concentration of IAF squadrons, as many as six out of the possible nine being engaged here during this campaign. Nos 4 and 9 Squadrons were already in the area. No. 2 Squadron arrived at Mambur, a satellite airstrip to Cox's Bazar, at the end of November 1944 and started operations on 1 December. It was a fighter reconnaissance squadron.[6]

The only Spitfire squadron in IAF, No. 8, came to the airstrip 'George', fifteen miles south of Cox's Bazar, towards the end of December and started operations on 3 January 1945. It was in this theatre only for a short while, being withdrawn in the last week of February to Baigachi for further training and to defend the Calcutta area.[7] They were replaced by 615 squadron. The last Indian squadron to arrive was No. 3, which reached Bawli North by 20 January 1945 and began operations on 4 February. It operated as a Hurri-bomber squadron until 19 April.[8]

On 30 November 10 Squadron prepared to move forward. Within 224 Group it was in 904 Wing under Group Captain Chater.[9] The diarist reported that the squadron was in high spirits as it loaded equipment onto the railway trucks. The pilots attempted to take as much personal kit as possible in the cramped space of their Hurricanes and took off in the early morning led by Bob and headed for Ramu. The advance party had managed to get the camp ready for them and there was a welcome meal waiting. Food was a different matter in forward bases, with bully beef the routine food. Bob considered himself fortunate to be in an Indian squadron as the Indian cooks were highly creative with rations and supplemented it with local provisions. Their curries were wonderful but the British missed their breakfasts. So Bob and twenty or so British men cooked their own breakfast. They took it in turns, including Bob, opening tins of bacon and putting it with the accompanying fat into a pan over an open fire. It was delicious when mopped up with chapattis.[10]

Meanwhile an officers' shop was found in the vicinity, the pilots busy themselves in buying camp beds, Hurricane lamps and other little odds and ends to make life as comfortable as possible for themselves in this forward area. Already the inevitable pin-up girls are beginning to show their faces in the bamboo bashas. Much briefing by group and intelligence and studying of maps.[11]

The squadron was to work in close cooperation with 9 Squadron IAF, who occupied the next strip. 'Many of the Indian pilots meet old acquaintances and they are as pleased to see us as we they.'[12] The newly appointed CO of 9 Squadron was Denis Adams, another Battle of Britain veteran. 9

Squadron had been formed at much the same time as 10 but was already on its third CO.

On 15 December the ground party finally arrived. It had come by boat and had been delayed when it was in collision with another craft. Bob managed to borrow a convoy of lorries from Wing HQ and everyone got stuck in to get the kit unloaded and taken up to the camp. Finally all was unpacked and sorted and the pilots could reconnoitre the Manndaw and Kaladan area. 'We had a look. It seemed peculiar that heavy fighting was going on below.' With the arrival of their first load of bombs there was a keen sense of anticipation and excitement. The narrative recorded that 'pilots can be seen by their respective planes washing, polishing and cleaning. Ground crew also excited, this the great day that they have waited for ever since the squadron was formed. Much talk is carried out and many speculative guesses.'[13]

10 Squadron IAF was the third Hurri–bomber squadron in the Arakan. Bob had at his disposal an establishment of thirty officers, of which he had as available pilots twenty-six officers and one NCO plus fourteen serviceable aeroplanes. Their operational start was to be on 23 December and even in the early dawn of a very cold morning the excitement was noticeable. As they waited and the hours passed with no call to action the men calmed down and they 'either play bridge (pilots), write witty pieces on the bombs (ground crew) or carry on with their normal work'.[14]

At last, just before 11.00, the telephone rang with a request for an attack on a bridge. They took off and attacked a bridge near Thayettabin, diving from 4,000 to 3,000 feet. They scored one direct hit on the bridge and one near miss.[15] Their campaign was well underway and from now on they operated each day on targets and took great pride in the accuracy of their bombing. Three days later the Myomaung ferry was the day's target. In their words it was 'well and truly duffed up, all the bombs landing in a square fifty yards by fifty yards'.[16]

The squadron was operating well and despite the war they did not forget that it was Christmas and due celebrations were held, assisted enthusiastically by their Group Commander, Bandon, who visited every squadron in his command. Beer was strictly rationed and was restricted to the British troops. Bob, not impressed that only a minor part of his squadron qualified, 'accidentally' noted all his Indian airmen as British. The Harvard was sent to Calcutta for other essential supplies such as Carew's gin and other comestibles for the Christmas table and a great time was had by all.[17] But after the celebrations the work began again.

To the frustration of the pilots, little was seen of any Japanese activity. All they had was reassurance from the Army liaison officer that even though they might never see the enemy, their bombing work was much appreciated. The pilots within the squadron were naturally competitive and Flying Officer Suri was one of their best pilots. When he disposed of a bridge with the first bomb 'the rest of the fellows took a dim view of being done out of their target like that so they moseyed around and came across some jetties and a warehouse which duly collected the lot'.[18]

The terrain was a major challenge, as Bandon described in a radio interview after the campaign:

The Arakan is a country of jungle with steep little hills – not so little, covered with jungle to their summit. I should have hated to walk up these hills even without a pack or a rifle, still less at the same time as hand grenades and such like were rolling down a hill towards me; so you can imagine the soldiers' difficulties. At first when we bombed these strong points we found that the Japanese would run off into the jungle only to return before the troops could get here.[19]

Tactics were adjusted from experience. The pilots of 10 Squadron began to climb higher over the target to 6,000 feet and then peel off into a seventy-degree dive, releasing the bombs at 3,000 feet. This was followed by a complete circuit and two strafing runs. Pictures were taken and debriefings held of each mission.[20]

On 29 December the squadron, led by Flight Lieutenant Jones, bombed and strafed a hill in the Kaladan valley where 200 or 300 Japanese were holding up the 'boys' advance'. The action involved two other IAF squadrons, 9 and 4, plus a USAAF squadron which flew Mitchells. The latter dropped delayed-action bombs, much to the disgust of the IAF squadrons who had to fly through them, strafing, 'while the bombs were going pop in every direction they looked'.[21]

Meanwhile, on New Year's Day 10 Squadron was suffering, but at least it was self-inflicted. The whole squadron, pilots and aircrew, had hangovers as a result of their New Year's Eve party. The next day there was eager anticipation as 9 and 10 Squadrons were selected to play a big part in a major offensive on Akyab. There was considerable disappointment when the island of Akyab was taken with little opposition. Bandon had suspected that the Japanese numbers had been reduced at Akyab so sent his staff officer Group Captain Dennis David, another Battle of Britain veteran, to fly over in a small light aircraft. He saw no enemy activity while flying low and so Bandon and Christison both flew in personally and landed. They were welcomed by locals who confirmed the Japanese had left, so the bombardment was called off. The Japanese may have vacated Akyab but they were holding on tenaciously to Kangaw and Taungup, which protected their forces in the Irrawaddy valley.[22] 10 Squadron returned to their regular attacking of rivercraft and hilltop positions. It was not without its risk and Bob's logbook on 3 January notes 'considerable' return fire.[23]

The Allies had air superiority, but this did not mean that there was no activity from the highly manoeuvrable Japanese Zeros. But if the risk from the enemy fighter aircraft was limited, flying over the jungle had its own dangers. Low flying was essential as the Japanese had mastered the art of remaining still and hidden within the cover of the thick jungle canopy. Neville Gill was a flying officer with 4 Squadron IAF and recalled the risks.

When we reported for duty at the Akyab Air Base in Burma, our Commanding Officer told us, 'there are 14 of you. At least four will be buried here – those are the statistics – so be careful.' This was mainly because we were part of a squadron that mainly carried out low-level flying, at about 500 feet, which meant that we were mostly flying at treetop level ... At that level, everything looked so green, like a smooth carpet, but the danger was that there were many tall trees that were bound to be a little higher, sticking out, and there would be very little time to avoid them. If we hit them, we had it – chances of survival were very little.

It was dangerous every time we went up – they used to fire with ammo-belts that contained five assorted bullets – the first would be an armour piercing round, the next a slightly bigger round, then a tracer, and so on, all in sequence, one after the other, so if we were hit, or our fuel tanks were hit, that was it.[24]

A crash through enemy fire, engine malfunction or some other accident was a constant risk. Landing a damaged aircraft in dense jungle was not viable so the aircrew were encouraged to bale out and everyone knew the likely consequences of falling into Japanese hands. On 8 January the squadron listened unusually intently to a lecture. Given by a staff officer, its subject was 'evasion and escape'. With suitable wartime understatement, the talk was judged 'very interesting indeed'.[25]

Considerable thought and planning had been put into the challenges of rescuing men from the jungle. It was essential to be able to reassure each pilot that despite the risks he had a good chance of surviving if he landed behind enemy lines. Just as mainland Europe had a series of well-organised escape routes for those who landed behind enemy lines, so too did Burma. Between November 1944 and May 1945, 'over 1,350 sorties were flown in which 2,100 tons of stores and 1,000 liaison officers were dropped behind enemy lines'. They were known as Force 136, and the officers included planters who had previously worked in Burma as well as local Burmese keen to assist the Allies.[26] The challenge for a pilot landing behind enemy lines was to distinguish between friend and foe, as some Burmese nationals supported the enemy and the Indian National Army was fighting alongside the Japanese.

Aircrew needed to be equipped and trained to survive. The lecture reassured them of the rescue organisation behind enemy lines and introduced them to their equipment. Apart from water bottles, rations, compass, heliograph, sewing kit, leech stick (loss of blood from leeches was a danger), salt tablets, commando dagger, machete and fishing tackle it also included chewing gum. The lecture anticipated the likely reaction of the pilots to the long list of equipment:

And here let us get one point straight. Even if you are slightly dazed at the assortment which you are apparently expected to carry into the air and even if you are wondering whether your aircraft will accommodate the unholy collection with which you are faced, it is sheer and absolute idiocy for you, in the depth of your ignorance, to try a little pruning and leave out such items as do not appear to you personally to be of much value. Your personal opinions at this stage of the game are not worth two hoots in a hollow, and the lifesaving equipment with which you have been issued, every item of it, is there because of opinion expressed by those who have had to learn the hard way. So don't be tempted to leave out items just because you don't quite see what use they are going to be.[27]

After listing the extensive amount of equipment to be carried personally in a specially adapted overall, the lecturer continued,

We shall now have a short pause for prayer or any other reaction which suggests itself to you as you survey this assorted pile of ironmongery and haberdashery. My personal reaction is that it would have been a kindly thought to have flung in the Dakota to lug it along because, and here is the point, it all has to go, every single item of it, unless you prefer to take a chance with your life when it comes to walking out.

The question is what are you going to do about it? If you attend [these lectures] with the firm intention of paying as little attention as possible and of obtaining the maximum amount of slumber in the back row, then there is little we can do for you ...you are in danger of becoming a complete write off or alternatively a cause of much unnecessary blasphemy as [we] struggle to rescue your valuable but brainless body from the jungle.[28]

The authorities knew just how essential this training was for all those who were daily asked to fly over the jungle knowing they might be forced to bale out, survive alone and evade a remorseless and pitiless enemy. It was an essential aid to morale as the Air Ministry was well aware. A report on jungle training facilities and the vital importance of jungle training concluded, 'Men are not afraid of that which they know, but only the unknown. The jungle can be looked upon as a friendly ally to help escape provided one has learnt to move about in it and how to use it as an aid to sustenance.'[29]

There was good reason for the squadron to sit up and take notice. On 31 January a Liberator crew crashed into the jungle. Six men survived and were tortured by the Japanese for information. All eventually died. A posthumous George Cross was awarded to the flight sergeant wireless operator.[30]

The weather was not making life easy either. For the early weeks of January, heavy rain delayed operations and the airstrip was totally waterlogged. As the Hurricanes risked sinking into the ground, considerable manpower was needed to push, pull and manhandle them to the hard ground outside the dispersal hut. There were also some personnel changes as men moved on for promotion or came to the end of their tour of duty. Bob's Canadian Flight Commander left and was replaced by an Indian officer, Ranjan Dutt. Bob soon found to his pleasure that Ranjan was a brilliant pilot and he and Suri became the leading pilots in the squadron. The other change was a new adjutant; replacing a British officer was G. S. Singh, who turned out to be Indian nobility as he was one of the princes of Bharattpore.[31]

There were changes, too, in armament as the Allies sought more ways of attacking the well-camouflaged and well-dug-in enemy positions. An armament officer from Group HQ arrived with an Army major who inspected the aircraft and finally informed the squadron that they were to test a 'frightfully hush hush parafaxe bomb'. Suri and Pye set off to test them on a nearby hill. Suri's released, but not all of those on Pye's aircraft did. After three unsuccessful attempts to shake them off, Pye had to return home knowing the risks of landing fully bombed up and with a new weapon. But as he came into land, the lowering of the flaps caused the bomb to fall off, landing just short of the strip. Not surprisingly, 'this bomb was quickly located by the group armament officer'.[32]

The next day Bob led his squadron on a strike against Kretsin village, in close support of 81st West African Division. The target was a Japanese supply point and the 'village felt rather sorry for itself when we left'. In the afternoon Flight Lieutenant Dutt led the squadron on a strike against Kwagon village but while over the target area Pilot Officer McKie developed an internal glycol leak and made a successful forced landing on a Dakota strip nearby. He was contacted after forty-five minutes by V Force and taken under their wing, fed and made as comfortable as possible for the night. His position was noted by Dutt and the squadron returned to base. McKie was speedily returned to base by a DC3 that was bringing reinforcements to 81st West African Division, who subsequently destroyed his stricken aeroplane.[33]

If the Japanese had withdrawn from Akyab they were holding on to Myebon and so a combined operation was launched on 12 January. As they flew to attack Myebon, which was at the extreme limit of their range, the pilots looked down on '100 tiny ships in a glassy sea shelling the mainland'. It was, they felt, a wonderful sight.[34] The next day they were bombing Myebon again and then in the afternoon Zingyawmaw. Messages from the 81st conveyed welcome congratulations on the squadron's bombing accuracy.

The squadron was to get to know the West African Division well. It was made up mainly of men from West Africa with mostly British officers. The brigadier, Jolly, had been commissioned in the Territorial Army. The other officers were Major Caiger-Watson and captains Seepes, Benson and Trowbridge. There was a British warrant officer, two British lance sergeants and the rest were African other ranks including two cooks, one for European cookery and one for African.[35] The division was heading southwards through the Kaladan valley, through the deep river valleys and rice fields. Their task was very hard when they came up against well-dug-in Japanese points on the hills and a particularly tough situation in January called for extreme measures.

Bob had been called up to Wing HQ to go to a forward strip to confer with Wg Cdr Smith and Brigadier Jolly. Bob flew Jolly in a light airplane, an L-5 Sentinel, to understand the situation.[36] The Japanese had halted the division and were bombarding them. The position was behind enemy lines and was right at the extreme range of the Hurri-bombers, who could therefore spend little time in attack. In this war front lines were fluid, as Eddie Sparkes explained in a letter home: 'This is a crazy war ... there is no front line, we and the Japs are all over the place and a forward landing strip can be a hundred miles in front of the most backward Japs.'[37]

Bob briefed the pilots on the task ahead. There were twelve pilots in their Hurricanes and one flew the Harvard. In addition they were joined by six aircraft from 9 Squadron IAF. Bob, as the senior commander, led the combined force. The task was to dislodge the enemy from the ridge at Paukpingwin. It had proved impossible to take the ridge by assault and other means had not been effective. What Bob knew and had previously agreed with Smith and Jolly was that the West Africans would create a temporary airstrip by flattening the mud walls between the paddy fields. Just three days later a 1,500-yard strip was ready for them. The pilots were to take just blankets and essential rations and fly in to land on the prepared strip. They would then operate for a day from there, which was just four miles from the Japanese HQ. The men all understood the risk of the task. They would be flying fully bombed-up onto an unknown temporary airstrip, spending the night there and would have to rely on the aircraft's internal battery starting up in the morning. Under normal circumstances they used large battery packs on trolleys as a more reliable means of starting up the engines. The pilots were told that any pilot whose Hurricane did not start in the morning would be left behind. Throughout the whole time they would be within range of the Japanese artillery.[38]

They set off with Bob leading the way and planned to use their now well-practised stream-landing technique. But as the 10 Squadron diarist wrote, 'Alas, alack the strip was very dusty indeed and when the cloud eventually settled down it was found that F/O H D Jarman had run off runway in D and landed up on his in a paddy field, while F/O David IAF had run into F/O Chrishna IAF writing them both off, much to everyone's disgust including their own.'[39] It wasn't what they had planned. Bob had landed first and when he walked back to investigate he discovered there was a hidden stream underneath part of the strip and the aircraft were simply too heavy. Fortunately the Army had plenty of manpower, and the aeroplanes were physically hauled out of the hole that had opened up.[40] The night was spent in foxholes especially dug for them by the Army. They were lined with supply parachutes, of which there were plenty, the accommodation being nicknamed the Hilton. The pilots settled in for the night but the shelling by the Japanese began at 22.00 and was continuous. Few of the pilots had experienced mortar fire and found it unnerving knowing they were sitting there as the targets. Just when their spirits were at a low ebb, a welcome invitation came from the division to join them in a local temple for a drink. It was explained that it was the only place that could be blacked out.[41]

The next morning they awoke to find the aircraft still remarkably unscathed despite the heavy shelling. The plan of campaign was explained and the pilots were on readiness as shells continued to fly over them. The target eventually came up and was dealt with successfully. Meanwhile the Harvard also took two trips back to base with what they could salvage from the three wrecked Hurricanes and flew it back to base in the Harvard.[42] The 81st Division were very grateful and gave both Bob and Squadron Leader Adams a carved Buddha as a memento.[43]

At the end of the day the remaining aircraft returned to their normal base at Ramu where a surprise awaited. A party had been arranged by Bob to celebrate the squadron's achievement. In the absence of the pilots, four officers had decorated the mess and Air Vice-Marshal the Earl of Bandon DSO had been invited. Bandon paid tribute to the men involved in this operation during his later radio broadcast from England. He described the work of the close support squadrons as

possibly even more important than the work of the transport squadrons. Without it the Army would have found it very difficult to move forward at all, and certainly could not have advanced rapidly. It seems to me that it was really the close support which made the advance possible and the transport squadrons that kept up the momentum.

The cooperation was so close that in one case when real close support was needed very early in the morning, we sent one of our squadrons of Hurricanes to work off a forward strip surrounded by jungle, which was under Japanese sniper and mortar fire. The troops looked after these aircrews like children, and almost tucked them in at night.

The Army appreciated this type of activity and made the aircrews realise the extreme difficulty and discomfort under which the army was advancing.[44]

Bandon also thoroughly enjoyed the party at the time and is quoted in the squadron diary as remarking that the 'Arakan coast had never seen a party such as this'.[45] There were, inevitably, a few heavy heads the next day but they were back on readiness. The two remaining pilots who were left at Paukpingwin were flown back to base by DC3 having destroyed the aircraft prior to leaving. They had not wasted their time while with the Army and had joined in with the return fire on the Japanese position.

The squadron went back to their normal operations but were also told they would shortly be moving temporarily to a forward position, Indin, to take part in a combined operation against Ramree Island. This time they were able to take their ground crew with them under the capable charge of the senior warrant officer, Warrant Officer Ware.[46]

While they waited to move forward, work went on as usual. The squadron were now being directed to their targets by a visual control post (VCP) under the call sign of Arcade. This post proved to be an invaluable aid.

On one occasion the Visual Control Post was right forward in a jeep and the jeep was being annoyed by being fired at by the Japanese. I should explain here that the Visual Control Post is a combined RAF and Army unit in which the RAF passes by wireless to the aircraft in the air any detailed information about the target they are attacking, when actually watching from the ground the attack of the aircraft taking place, to ensure that the attacks are as effective as possible. As I was saying, this VP or Visual Control Post was being attacked. The flight lieutenant rang up a squadron and said, 'Please strafe Japanese fifty yards north of my jeep.' Down came the fighter bombers in a flash … the Japanese no longer annoyed him.[47]

Force 136 was providing invaluable support to the tactical aircraft of 221 and 224 Groups. Many not only indicated targets but succeeded also in giving detailed reports of the results of attacks, while others assisted pilots who had been forced to bale out to return to the Allied lines.[48] There were two near casualties to serve as a reminder of the dangers. Pilot Officer Sujir returned to base on the way out to one operation due to engine trouble, while Flying Officer Ingle force landed one mile east of Ratedung due to lack of fuel. He was later flown back to base in an L-5.[49]

On 20 January, twelve aircraft and the invaluable runabout, the Harvard, took off for Indin. Nos 4 and 9 IAF squadrons were already there. The ground party had done a good job and they were on a reasonably comfortable tented site eating mainly tinned food. The next morning they were on readiness early and 'everyone on their toes waiting to be called on to play their part in the invasion of Ramree Island but once again the Navy had its own way meeting very little opposition that little having been quickly disposed of by themselves'.[50]

The squadron was again stood down from a potentially major operation, much to their disappointment. The Japanese were leaving the islands to the advancing Allies and did not seem to appreciate the strategic value of their use as forward airbases. The capture of Akyab and Ramree made possible the supply by air of the XIV Army. Until the capture of these bases, air supply had to be carried out from Chittagong northwards as there were no airfields further south from which they could operate.[51] But 10 Squadron was still needed in a strike in support of 'our old friends the 81st WA div.'. They continued to be praised on the accuracy of their bombing.[52]

A constant requirement for Bob, as CO of the squadron, was to keep his aircraft and pilots ready and fit for operations. The Hurricanes were elderly and getting spares was not easy and the tropical conditions made life very difficult. 'All aircraft are maintaining a high standard of serviceability due to the keenness of our ground crew and earn praise of their respective pilots.' The squadron was flying fifty to sixty hours daily, with up to thirty-six sorties a day. Bandon paid particular tribute to the ground crews: 'I really cannot speak too highly of the work these airmen did where sometimes the aircraft were too hot to touch and other times so wet that they could literally sail to their work in a dinghy across flooded paddy fields.'[53]

The ground crews were operating in very tough conditions and they rose to the challenge. The Harvard was the essential runabout for the squadron and was the only means of getting to and from Calcutta. The propeller was damaged by a bird strike, but although they managed to get a replacement, by simply pinching one from another, fitting it was a challenge of a different order of magnitude. They had previously had difficulties in servicing it as it was an American aircraft and now they needed specialist equipment to fit the propeller. Several palm trees were chopped down, a crane was made and the propeller was fitted successfully by eye. Bob was seriously impressed.[54]

The aeroplanes were in some ways the easy part – at least there was some control – but the health of the pilots was a different matter. Some health issues could be managed such as banning the pilots from swimming in dangerous waters. The water looked inviting but there were stingrays lurking for the unwary in some areas. One pilot had already been bitten and been out of action for twenty-four hours. Other illnesses were hard to avoid. Eddie Sparkes had been in hospital for some time and was now on sick leave, but Flying Officer Picken RCAF contracted a bout of malaria. He then developed pleurisy and was ordered to a hospital in Bombay prior to his embarkation for Canada. But before he was invalided to Bombay his promotion to flight lieutenant came through and Bob had the pleasure of informing him of the good news.[55]

Weapons were under constant review, and they were now carrying 500 lb bombs that made the aeroplanes even harder to fly but cleared 'an awful lot of forest'.[56] Bob even decided to experiment with bomb loads himself, convinced that the Hurricanes could carry bigger loads and be more effective in one sortie. Unfortunately he had not considered the aerodynamic effect and his experiment was a failure, at which point he recognised that he was not destined to be an aeronautical engineer.[57]

If Akyab was taken without a fight and Ramree Island was similarly taken, Kangaw was different, with the Japanese holding on to two well-fortified hills. Bandon switched all his available air forces to attack. This was the vital battle of the Arakan campaign. The landings were supported by Mitchells, Thunderbolts and Hurricanes, but the main battle did not take place until a little later when the Japanese were holding stoutly to two heavily wooded features behind the beachhead. The total effort between 22 and 31 January amounted to over fifty tons of bombs and 17,720 gallons of napalm being dropped on the two features.[58]

Considerable pride was felt by the whole squadron on the accuracy of their bombing. Sometimes their work involved the standard hill strikes, but they were also used as pathfinders for Liberators in Kangaw area. 'For this we received a tremendous strawberry from W/C Parker RAF.' The squadron continued to bomb effectively and their view was that the 'Japs must certainly be terribly tired of our air power while not one fighter of theirs even shows a nose'. But the Japanese were holding on tenaciously and indeed managed to counter-attack and regain lost ground briefly.[59]

Operations continued in the Kangaw area during February. Low cloud was often a problem but the squadron, determined to play their part, found on one occasion that even though the cloud base was only 1,000 feet by 'flying down the coast, and cutting across the lower Kaladan valley, we were able to find a beautifully clear spot over the target'. They returned the same way and were 'gratified to hear that we were the only Squadron to go on sortie today, the other having one look at the low clouds returning to base'. It was not all work; when no targets came through and they were stood down, much of the time was spent on the river in a rather rickety homemade boat. Training was not neglected and every opportunity was used to keep them active, with practice quarter attacks and tight formation. At last the squadron was due to move forward to Ramree Island. The ground section moved first as the strip was not ready for the aircraft. Meanwhile the rest of the squadron, nineteen pilots and seventy-eight ground crew, moved to Bawli Bazar, 'flying a very tight formation and accomplishing one of the best formation landings yet'. Here they settled into their latest temporary base.[60]

On 20 February the squadron celebrated their first birthday, although due to operations there was no actual party. Their pride was evident:

> During this last year we have been many places, and seen many things and we can look back on a very good record, and justifiable pride in our squadron. There are still many things we have to do, and we hope to accomplish these things in way that will make us top notch squadron of the Indian Air Force.[61]

Indeed, their pride was justified; all the squadrons on the front line, both IAF and RAF, had attained high standards and were operating at high pressure.

Few targets came up, but there were other enjoyable pursuits. They played cricket against 2759 Squadron (RAF Regiment) – despite their CO's prowess at the game 'they really duffed us up inside and out' – and enjoyed some 'marvellous swimming to be had in the Chaung by the side of dispersal'. There was little action, and Bob flew down to forward group in Akyab to determine the time of the move to Ramree. Meanwhile one of the pilots, Pilot Officer Evans RAAF, was driven in the truck to Cox's Bazar on an essential mission to collect the beer ration. On his return he swore that one bottle had been broken in transit. The diarist was understanding, 'but then again, it's a long and dusty road'. At last the message came through from Movement Control in Calcutta with the order to move and 'packing [was] renewed with a tremendous vigour'.[62]

902 Wing, comprising 4 and 10 Squadrons RIAF and 275 Squadron RAF, equipped with Spitfires, moved forward to Ramree Island. They were now the most forward wing of the campaign.[63] By March most of the squadron was based at Kyaukpyu on the north of the island. There was a

reminder of how far forward they were when a solitary Japanese bomber attacked the island and hit the hospital about a mile distant and injured five men. Life was a strange mixture of constant readiness, 'a morning spent pulling our fingers and listening to the knuckles crack' while waiting for targets to come up. Then when they were stood down they headed for the beach to unwind with a swim. Even here at this forward base entertainment had not been forgotten. George Formby and his wife Beryl arrived with a small group of entertainers and were given a tremendous welcome by an audience of nearly 2,000. Then a singer, Patrice Burke, also arrived to entertain them. 'All these shows good or bad are greatly appreciated as other means of amusing oneself are non-existent.'[64]

Gradually they settled in to yet another new base, laying floors in the tents, setting up a mess, and hearing the news on the wireless of the British breakthrough in the Mandalay area. This breakthrough was hailed as a major achievement by Churchill. Mandalay was the traditional heart of Burma but Churchill also noted his relief that it was one of the few places that could easily be pronounced. The squadron's accuracy remained a matter of great pride, making direct hits on targets indicated by the VCP, who congratulated the pilots on their accurate bombing and strafing. The latter at times took place only fifty to sixty yards from their own troops.[65]

Suddenly there was, in the jargon of the day, 'a big flap' as the Japanese were reported as having made a landing ten miles south of camp. The diarist described the scene. 'Everyone grabs a gun and steel bowler and started calculating how long it will take them to the strip. News flashes bring report that there are between 200–300 men but no one can decide if they are Japs or Burmese returning to the Island. Nothing materialises but the a/c are grounded awaiting results, and everyone is on his or somebody else's toes.'[66] It turned out to be a false alarm, the first of several. If their toes had been a problem it was their fingernails that were bitten in frustration when no targets came up and they watched 'while Liberators and Mustangs fill the sky, flying in the general direction of Rangoon'.[67]

After organised resistance ceased on Ramree Island 4 and 10 Squadrons were used in amphibious landings in Ruywa and Letpan where they flew cab rank patrols. Cab rank had been developed in the Normandy landings. Fighter bombers flew in orbiting positions close to the front line and could be called on in number to a given target by a forward air controller.[68] Cab rank patrols were heavy on fuel and not always effective. But soon the squadron was in action again against targets that included a gun position and tanks and there was a new rumour that they would shortly be using 'two entirely new types of bombs, and these sound to be not only deadly, but also unhealthy'.[69] Napalm had been developed in 1942 at Harvard University and was now to be used in Burma.

Spare parts were not easy to get, and the soft sand grounded the aircraft and caused those taxiing out to veer off onto their noses. The Harvard was still the essential runabout for the squadron, collecting people and spares, and on 9 March it was flown up to 'to collect the very welcome liquor' – it was the day before their commanding officer's twenty-fifth birthday – but it was also collecting something else. There had been a major problem with supply of fuses for the bombs. Bob had flown up to Group HQ and managed to get hold of a few hundred fuses. These only operated on air pressure when the bomb was released. This meant that they could not be armed as safe once loaded on the Hurricane so their normal way of bombing need some rethinking. Since the bombs detonated due to the build-up of air pressure, dive-bombing was not an option.[70]

We are using a new type of fusing today, and when a village came up we were all excited to find out the extent of the damage caused. Red section led by S/Ldr Doe paved the way followed at 5 min intervals by Yellow Section and Blue Section. Approaching the target the a/c moved into loose Vic formation and in a slight dive the word to release bombs was given by the respective section commanders.[71]

The bombs exploded about six inches above ground, giving the maximum possible blast effect. 'The north end of the town was flattened and left blazing while the south end felt pretty sorry for itself.' Bob recalled the moment:

Can you imagine standing on the ground watching twelve Hurricanes in formation approaching you at about three thousand five hundred feet, with the leader standing on alternate wingtips (so that I could see the ground and judge where to bomb) and then finding a very neat pattern of bombs all exploding at the same time.[72]

By mid-March, the squadron was frustrated by the lack of action: 'We thought when we came to a very forward airstrip such as this we would be over whelmed with targets, but in actual fact we are lucky if one mediocre effort comes up in a day. We are not sure if we are waiting for the war to catch up, or the war is waiting for us.' Pilots were beginning to look ahead to the monsoon period, when they might be able to take leave.[73]

A chance has been given by Group to let us buy a few luxuries at amazingly cheap prices, so the whole squadron has stepped in to take advantage of this offer, and also to spend some of the money which has been burning holes in pockets ever since we arrived here.[74]

The Indian Air Force had been a strong player through the war, particularly in the last two years, and recognition of its valiant efforts came when it was announced that King George VI had given them royal status. They were now officially the Royal Indian Air Force.

The squadron was to some extent marking time until the Army caught up and found them some close support targets. 'Close support definitely is our forte, and strawberries from various Army Commanders can be shown to prove that our good work is well appreciated.' They were still using diaphragm bombs, which they described as 'beautiful but dangerous', and Bob's scheme was now standard and was proving highly effective. They went straight for the target in a dive no steeper than thirty degrees with the aircraft in a tight formation, and when the leader said 'drop' all bombs were dropped.[75]

The Japanese may have relinquished the coastal bases, but they were defending their inland territory with ferocity. Supplies and communications came to them via the Burma–Siam railway with its infamous death bridge, through the rivers and along roads. These were all targeted by the Allies. A major road link was the road running east–west between Taungup and Prome. An order came through from Group HQ that the road was to be blocked and kept blocked at all times to prevent the Japanese from using this in their retreat eastwards. Bob and the commanding officers of 4 RIAF and 273 RAF squadrons held a conference and split the road between them in forty-mile sections. Road busting was a thankless task. Even with really accurate bombing, since the road was made entirely of loose sand and dust it could be refilled and made serviceable quickly and easily.[76]

The number of targets began to increase and now they were also using the new deadly 'incendiaries', which cleared vast areas on the ground. Rivercraft in the Taungup area were attacked and the squadron returned with some 'very nice claims of good shooting against long lines of sampans'. When the squadron was stood down they immediately rushed down to the beach for the 'ever welcome daily dip'.[77]

The Harvard continued its regular trips collecting some of life's essential supplies such as cigarettes. It was welcomed by 'practically the whole of the squadron rather tired of smoking woodbines and de Reskes and eager to lay their hands on the so-called 'good' Indian Players'.[78] Bob was a heavy smoker, rarely seen without a cigarette in his hands, and was very pleased to see these.

With limited opportunities for amusement, parties were held on many occasions. There were even high hopes on one occasion of persuading the nurses who served in the local hospital to join in. The Harvard was sent to Calcutta for supplies while at a late hour the squadron cheerfully took off to plaster a Japanese divisional HQ where an enemy VIP was supposed to be visiting. 'Plaster was the correct word as the whole area was razed to the ground.' Satisfied, they looked forward to the party, having worked hard to set it up. But despite high hopes, no nurses turned up. 'However members of 273 Squadron rolled along in full strength with a very enviable thirst. The food that was laid on was very good.'[79]

The squadron was operating at full stretch, with pairs of aircraft taking off at thirty-minute intervals to be directed by the VCP. Bombing and strafing continued and the targets included sampans, bashas, hill features, main roads and an ammunition dump. The risks were constant. Pilot Officer Chrishna had just turned for home when the Japanese opened fire on him. He returned rather hurriedly with his 'a/c looking like a well-worn sieve'.[80] The next day four aircraft were in the Irrawaddy valley on an offensive recce. Flying Officer Jarman struck a telephone tripwire which had been strung across a runway. With his engine vibrating badly, he managed to return home and landed on an already cleared strip. On inspection, fifteen feet of wire was found coiled around the shaft of the airscrew. A second Hurricane had both wing tips damaged by the same tripwire.[81]

Taungup fell on 16 April to the 26th and 82nd divisions after what the ground forces described as 'a very heavy and successful air strike' upon a dominating Japanese position in the neighbourhood. During the progress of Allied troops south down the coast to Taungup, their line of advance was through valleys dominated by jungle-covered heights that offered ample protection to enemy troops, observation points and gun positions.[82]

No 10 Squadron using the incendiary bomb in novel form of attack, smoked out the enemy with such satisfactory results that the advance of the Allied ground forces on Taungup was considerably accelerated. While the incendiary bomb was effective in built up urban areas it had hitherto not been of much use against dense, damp, monsoon jungle. But it was then at the end of the dry season and the scrub burnt well. One such attack was put in early in the morning by No 4 Squadron and with a favourable breeze from the sea the fire swept up the hillside, down the opposite slope, and up a still higher hillside. Planes on night patrol reported that it was still burning at midnight, sixteen hours after the initial attack.[83]

After the fall of Taungup there was a sense of the end of term as rumours were rife that the squadron was moving out, and the news was confirmed by Bob. With the monsoon season due, Bandon's 224 Group was to withdraw from the Arakan to southern India to re-equip and prepare for the invasion of Malaya. The campaign had been very successful, and it was time to count the losses. 224 Group had lost twenty-six men killed in action, twenty-seven killed on active service, sixty-four men were missing and twenty-six would be found as Japanese prisoners of war in Rangoon. Bob had brought his men safely through with just one casualty, Chackerbutty, who had been killed while training. Other Indian Air Force squadrons had not fared so well. The other two Hurricane squadrons, 2 Squadron and 9 Squadron, had lost eight and five men respectively.[84]

Packing commenced, photographs were taken of the squadron and goodbyes were said to those being left behind. A final football match was arranged against 273 Squadron which 'ended in rather a dismal failure for us. Never mind, there must be some team we can beat.'[85]

On 19 April, the squadron was finally stood down after four months of continuous operations in jungle conditions. They were to proceed to Yelahanka, near Bangalore, a trip of around 1,700 miles. As usual, the pilots were to fly by stages while the rest of the party proceeded by ship to Calcutta and then by train and road. On 21 April, after a short speech of thanks given by Group Captain Marvin and Wing Commander Smith from 902 Wing, the pilots were strapped into their respective Hurricanes and, led by Bob, they left Burma.[86]

9

POST-WAR RAF AND 25TH ANNIVERSARY OF THE BATTLE OF BRITAIN

As the pilots headed on their long journey to southern India and the ground party continued the job of packing up the equipment, the big news came through with an announcement by Winston Churchill: 'The war in Europe is at an end.' There was 'great rejoicing everywhere, but little for us, I am afraid as kit has to be loaded on to the train, and a great amount of work to be done.'[1] They did find time to celebrate with a few drinks and to speculate on how long the war with Japan might last. While Europe celebrated the German capitulation, there were 'hundreds and thousands of soldiers, sailors and airmen still confronting the Japanese in the Far East'.[2] Rangoon fell on 3 May and with no Japanese threat to the China supply lines the US forces left for China while the RAF concentrated on the drive for Singapore. Eastern Air Command was now wholly RAF. But there were still 50,000 Japanese troops fighting in Burma and this posed real challenges for the RAF after the loss of the US transport planes.

Bob led his pilots and sixteen Hurricanes and the Harvard in a series of stages to Trinchinopoly in southern India, near Bangalore. Gradually the squadron reduced as more men went on leave. They were to be re-equipped with Spitfires but, while the Hurricanes were moved away, the new aircraft did not appear. There was a sense of flatness after months of high activity. An education officer arrived and arranged lectures for the Indian other ranks who, with little to do, were getting restless and bored.

Those officers who were not on leave were persuaded to give talks on a range of subjects including the 'political and commercial future of India'.[3]

It was a tricky time to run a squadron as it required keeping the men committed and involved in this state of limbo. Their new base at Trichinopoly was in a beautiful setting and it seemed wholly untouched by the war. It was a lovely town, with its officers club and English-style lawns and flowerbeds. But the diarist noted,

Trichinopoly town offers practically no amusement whatsoever as there is only one small cinema that shows mediocre to poor films and there are no decent shops where anyone can replenish his sadly depleted wardrobe, depleted due to having been in the front for many months.[4]

Pre-war colonial attitudes still prevailed in Trichinopoly. The officers club 'didn't like dirty uniforms or Indian officers. All of which we had.'[5] Bob, who understood what it was like to feel outside a club, went with his officers to set up an 'Alternative Club' in a local Chinese restaurant.[6]

There was one final celebration for Bob and his men as news came through that Bob was to leave the squadron and go to Quetta, then in northern India, now Pakistan. Quetta was the Army Staff College and two naval and two RAF officers were selected for each course. Here he settled down to five months of lectures and exercises, which must have come as a relief after so many months on operations. In his spare time he indulged in his two hobbies, cricket and food. He captained the college cricket team and formed a private dining club with the college librarian.[7] Bob was well regarded by the college and his assessment summed him up thusly:

Although this officer has a somewhat casual manner he is pleasant helpful and keen. He has cooperated well and been an asset to the course. He has confidence and good powers of decision and initiative. Has a quick brain and thinks clearly. NOT liable to fluster. He has a broad outlook with plenty of common-sense. Appears very fit.[8]

While at Quetta he heard the news that the two atomic bombs were dropped on 6 and 9 August and Japan surrendered. The war was ending, although there were still large numbers of Japanese troops spread throughout Burma, Siam, Malaya and further east. Mass leaflet drops were organised to get the message through to them. There was other more personal news for Bob. He had been awarded the Distinguished Service Order.

He had impressed his superiors with his command of his squadron. His efficiency and tact were noted and his 'personal example has been an inspiration to all members of his squadron'. He was described as a 'magnificent leader both in the air and on the ground'.[9]

The citation referred to his 'unconquerable spirit and great devotion to duty'. It was a very significant award, even more so when the RAF in the Far East was seen as parsimonious with awards.[10] The recommendation for the DSO stated, 'Through his exceptional energy, resourcefulness, enthusiasm, and magnificent leadership, and in overcoming all the unusual difficulties in an RIAF unit, he brought his Squadron to a very high state of operational efficiency and discipline.'[11] Bob, aged twenty-five, certainly had a high reputation even among other squadrons, where it was noted that his men admired him but were somewhat in awe of his explosive temper. Leading an Indian Air Force squadron was a real challenge for a non-Indian at this time of political uncertainty. Several other commanding officers had not survived long and in some squadrons, such as 8 Squadron, there had been a considerable turnover of squadron leaders. A member of 8 Squadron recalled a poor atmosphere and intense anti-British feeling with the CO, a New Zealander, and the Bengali adjutant at loggerheads.[12] Bob, as commander of 10 Squadron, was the longest-serving leader of an IAF squadron at the end of the war. In total three DSOs were awarded to RIAF commanders: Squadron Leader Mehar Singh of 6 Squadron, Squadron Leader Geoffrey Stanton, RNZAF of 4 Squadron, and Bob.

With war at an end it was a time to pick up the pieces, as Bob was posted to Air Headquarters India at Delhi. There was much to do. Tokyo had officially surrendered on 2 September and on 12 September Mountbatten with his senior commanders held a formal surrender ceremony in Singapore of the Japanese forces in Burma, Malaya and Singapore.[13] Repatriating the Allied prisoners of war was high on the list and food, medical supplies and medical teams were dropped into the camps. By the end of October 71,000 people had been evacuated from south-east Asia, including 3,000 by air. Many of these went by Sunderland to Ceylon.[14] The living, and barely living, were the priority but the dead had to be buried and remembered. Cemeteries were created and the dead identified where possible, but it was no easy task. A memorial was erected on Singapore Island at Kranji with the names of 2,990 airmen who died in the war in south-east Asia and who have no known grave.[15] Previous conflicts were not forgotten, and on 15 September Bob led the Battle of Britain parade through Bombay and read the lesson in Bombay Cathedral.

Bob was in Air Staff Plans until April 1946 and then was part of the Commander-in-Chief's secretariat until September 1946. It was a huge operation to dismantle the war machine in India. It was one thing to manage the troops and equipment as it poured in, but a very different scenario to dismantle bases, salvage equipment and repatriate men who were now frustrated, weary and, in many cases, ill. The Far East did not take priority, as the end of the war in Europe was bringing its own challenges. Demobilisation had to be organised over time and those in the east became concerned as experienced men were leaving and the men left behind feared being at the back of the queue for jobs in Britain. There was an increase in theft and loss of service equipment, men got drunk and the court martial system saw a spike in activity. In Colombo, where Mountbatten had placed his HQ, the elimination of obsolete navigational charts, many dating from Singapore days, resulted in the clearance of approximately five tons of maps and charts.[16]

During this time Bob received his DSO from Viscount Wavell, the Governor General and Viceroy of India, in a ceremony that was 'far more impressive than the Buckingham Palace Investiture'.[17] He organised a major air display in Delhi, was involved in trying to sell surplus equipment, notably Spitfires, to the Afghan Air Force and had a big adventure with the Rolls-Royce belonging to the King of Afghanistan. He was asked to drive the car from Kabul to Delhi to get it repaired, together with his companions, a Rolls-Royce aero-engineer and a Hawker sales representative. On his return, Bob was at last given his ticket home and left India on 14 September to sail for England.[18]

Bob returned to England to be briefly reunited with his young daughter, Lynne, now aged three. His marriage had not survived the trauma brought on by his previous crash and the facial injuries. His absence in India had only served to widen the gap between him and Sheila. They separated and he would not see his daughter again until, to his great delight, she traced him via the RAF eighteen years later and invited him to her wedding.

On return Bob was posted to north Devon to the School of Combined Operational Training. His work in Burma had given him plenty of experience in this topic. The school had been planned in 1944 as a joint school for all three services to teach Army/Air support in its widest meaning. It was to replace the RAF School of Army Cooperation.[19] In a paper written in October 1944, some lessons were emerging from the war and inter-services training was seen as a priority. Plans were in place for a Joint Staff College, but did not go far enough. All services agreed that was essential for all officers to have inter-service knowledge.

In this war the need had been very evident for the personnel of all three Services to be better informed in the tactics and strategy of the other Services, and to have wider knowledge and greater sympathy with their limitations.

I think there is no doubt that it is essential that each service should at least accept the responsibility of training its own officers in the tactics of the others services, and that it should never again be left to the RAF to 'sell' its tactics to the Army and Navy on the basis of a poor relation.[20]

The school was established in 1946 at Fremington near Barnstaple in north Devon. There were two courses, one for staff officers and one for senior officers with a planned ratio of attendees of twenty from the Army and ten each from the Navy and RAF.[21] Bob was not impressed with the idea of teaching skills to the staff colleges and senior military schools that would be out of date in the next war. Such backward theoretical thinking was a waste of time in his view. It was better, he felt, to concentrate on the practical but expensive training in the skills that would always be needed such as shooting and bombing.[22] But there were other enjoyable aspects, such as resuming his great passion for playing cricket, going to parties and generally enjoying the very social life of the forces. It was while he was in Barnstaple that he met Gee, a widow with a two-year-old daughter, Susan. Gee owned and ran a nursing home in Barnstaple and they met at a party.[23]

After this tour of duty in Devon, Bob was posted to Headquarters Reserve Command as the Training Officer for the Auxiliary Air Force. Here he worked with Chris Foxley-Norris. The AuxAF had been established pre-war and had proved to be highly effective, notably earning its place in the Battle of Britain alongside the regular RAF and the RAFVR. After the war, twenty AuxAF squadrons were retained and they were rearmed with Meteor and Vampire aircraft in place of Spitfires. These weekend pilots were to be part of front-line squadrons alongside the regular squadrons of Fighter Command. It was recognised that the post-war situation was somewhat different from the 1920s and 1930s, where membership of the AuxAF was dominated by social position. But it still asked a great deal from those who were prepared to join. Training pilots and ground crew was very expensive and time-consuming. To achieve the required standards the RAF needed auxiliaries who would commit to regular and frequent attendance at drills, and particularly at weekends. For the men this meant they needed to be sufficiently enthusiastic to 'subordinate to their Squadron their hobbies and spare time interests'. They had to be willing to submit to the high standards of discipline and required sufficient energy to work hard in the squadron and in their primary occupation. It was also considered that they should have no 'ties or obligations (domestic or otherwise) which restricts their desire to give nearly all their spare time to the squadron (this almost excludes married men, except in small numbers)'.[24]

Bob travelled across the British Isles visiting the various squadrons that were located across the country. It was during this period in 1948 that he and Sheila finally divorced and Bob was married to Gee at Kensington Registry Office. Sheila also remarried a few months later. The big question now was whether to try to remain with the RAF or head for civilian life. For those that had careers before the RAF, were part of family firms or who had good civilian qualifications, a return to a known job was reasonably straightforward. For Bob, his life was the RAF. He had been moulded and shaped by a service career into roles unimaginable pre-war. His social position was a very different one now from that of his parents, who were living in a small tied cottage in Hampshire. Bob's only previous experience of work was at the *News of the World* and that had been in a fairly humble position. The RAF held more certainty and the possibility of action in the future. He decided to apply to stay on and he was granted a permanent commission in the RAF on 29 October 1948.[25]

His wartime record, such as his service in the Battle of Britain, was not forgotten and in September 1949 he was interviewed on television. The Air Ministry had initially resisted identifying successful fighter pilots of the battle and disliked the notion of encouraging the adulation of 'fighter aces'. The press had latched onto a few names, particularly Douglas Bader, who due to his disability and personal determination to overcome his disadvantages made a great story. Despite the difficulty of absolutely confirming kill claims, a senior Air Ministry official had published a list of the top-scoring pilots in a book in 1941 with a foreword by Trenchard; Bob was included in this list.[26]

From 1941 there were many books, films and newspaper articles that developed the status of the Few. Churchill had energetically used the image and the men in bringing the US into the war. Post-war the propaganda continued, and there were some sensitivities. One small paragraph in the *Daily Express* in November 1947 had feathers ruffled at a very senior level in the RAF. Commander Gaylor of the US Navy gave a speech to scientists in Washington in which he stated that only 20 per cent of fighter pilots in the battle shot down a German aircraft, that the rest 'hit nothing and served only to spread return fire'. There was general outrage by many readers who wrote to protest. It reached the Chief of Air Staff (CAS), Sir Arthur Tedder, who ordered an inquiry into the facts. The chief research officer and the chief intelligence officer were forced to admit they could not obtain accurate figures but only estimates. They refuted Gaylor's numbers and estimated that around 40 to 50 per cent failed to hit a German aeroplane rather than his view of 80 per cent. This was probably not quite the heroic figure CAS wanted. However, they did cast doubts on the source of Gaylor's figures as the information had apparently been derived from the assessment of films from camera guns. The problem was that only 15 per cent of aeroplanes carried these guns and only 6 per cent of the film was analysed. In the end it was decided not to say anything official to journalists in reply but to let it quietly go away. Tedder, however, did reply to one concerned correspondent and managed to reassure him that 'the average number of aircraft shot down by each pilot throughout the period of the battle was somewhere between 0.72 and 0.82'.[27] So much for statistics. But the battle was still very much a key topic, and BBC Television knew that wartime tales were popular viewing. One programme in 1949 featured a debate between Bob, Douglas Bader and Johnny Kent on the pros and cons of the Spitfire *versus* the Hurricane. Douglas Bader had flown Hurricanes during the battle and Johnny Kent flew Spitfires, notably leading 303 (Polish) Squadron, while Bob was one of the rare pilots who had flown both aircraft during the battle.[28]

After the adrenalin rush of the war and a quiet time in his previous post, Bob found his role with the auxiliaries 'a pleasant occupation, but not terribly productive'. He was keen to get something with a bit more action so he applied for an overseas posting. It came through in 1950 and he had a posting to Oman to take charge of the RAF unit there. In May 1950 he and his new family – Gee, Susan and their eleven-month-old daughter, Helen – were on board the *Empire Fowey* heading for Port Said. They never reached Oman as Bob's essential skills were badly needed in Egypt. Just outside Port Said, a launch headed for the ship and a voice bellowed across the water. 'Bob Doe! You can't play cricket for us in Oman, so you're going to Egypt.'[29] This was confirmed when they landed; he was to stay in Egypt and he was posted to Air Plans in 205 Group. Here he remained for two years and he did indeed play a lot of cricket, representing the RAF against the Army. He was not particularly keen on desk work but was appreciated as an intelligent, well-informed, likeable and efficient officer. Air Vice-Marshal David Atcherley was posted to command the group in February 1952. Atcherley, described as a 'ball of fire' by Bob, had been Bob's commanding officer at some time during the war and Atcherley had a very high opinion of him as an officer and remarked on his 'markedly good personal qualities'.[30]

It was a complex political period in the Middle East. The State of Israel was established in May 1948 and was not recognised by the Arab states, while in Egypt, which had always been seen as a major British partner, there was fury at the British support for the establishment of the State of Israel. The Israeli Air Force had rapidly expanded, there were reports of Jewish advances into Egyptian territory and just before Bob arrived in Egypt several RAF aeroplanes had been shot down by the Israelis. Britain had a major military presence within the Canal Zone. Over 80,000 personnel were based there to protect the vital lifeline that was the Suez Canal. This had been the gateway to Britain's Far East territories, but post-war it was becoming the essential through route for the movement of oil. Sir Erik Bennett, a Middle East expert who worked extensively with both the Jordanian and Omani air forces, was a flight lieutenant in the RAF in Egypt at that time and, looking back, he saw it was the twilight of the British Empire as Britain gradually made the transition away from imperial power. This resulted in a disconnect between the London view of the situation and that on the ground. The Egyptians wanted the British out of their country and there was considerable civil unrest. The Egyptian authorities were impeding the movement of shipping through the canal and restricting the use of British airfields within the zone.[31]

In October 1951, tension was increasing. Protesters disrupted work where they could and intimidated those Egyptians working for the British services. Shooting broke out on several occasions and orders were given to move British families from Ismailia into Army compounds and some were repatriated.[32] The Egyptians were building up an armoured force close to the centre of the Canal Zone. It was considered too provocative to use operational aircraft so Bob volunteered to fly a Proctor in a reconnaissance flight. Accompanied by Flying Officer Davies, he flew on 16 October along the canal for two hours locating Egyptian forces. The next day he was out again, this time piloting a Valetta with Group Captain Henry and a Captain Gingell on board. On 18 October, back in a Proctor with Wing Commander Bushel and Flying Officer Davies, they had their first sight of an 'armed force approaching Fayid' (very close to Group HQ). Bob flew back and forth to ensure that the force knew they had been seen. The following day as he headed out he witnessed them withdrawing.[33]

It was very clear that Bob's heart lay in flying and operations, so Atcherley asked him if he would take over the command of 32 Squadron. Bob accepted with alacrity, but there was a bit of a problem. 32 Squadron were equipped with Vampire jets and he had never flown one. The accident rate was high as the air force moved into the new jet age. It was a major change; Erik Bennett recalls that 'everyone was learning and there were horrendous accidents'. Between 1952 and 1953 the fatal accident rate for jets was four times as high as that for piston-engined aircraft. There were 200 fatal accidents each year. The young pilots were learning on jets but their leaders, who learnt their skills in very different aircraft in wartime situations, needed to catch up. There simply was no pool of older, experienced officers with jet knowledge.[34] It was predictable of Bob that he set about ensuring that he could arrive having already flown one. Kasferet was the maintenance unit and it had some Vampires. After exerting both his persuasive charm and several beers on the test pilot, Bob managed get a half-hour flight in a Vampire that afternoon. He found it a 'normal and very nice aeroplane'. It was not that simple, as many other older RAF pilots found the transition harder. But after thirty minutes, Bob, now satisfied he could fly a jet, headed for Deversoir to meet his new squadron.[35]

Dickie Dicken was a young sergeant pilot and recalls his CO. His first memory was that Bob had the only car on the station, a 'posh, open tourer'.

As Deversoir was a fair way out of town a car was handy. Being based in the Canal Zone was no picnic as living conditions were very basic. The squadron's role was air defence and Bob's way of keeping his pilots sharp just before operations was to get them to play five-minute chess. Playing a fast game of chess just before operations helped to keep them 'ticking over'. Stream landings were practised and speed was essential, particularly late in the day as the sun set so rapidly there was little time to achieve a landing. Jet landings were again different, and as the aircraft landed within seconds of each other there were occasional problems with jet wash in the final stages of the approach.[36] Dickie's memory of his former CO was of a kind man, 'easy going' with an ability to 'walk with you, put his arm around your shoulders and gently get you to do something'. The squadron, while operating in a tense situation, was operating in peacetime, and the young Dickie observed the very close relationship between those men who had served during the war. These older men, many still only in their early thirties, were impressive role models to the young pilots. In Dickie's words, he saw these veterans stick 'together like glue' with an innate understanding from which the younger generation were excluded. Bob could very occasionally be persuaded to say a little about his experience, such as his lack of aerobatic ability and the use of cloud cover.[37]

His assessment in June 1953 described Bob as an 'excellent officer with a great zest for life who throws himself with maximum enthusiasm into all that he does, strong willed and well-disciplined himself. He is rightly proud of his squadron and has maintained a good *esprit de corps* in it.' This is in contrast to his previous assessment as a staff officer where he had been found to be very good but someone who did not 'seek out work, but let it come to him'.[38] Bob much preferred an active operational role to driving a desk. He was not unusual in that; the peacetime RAF had many such war veterans.

At the end of his overseas tour of duty, Bob and his family returned to England in May 1953 and were instantly struck by the greenness of the countryside after the years in Egypt. Bob's next posting was back to RAF Leconfield, where he had joined his first squadron in 1939. This time, however, he was to take over as the officer commanding a squadron in the Fighter Gunnery Wing at the Central Gunnery School. Their role was to maintain and improve standards of fighter gunnery in the RAF.

The station's cricket team was significantly boosted by Bob's arrival and the operations record book reported a very successful season. It shared the lead in Division II of the East Riding amateur league, 'having won the last 6 matches in succession', and it reached the semi-final of the RAF Cup. Sport aside, Bob enjoyed his training role. In July 1953 he led a formation of three Vampires and six Meteor aircraft in a Battle of Britain day flypast. A few months later he was very pleased to meet three officers of the Indian Air Force who arrived on the unit for Meteor conversion and then went on gunnery courses. The school also led visits to squadrons based overseas to demonstrate a range of weaponry and Bob commanded a fixed gunnery liaison team on a tour of the Far East in late 1953.[39]

From 1955 to 1959 he had a series of staff roles. Bob's career was still in the ascendant; he attended the Joint Services Staff College in August 1955 and on 1 January 1956 he was promoted to wing commander. He was assessed as a good judge of men, practical and hard working with a 'clear thinking brain'.[40] He then went to the Administrative Staff College at Henley in 1959. By November 1960 he was in HQ Fighter Command, where he continued to impress, and he was being presented by his superiors as fit for promotion to group captain. His air vice-marshal described him as 'full of vitality and enthusiasm, mentally quick and a sound staff officer', while his air marshal supported this view, adding that he was 'a very loyal and conscientious officer. He is steady and able with a good grasp of his job and now fit for Grp Captain rank.'[41]

Bob was now happily settled with his wife and three daughters in Tunbridge Wells, Kent. His wife, Gee, worked for a cosmetics firm, Beauty Counsellor, and travelled considerably across the county. She came home one day and commented to Bob that she was concerned that she was being followed, having seen the same car on several days in different places. It transpired that the car was driven by a private detective who had been hired by the Ministry of Defence. Bob, and his wife, were being security vetted as he had been selected for a special role in the Chiefs of Staff Secretariat.

The Chiefs of Staff (COS) Committee was part of the Ministry of Defence and reported to the Cabinet. It was collectively responsible to the Secretary of State and government for professional advice on strategy and operations, advising on the capabilities and activities of each of the three armed service as well as coordinating their work. The committee was made up of the Chief of the General Staff (CGS) representing the Army, the Chief of the Naval Staff and First Sea Lord (CNS) and the Chief of the Air Staff (CAS). Other members included the Chief Scientific Adviser and the Permanent Under-secretary to the Secretary of State for Defence, who advised on financial, political and parliamentary matters. The committee was permanently chaired by the Chief of the Defence Staff (CDS), who did not represent the interests of any one service, and who was therefore seen as an independent source of advice. Prior to this date, the Chiefs of Staff would alternate the chair. When Bob took up his post, the CDS was Mountbatten.[42] Bob had great admiration for Mountbatten, having experienced his leadership in close action in India and Burma, so this new appointment in June 1961 was very exciting.

There was a major event at a very early stage. Just a few weeks into his job, one Friday evening, 30 June 1961, the most senior civil servant at the Foreign office, the Permanent Under-secretary, walked into Bob's office at the COS Secretariat and uttered the words, 'Good evening Bob, all the indicators are down on Kuwait.'[43] This meant that Operation Vantage was to be implemented. In the 1960s, Kuwait was essential to Britain's oil supply as it supplied around half of the nation's requirements. Additionally, British oil companies based in Kuwait made a major contribution to the balance of payments. Plus, it was strategically placed within the Middle East and Gulf airbases were important staging posts on the way to Britain's Far East territories. With increasing instability in the region, contingency plans for the defence of Kuwait were made and these depended heavily on air power to get troops there in an emergency. After the Suez Crisis in 1956, several states refused to allow Britain the right to overfly their countries.[44]

The Amir of Kuwait formally requested British support after serious reports that forces from neighbouring Iraq, led by Abdul Karim Qasim, were heading for Kuwait and that Radio Bagdad had asserted Iraq's claim to Kuwait.[45] That evening Bob rang the War Office, the Admiralty and the Air Ministry to alert them that Operation Vantage was about to be put into action. After sending a signal to Aden to tell them it was now in operation he sat back and, in the days of well-stocked drinks cabinets in offices, poured himself a gin. Then the phone rang and it was a young squadron leader from the Air Ministry checking that it was indeed all part of an exercise. Bob's response was clear, effective and unprintable and told him to get the Assistant Chief of the Air Staff (Operations) on the phone so the situation could be explained. This individual was at a cocktail party and did not wish to be disturbed. Bob's method of persuasion was to threaten a court martial, which 'seemed to do the trick'. After speaking to ACAS (Ops) he settled back for another gin.[46]

The next challenge was a signal from Aden saying the plan had changed but that they had not had time to send a copy to the United Kingdom. Bob was at his happiest in these challenges, and by now he was not alone in the office. They called up all the drivers to collect nearby security-cleared typists, although it was by now nearly midnight. Then they organised a secure line to Aden, utilised the old Cabinet War Rooms where there was a special screen to show text and by nine the next morning there were sufficient copies of the new plan in the right hands.[47] The Commander-in-Chief Middle East, Air Marshal Sir Charles Elworthy, had formally put Vantage into operation at 07.00 that morning, several hours after it had actually been in effect. British troops were swiftly deployed into the area and Qasim's troops never appeared. Operation Vantage was hailed as a political success as part of Britain's policy of deterrence. Lessons were learnt for future situations, as Iraq's claim to Kuwait remained a permanent feature of the political view across all parties in Iraq. But it was one of the last gasps of British imperial policy. The British forces in Kuwait subsequently withdrew and were replaced by those from the Arab League.[48]

After that brief excitement, matters did not go so well for Bob. He may have been working in the most senior staff levels in the services, but he had not reckoned on the deadly hand of bureaucracy at this level. The minutes of the COS Secretariat for this period are a strange mixture of subjects. News from the Americans about the Cuban crisis, with a telephone call from President Kennedy to the Prime Minister, Harold Macmillan, might be next to an item about the planning for Churchill's funeral. The Chiefs of Staff were most exercised about the precedent in the funeral procession. In which order should they march? The decision from the Earl Marshal's office was that it was one of seniority of the post holder and not the service.[49]

It was, Bob later admitted, 'the most difficult two years' of his career and, apart from it being wholly desk-based, the personalities involved were difficult. The main secretary to COS was an Army general who 'nitpicked' and his assistant was weak. Bob began to lose faith seriously in himself.[50] It was not helped by a disastrous rating in January 1962 by his boss, Commodore Watkins. Watkins did not find Bob had reached the 'required standard' and placed an adverse report on his personnel file. The air commodore in personnel put another note on the file to balance the apparently damning view: 'It should be noted that this was the third officer in succession to be found wanting by the reporting officer in this appointment.'[51] Two previous wing commanders had also received adverse reports from Watkins. Bob was moved to a new post as secretary to a specialist scientific committee. Joint Inter-Service Group for Study of All Out Warfare (JIGSAW) was part of the Joint Services Scientific Committee (JSSC) and had been set up by Sir Solly Zuckerman, who was the Chief Scientific Advisor to the government. Zuckerman was a close friend of Mountbatten, with whom he conducted a running debate on nuclear warfare. Mountbatten was not a proponent of Britain engaging in a nuclear arms race; he and Zuckerman saw controlled disarmament as necessary. Although this is now a well-accepted view, in 1960 'it was heretical'.[52] Zuckerman was a brilliant man, described as 'a complicated man, often secretive, irascible and dismissive of those whose abilities and perceptions failed to match his own. Of some men it is said that they "did not suffer fools gladly"; Solly declined to suffer them at all.'[53]

The primary aim of the JIGSAW committee and staff was to carry out global war studies including nuclear disarmament and the practicalities of disarmament, such as the requirement for an international force 'to guarantee the authority of the inspecting teams'.[54] So unknown to the Campaign for Nuclear Disarmament, which was organising major sit-down protests and marches, the committee, with Bob as its secretary, was considering the practical and political difficulties. These included the minimum inspection necessary to ensure that the declaration by the parent country was valid and whether it would be 'unacceptable to that country for its commercial and industrial secrets to be discovered before they were marketed'. There were briefings on new weaponry such as the neutron bomb, which released ten times more radiation.[55] Then there was the Cuban missile crisis of late 1962, which served as a reminder of the risk to the world from nuclear weapons. Bob, who had left school at fifteen without formal qualifications, enjoyed his time with the scientists, among whom was the chairman, Dr A. C. Kendrew, who shared the 1962 Nobel Prize for chemistry.[56] The rest of the group was made up of four more leading scientists and three serving officers, including Captain N. L. Jewell, who was director of the RN Staff College at Greenwich. Jewell was most famous for his part in Operation Mincemeat, the very successful disinformation mission which convinced the Germans that the Allies were about to invade Greece.[57]

After enjoying his time with the scientists, it was back to 'run-of-the-mill staff jobs which bored me to tears'.[58] This included a brief time as the board president at Biggin Hill aircrew selection centre, but he was not ideal for the job. The RAF had changed in a major way. The RAF of the Cold War was a more cerebral organisation. The recruits were vastly different in background, schooling and experience and were not part of any call-up process. Bob and his wartime contemporaries had been forced to make instant decisions about the men they flew with at a time when trust in your flying companions was a matter of life and death. Bob was quick to make up his mind about people and preferred an instinctive decision to the more fact-based, paper-led decisions favoured by the RAF in the new era of psychological assessments.[59] Then for two years he was based at White Waltham, where he was Senior Personnel Staff Officer in Flying Training Command and he became president of the Mess Committee at Shinfield Park near Reading. This was a role in which he could enjoy some independence and use his flair for organisation.

Meanwhile, in the Air Ministry serious planning began early for the twenty-fifth anniversary of the Battle of Britain. It would culminate in the service at Westminster Abbey in September. The queen rarely came to London in September, but a letter from her private secretary confirmed her attendance as she regarded the twenty-fifth anniversary of the Battle of Britain as 'an occasion of national importance'.[60]

An official booklet was issued to commemorate the event. This gave a view of the Luftwaffe and RAF losses during the battle and it also provided a list of the leading pilots of the battle with their scores. These are listed here and in brackets are the scores given by the booklet plus the generally accepted scores today: leading pilots Flight Lieutenant E. S. Lock (20/21), Squadron Leader A. A. McKellar (20/19), Sergeant J. Frantisek (17/17), Squadron Leader W. Urbanowitcz (17/15), Flight Lieutenant J. H. Lacey (16/18), Wing Commander H. M. Stephen (15), Group Captain A. G. Malan (14), Group Captain C. F. Gray (14/14.5) and Wing Commander M. N. Crossley (14). Missing from this list were Flying Officer Brian Carbury from New Zealand, with fifteen and one-third kills; Bob's mentor Flight Lieutenant Patterson Hughes from Australia, who had over fourteen; and Bob.[61]

Conscious of the press interest, for whom Bader and Tuck were the big names, the booklet went on to list 'other leading pilots who fought in the battle'. These included Group Captain D. R. S. Bader (11), Wing Commander R. R. Stanford Tuck (10), Flight Lieutenant G. Allard (10), Air Commodore A. C. Deere (9.5), Group Captain F. R. Carey (7), Group Captain P. H. Hugo (5.5) and Wing Commander D. E. Kingaby (5).[62]

The service in the abbey needed some careful thinking as there was a realisation of time marching on. The young men who had fought in the battle were now in their forties and fifties so subsequent major anniversaries would not be able to feature them in any active role. Normally the RAF ensign was marched up the aisle, borne by a serving Battle of Britain pilot, and it was decided that the tradition would need to be broken after this year. It was agreed that the last serving Battle of Britain pilot to carry the ensign would be Wing Commander Matthews, escorted by two flight lieutenants from Fighter Command.[63]

It was further decided that a group of twenty ex-Battle of Britain aircrew would be selected to represent the Few and they would follow the ensign up the aisle and back again at the conclusion of the service. They would then be presented to Her Majesty the Queen.[64] The Director of Personnel Services for the RAF wrote to Air Commodore A. MacDonell, now retired, who was the Chairman of the Battle of Britain Association, to ask for his help in identifying twenty aircrew:

> I feel that these should be as widely representative as possible and selected from all ranks who took part in the Battle. I hope that you might select a few serving ex Battle of Britain officers and airmen, and I wondered if you might consider one or two ex-aircrew who are not actually members of your Association. In this respect I appreciate that the latter do not come under the terms of your Association, but I believe that you do have a list of all those who served in the Battle.[65]

MacDonell pondered the issue and drew up his personal list. In writing to the invited men he explained that he had been asked to select the twenty to take part in the ceremony and be presented to Her Majesty. But that 'this has been no easy task ... I have drawn up a list of names representing as far as possible a cross-section of those who fought in the Battle as possible. Your name is on my list.'[66] Bob was on the initial list of twenty drawn up by MacDonell, although he was not a member of the association at that time. By 13 August there were sixteen acceptances, including Bob. Some of the nominated men were unable to attend for good reasons, while Douglas Bader simply refused. In the end there were twenty aircrew, of whom one was naval (Braham), one Polish (Kowalski), two Australian (Olive and Cock) and one a warrant officer from New Zealand (Campbell). There was great pleasure that Kowalski was attending to represent the many Polish pilots. The Czech pilot had not replied; he was behind the Iron Curtain.[67]

The added complication to the whole organisation of the event was the determination of the abbey authorities to put their own mark on it. Winston Churchill had died aged ninety in January and they wanted to combine the event with the unveiling of a commemorative stone to him, particularly as the queen was to be there. But they did not stop at that. At a meeting on 30 June between the abbey and the RAF, represented by Wing Commander 'Pancho' Villa, radical changes were proposed by the abbey. They wished to make the service change from one with a predominately Battle of Britain theme to one with a more national flavour. Fortunately 'Villa was in good batting form and put up a good show to such an extent that only minor alterations have been made. Nevertheless we should take this as warning that the ecclesiastical authorities are not averse to going back on their agreement.'[68]

In addition to nearly 200 Battle of Britain aircrew and a large number of next of kin of those who were killed, the congregation would include the great and the good, including the Prime Minister Harold Wilson, the opposition leader Edward Heath, the leader of the Liberals Jo Grimmond, ministers, senior serving officers and representatives from many Commonwealth countries. Air Chief Marshal Hugh Dowding was there, at the age of eighty-three, to be with his 'fighter boys' and to remember those who were not present.

Each of the twenty pilots was asked to complete a form and return it to the Ceremonial Branch with their full name, rank and decorations, Battle of Britain history including a brief account of squadrons in which they served, decorations awarded during the battle and any other points of interest. It also asked for their present employment. They make interesting reading. Some went into great detail about their experiences in the battle; indeed, one officer thoughtfully provided an extra page of detail. But

Bob and Stanford Tuck were very brief, simply noting their squadrons. For some such as Bob, 'shooting a line' was still not the done thing. The peacetime occupations included ladies' hairdresser, managing director of a Rolls-Royce hire firm, TSR2 test pilot, local councillor, mushroom farmer and designer of agricultural machinery. It is also noticeable that many of those retired from the RAF were now in some type of sales role. The forms were typed up, edited and sent as a briefing to the palace via the Lord Chamberlain's office on 16 September. It did not include the numbers of enemy aircraft credited as destroyed because 'when I went into it in detail I found that there were no official record of such claims and the numbers credited varied in different books, and also with information supplied by the individuals!'[69]

It was a high-profile occasion and there were anxieties, particularly as it was to be televised. Mr Johnson of the Royal Air Force Association (RAFA) had a sensitive matter to discuss. He approached Air Commodore Roberts and asked if it would be possible to make an official request to have RAFA standard bearers placed under RAF orders. It was, he said, a 'delicate business for RAFA representatives to issue orders to RAF standard bearers as this was often resented, but he thought they would not be offended if the orders came from a serving RAF NCO'. The request was duly made.[70]

Meanwhile, all the aircrew attended a rehearsal, uniforms were pressed, medals polished (in Bob's case by his daughter) and swords were to be worn. On the day, the pilots arrived early and, as planned, followed the ensign to the altar, the twenty Battle of Britain aircrew taking special seats at the side of the aisles for the rest of the service. At the conclusion the ensign was marched out again followed by the aircrew. The queen unveiled the commemorative stone to Sir Winston Churchill and then spoke to Lady Churchill, who was there with several members of her family. Then Air Chief Marshal Sir William MacDonald presented the aircrew to the queen and Prince Philip. The whole proceedings were filmed by both the BBC and ATV.

There were a few problems. Much to the annoyance of the organisers, the sermon ran over time and this caused a knock-on effect with the timing of the flypast of Lightnings due at 12.30. HQ Fighter Command complained that the formation leader received a message requesting a ten-minute delay at 11.53, just two minutes before starting engines, and after the engines had been started a second message arrived delaying things by a further five minutes. The weather was excellent so the formation leader took a calculated risk; the flypast was spot on time at 12.45 and the jets landed with 400 lbs below the accepted fuel level. 'Pancho' Villa was suitably apologetic: 'Despite some misgivings we were assured by the abbey authorities that the service would run to time. You can rest assured that, after the nervous tension experienced in the abbey when the sermon exceeded the expected duration, we shall never again accept timings given to us by a civil authority.'[71]

A letter of complaint was sent to the editor of *RAF News* about the misspelling of a name and an unfortunate photograph. The editor apologised for the misspelling but was robust in his defence of the photograph:

Incidentally I must contest your statement that the escort to the ensign in the photo you mention was out of step. Examination of the original Press Association print reveals quite conclusively that he was not. What you – and several other readers – have mistaken for a foot is in fact flash-shadow. Apart from this, however, the crease on the sergeant's trouser show that his left leg was unmistakably behind his right and that he could not have been out of step. You may be amused to hear that an ex-photo-interpreter also came on to us with the advice that the sergeant was a cripple with one foot one yard long and two-foot-six inches wide.[72]

The problem was that they *were* out of step. Bob had returned from the rehearsal much amused by the efforts of the twenty to march in step as many of them had been retired for some years. They were all well aware of the television cameras and the particular problem was the need for a change of pace. So the position of the cameras was carefully noted and the change was made hidden from view under the proscenium arch. But overall it was considered a great success. Roberts wrote to MacDonell to thank him for his efforts. 'I thought all the Battle of Britain aircrew looked very impressive and they performed magnificently. The Guildhall reception went off splendidly too and I cannot recall having been present at a more animated occasion.'[73]

It was a high point for Bob and the following year he decided to retire early from the RAF. His final assessment described him as a 'loyal and likeable man who will be a loss to the service when he retires. More at home in a cockpit than behind a desk.'[74] It was a good assessment. The young man who dreamt of flying and of emulating his hero Biggles had done well, better than he ever imagined. He had joined the RAF despite his complete lack of formal qualifications, his talent had been seen early and he was one of the tiny percentage who were commissioned as regular officers from the RAFVR. Despite his lack of aerobatic skill, which had him marked out for bombing, and his personal lack of confidence in his own abilities, he became a highly successful fighter pilot. He survived a major crash to fly again and proved his worth in a completely different and hostile environment in Burma with a very different task.

As a leader he had used his experience of the leaderless 234 Squadron and watched and learned from good leaders such as Pat Hughes. He may not have had a great education but he was a man who thought a great deal, analysed matters and learned from his mistakes. What made him such a good hunter-killer? He was physically very fit, he had great eyesight, superb eye and hand coordination, which made him successful at all ball games, and very good peripheral vision as he turned his head to scan the sky. His tall, large frame just fitted into his aircraft. It was as if he had wings strapped to him. His mother's insistence on early violin lessons gave him a light touch on the controls. He was also extremely competitive, with a need to prove himself. All of these combined with an innate sense of what was happening in the sky and a fierce determination to defend his country and his mother's backyard. He was a very British hero and in many ways an unexpected one, although he did not see himself as a hero; true heroes rarely do. He, and the surviving Battle of Britain aircrew, were and are still determined that those who did not return should be remembered. As the post-war publicity continued to build around 'the Few', it was Bob who spoke for many of them when he said,

We don't want to be remembered as heroes, we just want to be remembered for what we did.

Wing Commander R. F. T. Doe, DSO, DFC and Bar

1920–2010

APPENDIX I: PILOT COLLEAGUES IN 234 SQUADRON

Name	Period of service in 234 Squadron	Reason for leaving/date of death
Sergeant Bailey	4 May 1940–10 September 1940	Posted to 603 Squadron
Squadron Leader Barnett	2 November 1939–13 August 1940	Relinquished command
Sergeant Boddington	November 1939–February 1941	Commissioned in October 1941
Pilot Officer Ken Dewhurst	6 November1939–1946	Remained with 234 Squadron
Pilot Officer Bob Doe	6 November 1939–22 September 1940	Posted to 238 Squadron at Middle Wallop
Pilot Officer 'Scotty' Gordon	July 1940–6 September 1940	Killed in action
Pilot Officer Geoffrey Gout	6 November 1939–25 July 1940	Crashed at Porthtowan, cause unknown
Pilot Officer Richard Hardy	6 November 1939–15 August 1940	Forced to land near Cherbourg and became a prisoner of war
Sergeant Alan Harker	5 November 1939–19 May 1941	Crashed 1941 but survived
Sergeant W. H. Hornby	6 November 1939–4 September 1940	Crashed and injured
Pilot Officer Pat Horton	6 November 1939–November 1940	Killed flying from HMS *Argus*
Flight Lieutenant Pat Hughes	30 October 1939–7 September 1940	Killed in action
Pilot Officer Igglesden	July 1940–7 August 1940	Resigned commission
Sergeant Klein	6 August 1940–5 October 1940	Posted to 152 Squadron Warmwell. KIA 28 November 1940
Pilot Officer Ken Lawrence	6 November 1939–9 September 1939	Posted to 603 Squadron
Pilot Officer Mortimer-Rose	6 November 1939–November 1940	Killed in accident 1943
Pilot Officer Parker	July 1940–15 August 1940	Crashed into sea and prisoner of war
Sergeant Sharpley	July 1940–16 November 1940	Crashed into sea off Cornwall
Flight Lieutenant J. G. Theilmann	30 October 1939–7 August 1940	Non-effective sick
Sergeant Thompson	April 1940–31 July 1940	Crashed after night patrol. Did not fly again
Squadron Leader O'Brien	17 August 1940–7 September 1940	Killed in action
Flying Officer Z. Olenski	14 August 1940–5 September 1940	Posted to 69 Squadron
Pilot Officer Zurakowski	August 1940–5 October 1940	Posted to 609 Squadron
Sergeant Josef Szlagowski	3 August 1940–21 October 1940	Posted to 152 Squadron

Note: The sources for this are TNA: AIR 27/1439 234 Squadron ORB and Wynn, *Men of the Battle of Britain*.

APPENDIX II: LIST OF BATTLE OF BRITAIN ESCORT AT 25TH ANNIVERSARY OF THE BATTLE

Extracted from briefing note sent to Lord Chamberlain on 16 September 1965.

* indicates the original information from the individual was edited down, in some cases considerably.

All are available in TNA: AIR 20/11289.

1. Air Vice-Marshal F. E. Rosier CB, CBE, DSO, DFC
Commanded 229 Squadron (Hurricanes) at Northolt
Present employment: Senior Air Officer Staff, Transport Command

2. Air Commodore A. R. D. MacDonell CB, DFC, RAF (retired)*
Commanded 64 Squadron for July 1940 until March 1941 when became POW. Awarded DFC August 1940
Present employment: Head of Operational Research with constructors John Brown Ltd

3. Group Captain W. D. David CBE, DFC, and Bar, AFC, RAF
Served with Nos 87, 213 and 152 Squadrons. Awarded DFC and Bar during battle
Point of note: Saved Squadron Leader Cock's (see entry 14) life on one occasion
Present employment: Serving officer at Ministry of Defence

4. Commander H. G. K. Bramah, RN (retired)*
Seconded to Fighter Command, No. 213 Squadron (Hurricanes). Shot down, badly injured and picked up by Navy in the Channel, and spent many months in hospital
Present employment: Director of two Burnett and Hallamshire companies, director of two other companies

5. Wing Commander R. R. S. Tuck, DSO, DFC and two Bars, USA DFC, RAF (retired)
Served with No. 92 Squadron and commanded No. 257 Squadron. Awarded DSO, DFC and 2 Bars
Present employment: Mushroom farmer

6. Wing Commander R. P. Beamont, DSO and Bar, OBE, DFC and Bar, RAF (retired)*
Served with No. 87 Squadron (Hurricanes) Exeter. Awarded DFC
Present employment: Director and Manager of Flight Operations, British Aircraft Corporation. Late project test pilot for TSR2. In current flying practice on Lightnings

7. Wing Commander J. Kowalski, DFC (also holds Polish awards VM and KW)*
Served with No. 302 Squadron, the first Polish squadron to be formed. Flew in Polish Air Force during Polish campaign, captured by Russians, escaped to France and flew with French Air Force at defence of Dunkirk and Paris
Present employment: Designer of agricultural machinery

8. Wing Commander P. P. C. Barthropp, DFC, AFC, RAF (retired)
Served in No. 602 Squadron. Awarded DFC
Present employment: Chairman of Patrick Barthropp Ltd, Rolls-Royce hire

9. Wing Commander D. H. Grice MBE, DFC, RAF (retired)*
Served with No. 32 Squadron (Hurricanes) from Biggin Hill as flying

officer. Shot down three times and burned about face and wrists on last occasion. Surgery performed by Sir Archibald McIndoe
Present employment: Partner in firm of London solicitors

10. Wing Commander R. F. T. Doe, DSO, DFC and Bar, RAF
Served with 234 Squadron. Awarded DFC
Served with 238 Squadron. Awarded Bar to DFC
Present employment: Still serving in RAF at Ministry of Defence

11. Wing Commander C. G. C. Olive, DFC (from Australia)
Served in No. 65 Squadron at Hornchurch, Southend and Manston. Awarded DFC in September 1940. Appointed Honorary ADC (RAAF) to Her Majesty the Queen 1962, 1964
Present employment: Sales manager with Rhee Australia Proprietary Ltd, steel manufacturers

12. Wing Commander D. L. Clackson, MBE, RAF (retired)
Served with No. 600 (City of London) Squadron
Present employment: Newspaper representative, councilman of the City of London

13. Wing Commander I. B. Westmacott, DFC, RAF (retired)*
Served with No. 56 Squadron. Shot down in August 1940 and hospitalised
Present employment: Assistant secretary of RAF Benevolent Fund

14. Squadron Leader J. R. Cock, DFC (from Australia)
Served with No. 87 Squadron
Present employment: Sales manager, Preston Motors, Melbourne, Australia

15. Squadron Leader D. R. Turley-George, DFC (also holds King Haakon 7th Freedom Medal, Norwegian)*
Served with No. 54 Squadron, Hornchurch. Shot down twice and blinded in right eye on second occasion

Present employment: Sales executive of Decca Navigator Co., Ltd. Civilian
test pilot 1950–64

16. Flight Lieutenant A. B. Tucker, RAF (retired)*
Served with No. 85 Squadron at Debden and No. 151 Squadron at North
Weald. Shot down and in hospital for some months
Present employment: Was in Design Office in Vickers Aircraft Ltd. Retired
to devote time to voluntary work as councillor and manager/governor of
local primary and secondary schools

17. Flight Lieutenant J. H. Duart, FCA
Served with No. 219 Squadron
Present employment: Chartered accountant, assistant secretary and
accountant, Sutton District Water Company

18. Flight Lieutenant F. J. Tritchett, RAF (retired)
Served with No. 43 Squadron (Hurricanes), Unsworth and No. 229
Squadron, Northolt as Sergeant Pilot
Present employment: Sales manager for Remington Rand, Ltd, Holborn
Viaduct, London

19. Flight Lieutenant G. G. Griffiths, DFM (also holds Chevalier de
L'Ordre du Leopold II avec Palme and Croix de Guerre avec Palme)*
Served with No. 17 Squadron in France before battle and in same
squadron in Debden, Martlesham Heath, North Weald and Tangmere.
Awarded DFM in November 1940
Present Employment: Deputy engineer in the Epsom Group of Hospitals

20. Warrant Officer D. R. Campbell, DFM (from New Zealand)*
Served in No. 23 Squadron (Blenheim) as Sergeant Air Gunner from
August 1940
Present employment: Ladies' hairdresser

APPENDIX III: LIST OF AIRCRAFT FLOWN BY BOB DOE FROM A LIST IN HIS LOGBOOK

Blackburn II

Miles Magister

Avro Tutor

Tiger Moth

Miles Magister I

Hawker Hart

Avro Anson

Gloucester Gauntlet

Bristol Blenheim

Fairey Battle

Spitfire I

Spitfire IIa

Spitfire IIa long range

Spitfire IIb

Master III

Wellington I

Dominie

Proctor

Harrow

P/398 Lockheed
   Lighting

Spitfire XI

Mustang I

Spitfire Vb

Vega Gull

Hurricane II

Harvard

Twin Beechcraft

Valentia

Stearman

Ryan

Spitfire VIII

Hurri-bomber

Expeditor

Auster I

L 5 Sentinel

Dakota

Auster V

Avro XIX

Oxford

Fairey Jnr

Prentice

Chipmunk

Valetta

Vampire VIIX

Hastings

Venom

T II

Meteor VII

Meteor VIII

Lincoln

Sunderland V

NOTES

CA: Churchill Archive
IWM: Imperial War Museum
SHC: Surrey History Centre
TNA: The National Archives

1 Early Years and Early Influences

1. *Daily Telegraph* 22 February 2010.

2. *The Times* 22 February 2010.

3. John Willis, *Churchill's Few: The Battle of Britain Remembered* (London: Michael Joseph, 1985).

4. Bob Doe, *Bob Doe, Fighter Pilot* (Tunbridge Wells: Spellmount, 1991), pp. 1–3.

5. http://www.thechildrenstrust.org.uk/page.asp?section=34 [accessed 20 January 2013]

6. House of Commons Library: SN/SG/3339, M. Keep, *Agriculture: Historical Statistics*, 18 December 2009.

7. Doe, *Bob Doe, Fighter Pilot*, p. 1.

8. Willis, *Churchill's Few*, p. 24.

9. *Ibid.*

10. http://www.waltonheath.com/Heritage/Politicians.aspx [accessed 20 January 2013]

11. The National Archives (TNA): ED 161/11756 1900-71 Walton on Hill, Banstead C. of E. School.

12. TNA: ED 21/40436 Jan 1928 to Dec 1933 Walton on Hill, Banstead C. of E. School.

13. *Ibid.*

14. *Ibid.*

15. TNA: ED 161/11756 Walton on the Hill School.

16. IWM: Interview Doe.

17. Doe, *Bob Doe, Fighter Pilot*, p. 1.

18. Stafford Somerfield, *Banner Headlines* (Shoreham: Scan Books, 1979), p. 76.

19. Gail L. Savage, 'Social Class and Social Policy: The Civil Service and Secondary Education in the Interwar Period', *Journal of Contemporary History*, 18(2) (1983), 261–80, p. 262.

20. *Ibid.*, p. 273.

21. Theodore Frank Yuhas, 'Development of Education for Adolescents in England', *History of Education Journal*, 51(1953), 30–33, p. 32.

22. Surrey History Centre (SHC): Leatherhead Central School Admission Register April 1932.

23. Linda Heath, *Of Good Report: The Story of the Leatherhead Schools* (Leatherhead: Leatherhead & District Local History Society, 1986), p. 73–74.

24. *Ibid.*

25. *Ibid.*

26. Personal collection: Newspaper cutting, undated.

27. Willis, *Churchill's Few*, p. 25.

28. SHC: 8928/2/1/1 Leatherhead Central School Play programme.

29. W. R. Garside, 'Juvenile Unemployment and Public Policy between the Wars', *Economic History Review*, 30(2) (1977), 322–39, p. 325.

30. Garside, 'Juvenile Unemployment', p. 325.

31. Pers. com. to author.

32. Heath, *Of Good Report*, p. 73.

33. *Aberdeen Journal* 3 January 1935; *Western Daily Press* 3 January 1935.

34. *Western Daily Press* 3 January 1935.

35. *Chelmsford Chronicle* 16 August 1935.

36. http://www.theshipslist.com/ships/lines/bisn.html [accessed 3 March 2013]

37. *Aberdeen Journal* 3 January 1935.

38. *Ibid.*

39. Garside, 'Juvenile Unemployment'.

40. Dudley Baines & Paul Johnson, 'In Search of the "Traditional" Working Class: Social Mobility and Occupational Continuity in Interwar London', *Economic History Review*, 52(4) (1999), 692–713.

41. Cyril Bainbridge & Roy Stockdill, *The News of the World Story* (London: Harper Collins, 1993), p. 72.

42. *Ibid.*, pp. 100–1.

43. *Ibid.*, pp. 103–4.

44. Somerfield, *Banner Headlines,* p. 107.

45. Bainbridge & Stockdill, *The News of the World Story*, pp. 100 fwd.

46. Extract from 'Heather and Heaven', Walton Heath Golf Club centenary book. http://www.waltonheath.com/Heritage/Politicians.aspx [accessed 24 June 2013]

47. Bainbridge & Stockdill, *The News of the World Story*, p. 78; Somerfield, *Banner Headlines*, pp. 77–8.

48. Bainbridge & Stockdill, *The News of the World Story*, pp. 116–19.

49. *Ibid.*, p. 78.

50. SHC: 7894 Walton Heath Golf Club records.

51. Selina Todd, 'Young Women, Work and Leisure in Interwar England', *Historical Journal*, 48 (3) (2005), 789-809, pp. 789, 792–3.

52. Bainbridge and Stockdill, *The News of the World Story*, p. 117.

53. Todd, 'Young Women, Work and Leisure', p. 798.

54. *Ibid.*, p. 794.

55. Tel. con. Nick Mays archivist, News International 19 October 2012; SHC: 7894 Walton Heath Golf Club Records.

56. Pers. com.; Letter Richard Smith to Bob Doe undated, *c.* 2006.

57. Churchill Archive (CA): CHAR 8/511 Winston Churchill to Major Davies 13 May 1935, Davies to Churchill 15 May 1935.

58. CA: CHAR 8/533 Emsley Carr to Winston Churchill 4 February 1936.

59. CA: CHAR 8/551 Davies to Churchill 3 February 1937.

60. CA: Char 8/629 Carr to Churchill 11 July 1939.

61. News International Archive: *News of the World* staff card.

2 Preparation for Battle

1. The trophy is now held in the Science Museum, London.

2. IWM: Interview Doe.

3. www.biggles.com

4. IWM: Interview Doe.

5. Kenley airfield history. http://www.kafg.org.uk/airfrafkenley.htm [accessed 26th April 2013]

6. *Gloucester Echo* 8 October 1932.

7. *Cornishman* 7 June 1934.

8. *The Times* 16 August 1933.

9. A. Mansell, 'Flying Start: Educational and Social Factors in the Recruitment of Pilots of the RAF in the Interwar Years', *History of Education*, 26(1) (1997), 71–90, p. 78.

10. *The Times* 24 May 1935.

11. Mansell, 'Flying Start', p. 74.

12. Ancestry.co.uk: British Army WW1 Service Records.

13. *Ibid.*

14. Vivian John, 'Order of Battle of Salonika Army', *The New Mosquito*, 12 (Sept. 2005).

15. John, 'Salonika Army'.

16. James Holland interview with Bob Doe 12 March 2002. http://www.griffonmerlin.com/ww2_interviews/bob-doe/ [accessed 24 January 2012]

17. Mansell, 'Flying Start', p. 86.

18. *Ibid.*

19. *Ibid.*

20. TNA: AIR 32/15 History of Flying Training Part II.

21. *Ibid.*

22. *Ibid.*

23. *Ibid.*

24. *The Times* 13 March 1937; *Guardian* 14 March 1937; *Derby Daily Telegraph* 19 December 1938.

25. Mansell, 'Flying Start', p. 87.

26. *Derby Daily Telegraph* 19 December 1938.

27. Mansell, 'Flying Start', pp. 75 & 78.

28. TNA: AIR 32/15 History of Flying Training Part II.

29. TNA: AIR 2/1630 RAFVR Application Form.

30. *Ibid.*

31. TNA: AIR 32/14 History of Flying Training: Training of Pilots 1914–1945.

32. Tim Sherwood, *Coming in to Land: A Short History of Hounslow, Hanworth and Heston Aerodromes 1911–1946* (Hounslow: Heritage Publications, 1999).

33. *Flight* 3 June 1937.

34. IWM: Interview Doe.

35. Doe Logbook.

36. Doe Logbook.

37. *The Times* 15 August 1938.

38. Mansell, 'Flying Start', p. 82.

39. *Ibid.*, pp. 76–77.

40. *Ibid.*, p. 80.

41. 'Committee on Preliminary Education of Candidates for RAF Commission' quoted in *Ibid.*, p. 73.

42. *Ibid.*, p. 74; G. Campion, *The Good Fight: Battle of Britain Propaganda and the Few* (Basingstoke: Palgrave Macmillan, 2009), p. 44.

43. Mansell, 'Flying Start', p. 74.

44. TNA: AIR 2/2075 War Time Entrants Commissions, Conditions of Service and Promotion.

45. *Ibid.*

46. TNA: AIR 20/8992 Report on Recruiting for the RAF during War Period.

47. TNA: AIR 2/2075 War Time Entrants Commissions, Conditions of Service and Promotion.

48. Campion, *The Good Fight*, p. 45.

49. TNA: AIR 2/2075 War Time Entrants Commissions, Conditions of Service and Promotion.

50. *Ibid.*

51. TNA: AIR 2/2075 Letter from HQ Reserve Command 9 Oct 1939, Selection of Pilots, Observers, W/T operator, Air Gunners for Commission.

52. *Ibid.*

53. Campion, *The Good Fight,* p. 45.

54. TNA: AIR 41/69 Air Historical Branch monograph Flying Training Vol. I Basic Training.

55. Fenton, 'Aquarius: The Man Who Held the Watering Pot', unpublished memoirs, p. 20. With thanks to Jon Fenton.

56. Doe Logbook; Doe, *Bob Doe, Fighter Pilot*, p. 21.

57. Letter from Triptree to Bob Doe, undated.

58. *Flight* 11 May 1939.

59. Doe, *Bob Doe, Fighter Pilot*, pp. 8–9.

60. W. A. Wilkinson, *One Pilot's War: The Battle of Britain and Beyond* (Windsor: Windsor Books Ltd, 2010), p. 38.

61. Fenton, 'Aquarius', p. 7.

62. Doe, *Bob Doe, Fighter Pilot,* p. 9.

63. TNA: AIR 2/2075 War Time Entrants Commissions, Conditions of Service and Promotion.

64. Wilkinson, *One Pilot's War,* p. 41.

65. *Ibid.*

66. Fenton, 'Aquarius', p. 8.

67. *Ibid.*

68. H. R. Allen, *Fighter Squadron: A Memoir 1940–1942* (London: Harper Collins, 1982), p. 15.

69. Mansell, 'Flying Start', p. 80; Allen, *Fighter Squadron*, pp. 29–32.

70. Doe, *Bob Doe, Fighter Pilot*, p. 9.

71. *Ibid.*

72. Doe Logbook.

73. Fenton, 'Aquarius', p. 9.

74. Wilkinson, *One Pilot's War*, p. 44.

75. *Ibid.*, p. 53.

76. *Ibid.*, p. 57.

77. *Ibid.*, p. 52.

78. *Ibid.*

79. IWM: Interview Recording 28605 Judy Chard.

80. Doe, *Bob Doe, Fighter Pilot*, p. 9.

81. TNA: AIR 2/2075 War Time Entrants Commissions, Conditions of Service and Promotion.

82. TNA: AIR 29/558 6 FTS Little Rissington Operational Record Book (ORB).

83. Doe, *Bob Doe, Fighter Pilot*, p. 9.

84. Wilkinson, *One Pilot's War*, p. 46.

85. CA: Char 8/629. 24 Sept 39 Churchill to Davies.

86. *Ibid.*

87. Wilkinson, *One Pilot's War*, pp. 47–8.

88. *Ibid.*, p. 49.

89. Allen, *Fighter Squadron*, p. 23.

90. *Flight* 8 August 1929.

91. Doe Logbook.

92. Richard Overy, *The Battle of Britain* (London: Penguin, 2000), p. 13.

93. TNA: AIR 29/547 9 Air Observer School Penrhos.

94. IWM: Interview Doe.

95. Doe Logbook.

3 The Battle Begins and Leadership Lessons

1. Doe, *Bob Doe, Fighter Pilot*, p. 11.

2. TNA: AIR 28/448 SHQ RAF Leconfield.

3. Nigel Walpole, *Dragon Rampant: The Story of No. 234 Fighter Squadron* (London Colney: Merlin Massara, 2007), pp. 1–10.

4. 234 Squadron records incorrectly say they all came from 6 FTS.

5. TNA: AIR 27/1439 234 Squadron ORB 1939 Oct to 1943 Dec.

6. *Ibid.*

7. Kenneth Wynn, *Men of the Battle of Britain: A Biographical Directory of the Few* (Norwich: Gliddon Books, 1999), p. 23.

8. Wynn, *Men of the Battle of Britain,* pp. 203 & 399; TNA: AIR 27/1439 234 ORB.

9. TNA: AIR 27/1439 ORB 234 Squadron 18/11/39.

10. Keith Lawrence interview 2012.

11. TNA: AIR 27/1439 234 ORB 540 15 Dec.

12. Keith Lawrence interview.

13. *Ibid.*

14. TNA: AIR 27/1439 ORB.

15. G. Campion, *The Good Fight: Battle of Britain Propaganda and the Few* (Basingstoke: Palgrave Macmillan, 2009), p. 48.

16. Stephen Bungay, *The Most Dangerous Enemy: A History of the Battle of Britain* (2001 edn; London: Aurum, 2000), p. 255.

17. Doe, *Bob Doe, Fighter Pilot,* p. 12.

18. John Terraine, *The Right of the Line: The Royal Air Force in the European War, 1939–1945* (London: Hodder and Stoughton, 1985), p. 110.

19. Keith Lawrence interview.

20. TNA: AIR 27/2126 616 Squadron ORB; AIR 27/1439 234 Squadron ORB.

21. Holland Interview Bob Doe.

22. Keith Lawrence interview.

23. IWM: Interview Doe.

24. Doe, *Bob Doe, Fighter Pilot,* p.12.

25. TNA: AIR 27/1439 ORB.

26. Keith Lawrence interview.

27. *Ibid.*

28. IWM: Interview Doe; Holland Interview Bob Doe.

29. TNA: AIR 27/1439 234 Squadron ORB.

30. Terraine, *The Right of the Line*, p. 130.

31. *Ibid.*, quoted on p. 140.

32. *Ibid.*, p. 151.

33. TNA: AIR 27/2126 616 Squadron ORB.

34. Terraine, *The Right of the Line*, pp. 156–7.

35. Doe, *Bob Doe, Fighter Pilot*, p. 13.

36. Terraine, *The Right of the Line*, p. 159.

37. Overy, *The Battle of Britain*, p. 32.

38. TNA: AIR 27/1439 234 Squadron ORB.

39. *Ibid.*; AIR 28/732 St Eval ORB.

40. *Ibid.*

41. G. H. Bennett, '"The Scars of War" – Displacement, Dislocation and the Aircrew of the Forces Aériennes Françaises Libres 1940–44: Towards a Quantitative and Qualitative Analysis', *War & Society*, 33(3) (August 2014), 194–207, p. 195.

42. Capitaine Francois de Labouchere, served in 249 and 615 Squadrons, killed in action 5 September 1942. Quoted in Laddie Lucas, *Wings of War* (London: Hutchinson, 1983), p. 66.

43. Bennett, '"The Scars of War"', p. 195.

44. TNA: AIR 27/1439 234 Squadron ORB; AIR 28/732 St Eval ORB.

45. Doe Logbook.

46. TNA: AIR 27/1439 234 Squadron ORB.

47. Jean Shapland, *The Memories Linger On: A Collection of Reminiscences of Wartime RAF St Eval* (Cornwall, 1989), p. 5.

48. H. A. Fenton, 'Aquarius: The Man Who Held the Watering Pot', unpublished, pp. 25–26.

49. TNA: AIR 27/1439 ORB 234 Squadron ORB; AIR 28/732 St Eval ORB.

50. TNA: AIR 28/732 St Eval ORB 1 July 1940.

51. Terraine, *The Right of the Line*, p. 174.

52. Wood and Dempster, *The Narrow Margin*, pp. 88–90 quoted in *ibid.*, p. 179.

53. TNA: AIR 25/182 10 Group ORB.

54. C. J. B. Joseph, 'Brand, Sir (Christopher Joseph) Quintin (1893–1968)', *Oxford Dictionary of National Biography* (Oxford University Press, 2004).

55. TNA: AIR 28/732 St Eval ORB.

56. TNA: AIR 28/732 Fighter Sector HQ St Eval.

57. Doe Logbook.

58. TNA: AIR 27/1439 234 Squadron ORB.

59. Keith Lawrence interview.

60. Jeremy. A. Crang, 'Identifying the "Few": The Personalisation of a Heroic Military Elite', *War & Society*, 24(2) (2005), 13–22, p. 14.

61. IWM: Interview Chard.

62. TNA: AIR 81/1200 Casualty File Gout, Letter to Mrs Gennart 3 August 1940.

63. Holland Interview Bob Doe.

64. Holland Interview Bob Doe.

65. Doe, *Bob Doe, Fighter Pilot*; Doe Logbook – 15 July logbook shows convoy patrol in P 9378 out for 2 hrs. Most sorties were 1.35 hrs.

66. Wynn, *Men of the Battle of Britain*, p. 402.

67. Doe Logbook; TNA: AIR 27/1439 234 Squadron ORB.

68. TNA: AIR 27/1439 234 Squadron ORB 7 & 8 August 1940.

69. Peter Devitt, '"Repeat, Please!" Poles and Czechoslovaks in the Battle of Britain', *Proceedings of the Royal Air Force Historical Society*, 49 (2010), 35–57.

70. Joseph, 'Brand, Sir Quintin'.

71. TNA: AIR 25/182 10 Group ORB.

72. Joseph, 'Brand, Sir Quintin'.

73. TNA: AIR 27/1439 234 Squadron ORB.

74. Wynn, *Men of the Battle of Britain*, p. 209.

75. With grateful thanks to Dr and Mrs Tony Wright for this information.

76. TNA: AIR 27/1439 234 Squadron ORB.

77. *London Gazette* issue 36524 page 2340 23 May 1944; Wynn, *Men of Battle of Britain*, p. 399; *Flight* 8 August 1952, 10 March 1949, 9 October 1947.

78. Keith Lawrence interview.

79. John Ray, *Battle of Britain; New Perspectives: Behind the Scenes of the Great Air War* (London: Brockhampton Press, 1994), p. 22; TNA: AIR 27/1439 234 Squadron ORB.

80. TNA: AIR 2/8591 AVM Park to Air Ministry 22 May 1940. The pilot in question remained in the RAF and subsequently became a group captain.

81. TNA: AIR 27/1439 234 Squadron ORB; AIR 28/732 St Eval ORB; Wynn, *Men of the Battle of Britain*, p. 23.

82. Doe Logbook.

4 In the Heat of the Battle and the Move to Middle Wallop

1. TNA: AIR 25/182 10 Group ORB.

2. Doe, *Bob Doe, Fighter Pilot*, p. 21.

3. IWM: Interview Recording 26966 Joe Roddis 2006.

4. TNA: AIR 28/545 Middle Wallop Station ORB.

5. TNA: AIR 50/89/5 Sgt Michael Boddington Combat Report; TNA: AIR 28/545 Middle Wallop Station ORB; AIR 27/1439 234 Squadron ORB. Note: Chris Goss, *Brothers in Arms* (Crecy Publishing, 1994), p. 53 has an alternative view.

6. TNA: AIR 28/545 Middle Wallop Station ORB.

7. Stephen Bungay, *The Most Dangerous Enemy: A History of the Battle of Britain* (London: Aurum, 2000), p. 209.

8. TNA: AIR 28/545 Middle Wallop Station ORB.

9. TNA: AIR 29/2102 609 Squadron ORB.

10. Bungay, *The Most Dangerous Enemy,* p. 218.

11. IWM: Interview Doe.

12. IWM: Interview Doe.

13. Herbert K. Weiss, 'Systems Analysis Problems of Limited War', quoted in Bungay, *The Most Dangerous Enemy,* p. 239.

14. Bungay, *The Most Dangerous Enemy,* p. 239.

15. Bungay, *The Most Dangerous Enemy,* p. 239 ff.

16. IWM: Interview Doe.

17. TNA: AIR 50/89 Combat Report. Note Jaguars were Me 110s.

18. Bob Doe letter to Gerry Burke 20 August 2005.

19. TNA: AIR 50/89 Mortimer-Rose Combat Report.

20. TNA: AIR 81/1444 Casualty Report 19 August 1940.

21. Kenneth Wynn, *Men of the Battle of Britain: A Biographical Directory of the Few* (Grafton Books, 1999).

22. TNA: AIR 28/545 Middle Wallop Station ORB.

23. TNA: AIR 81/1444 Casualty file Cecil Hight.

24. Doe, *Bob Doe, Fighter Pilot*, p. 22.

25. *Ibid.*

26. TNA: Air 50/89 Doe Combat Report.

27. Doe, *Bob Doe, Fighter Pilot*, p. 23.

28. *Ibid.*

29. IWM: Interview Doe.

30. Bungay, *The Most Dangerous Enemy*, pp. 242–3.

31. *Ibid.*

32. *Ibid.*

33. J. K. Rowling, *Harry Potter and the Goblet of Fire* (London: Bloomsbury, 2004).

34. AIR 27/1439 234 Squadron ORB.

35. Doe, *Bob Doe, Fighter Pilot*, p. 39.

36. AIR 27/1439 234 Squadron ORB; AIR 50/89 Doe Combat Report.

37. AVM F. D. S. Scott-Malden in Lucas, *Wings of War*, p. 83.

38. IWM: Interview Doe.

39. Bungay, *The Most Dangerous Enemy*, p. 190.

40. Mary Pollock, 'The Solving of a Mystery', *Hampshire Magazine* April 1997.

41. *Ibid.*; see also Andy Saunders, *Finding the Foe: Outstanding Luftwaffe Mysteries of the Battle of Britain and Beyond Investigated and Solved* (London: Grub Street Publishing, 2010).

42. *Southern Daily Echo* 22 August 1940.

43. F. K. Mason, *Battle over Britain* (London: McWhirter Twins, 1969), p. 290.

44. Army Air Museum, Middle Wallop: Letter 3 August 1982 W. Blake to Captain J. R. Cross, Librarian.

45. TNA: Air 50/89 Doe Combat Report.

46. Doe Logbook.

47. Doe, *Bob Doe, Fighter Pilot*, p. 25.

48. *Ibid*.

49. Bungay, *Most Dangerous Enemy*, p. 272.

50. Matthew Freudenberg, *Negative Gravity; A Life of Beatrice Shilling* (Charlton Publications, 2003), pp. 41–2.

51. Doe Logbook 26 August 1940.

52. TNA: AIR 50/89 Doe Combat Report.

53. Doe, *Bob Doe, Fighter Pilot*, pp. 26–27.

54. *Ibid*.

55. Chris Goss, 'Who shot Rolf?', *Britain at War* 2013; Mason, *Battle over Britain*, p. 421; Doe Logbook.

56. Doe, *Bob Doe, Fighter Pilot*, p. 38.

57. Bungay, *Most Dangerous Enemy*, p. 272.

58. IWM: Interview Doe.

59. Doe, *Bob Doe, Fighter Pilot*, p. 25.

60. TNA: AIR 28/545 Middle Wallop Station ORB.

61. Doe, *Bob Doe, Fighter Pilot*, p. 13.

62. Doe, *Bob Doe, Fighter Pilot*, p. 38.

63. IWM: Interview Doe.

64. Richard Overy, *The Battle of Britain* (London: Penguin, 2000), pp. 82–83.

65. Overy, *The Battle of Britain*, p. 71.

66. Ibid., p. 29.

67. Ibid., p. 40.

68. Ibid.

69. TNA: AIR 1439 234 Squadron ORB August.

70. TNA: AIR 50/89 Doe Combat Report.

71. Doe, *Bob Doe, Fighter Pilot*, p. 31.

72. TNA: AIR 27/1441 234 Squadron ORB; AIR 50/89 Doe Combat Report.

73. TNA: AIR 27/1439 234 Squadron; *Aberdeen Press & Journal* 4

June 2003. Gordon's remains were discovered still in his Spitfire by archaeologists in 2003.

74. Doe, *Bob Doe, Fighter Pilot*, p. 40.

75. TNA: AIR 27/1441 234 Squadron ORB; AIR 50/89 Doe Combat Report.

76. Terraine, *The Right of the Line*, p. 207.

77. Overy, *The Battle of Britain*, p. 96.

78. Angels was the term for 10,000 feet, so Angels 20 was 20,000 feet.

79. Doe, *Bob Doe, Fighter Pilot*, p. 34.

80. TNA: AIR 27/1439 234 Squadron ORB August. Note: the Heinkel was probably mistaken identity for another German fighter aircraft. See Overy, *Battle of Britain*, p. 53.

81. TNA: AIR 50/89 Doe Combat Report.

82. TNA: AIR 27/1441/2 234 Orb appendices.

83. TNA: AIR 50/89 Harker Combat Report.

84. Kristen Alexander, *Australia's Few and the Battle of Britain* (Sydney: NewSouth Publishing, 2014), pp. 259–261.

85. Alexander, *Australia's Few*, pp. 31, 52 & 65.

86. Bob Doe letter to Gerry Burke 20 August 2005.

87. http://www.youtube.com/watch?v=SBXonwHCCD4 [accessed 12 February 2014]

88. John Willis, *Churchill's Few: The Battle of Britain Remembered* (London: Michael Joseph, 1985), p. 140; IWM: Interview Doe.

89. The names of all men serving as pilots on squadrons are not always easy to pin down.

90. Pers. com.

91. TNA: AIR 2/8591 Aircrew who refuse or are unfit to fly: disposal policy 1940-42.

92. *Ibid*.

93. TNA: AIR 2/8591 AVM Park to Under Secretary of State Air Ministry 7 October 1940

94. *Ibid*.

95. Martin Francis, *The Flyer: British Culture and the Royal Air Force, 1939–1945* (New York: Oxford University Press, 2008), p. 125.

96. Terry Kane conversation 2013.

97. TNA: AIR 27/1439 234 Squadron ORB.

98. Bob Doe Service Record.

5 The Battle Continues with a New Squadron and a New Aircraft

1. Doe Logbook.

2. Wynn, *Men of the Battle of Britain*, pp. 133–34; Fenton, 'Aquarius'.

3. Wynn, *Men of the Battle of Britain*, pp. 133–34.

4. TNA: AIR 27/1453 238 Squadron ORB; Wynn, *Men of the Battle of Britain*.

5. Air Commodore John Ellacombe recollections. http://war-experience. org/collections/air/alliedbrit/ellacombe/default.asp [accessed 20 September 2014]

6. Doe, *Bob Doe, Fighter Pilot*, p. 29.

7. A Mansell, 'The Origins of Aircrew Who Fought in the Battle of Britain', *Proceedings of the Royal Air Force Historical Society*, 34 (2006), 67–79, p. 69.

8. TNA: AIR 27/1453 238 Squadron ORB.

9. Fenton, 'Aquarius'.

10. Eleanor M. Lockyer, *Memories of Chilbolton Airfield, 1940–41* (Andover, n. d.).

11. TNA: AIR 27/1453 238 Squadron ORB.

12. Fenton, 'Aquarius', p. 30.

13. TNA: AIR 27/1453 238 Squadron ORB.

14. Lockyer, *Memories of Chilbolton Airfield*, p. 29; Caroline Freeman-Cuerden, *Veterans' Voices: Coventry's Unsung Heroes of the Second World War* (ISIS Publishing, 2007).

15. Holland Interview Bob Doe.

16. TNA: AIR 27/1453 238 Squadron ORB.

17. TNA: AIR 27/1453 238 Squadron ORB.

18. Terraine, *The Right of the Line*, p. 207.

19. Doe, *Bob Doe, Fighter Pilot*, p. 43.

20. TNA: AIR 27/1453 238 Squadron ORB.

21. Doe, *Bob Doe, Fighter Pilot*, p. 44.

22. TNA: AIR 27/1453 238 Squadron ORB.

23. Doe, *Bob Doe, Fighter Pilot*, p. 44.

24. TNA: AIR 27/2102 609 Squadron ORB.

25. Doe, *Bob Doe, Fighter Pilot*, p. 44.

26. TNA: AIR 27/2102 609 Squadron ORB.

27. TNA: AIR 27/1453 238 Squadron ORB.

28. E. R. Mayhew, *The Reconstruction of Warriors* (Greenhill Books, 2004), pp. 48–49; Stephen Bungay noted the considerably higher number of deaths in Hurricanes.

29. IWM: Interview Doe.

30. TNA: AIR 27/1453 238 Squadron ORB.

31. Spink Sale Catalogue London 25 November 2010, p. 21.

32. TNA: AIR 27/1453 238 Squadron ORB.

33. Fenton, 'Aquarius', p. 31.

34. Winston G. Ramsey (ed.), *The Battle of Britain: Then and Now* (Old Harlow, Essex: Battle of Britain International Ltd, 2011), p. 678.

35. TNA: AIR 50/91 Doe Combat Report.

36. Bentley Priory: Sigurd Hey letter 25 Jan 1985.

37. Doe, *Bob Doe, Fighter Pilot*, p. 44.

38. *Ibid.*, p. 46.

39. Holland Interview Bob Doe.

40. *Flight* 28 November 1940.

41. TNA: AIR 27/1453 238 Squadron ORB.

42. Wedding certificate.

43. TNA: AIR 27/1453 238 Squadron ORB.

44. *Ibid.*

45. *Ibid.*

46. Wynn, *Men of the Battle of Britain*, p. 435.

47. TNA: AIR 27/1455 238 Squadron ORB; Lockyer, *Memories of Chilbolton Airfield*, p. 45.

48. Lockyer, *Memories of Chilbolton Airfield*, p. 37.

49. TNA: AIR 27/1453 238 Squadron ORB.

6 A New Face and a New Reality

1. TNA: AIR 28/888 Warmwell ORB.

2. TNA: AIR 27/2102 609 Squadron ORB.

3. *Ibid.*

4. *Ibid.*

5. TNA: AIR 27/1453 238 Squadron ORB; Fenton, 'Aquarius', p. 27.

6. TNA: AIR 27/1453 238 Squadron ORB; Caroline Freeman-Cuerden, *Veteran's Voices: Coventry's Unsung Heroes of the Second World War* (History Press, 2005); Holland interview Bob Doe.

7. Holland interview Bob Doe.

8. Fenton, 'Aquarius', p. 33

9. TNA: AIR 28/888 Warmwell ORB.

10. IWM: Interview Doe. Note in his book Bob refers to the Laurence of Arabia tale re: the cottage hospital but T. E. Lawrence died at Bovingdon Camp hospital. *Guardian* 19 May 1935. It is possible that Bob was in just one hospital, probably Bovingdon.

11. Pers. com.; *Guardian* 19 May 1935.

12. http://www.biotopics.co.uk/g11/antibiotics.html [accessed 29 July 2013]

13. To understand the incredible work of the many specialists read Murray C. Meikle, *Reconstructing Faces: The Art and Wartime Surgery of Gillies, Pickerill, McIndoe and Mowlem* (Otago: Otago University Press, 2013).

14. *Ibid.*, pp. 120–21.

15. *Ibid.*, p. 125.

16. *Ibid.*, p. 174.

17. *Ibid.*; *The Times* 12 September 1960 Gillies obituary.

18. *The Times* 12 September 1960 Gillies obituary.

19. Meikle, *Reconstructing Faces*, p. 179.

20. Doe, *Bob Doe, Fighter Pilot*, p. 56.

21. *Ibid.*, p. 58.

22. *Ibid.*

23. Meikle, *Reconstructing Faces*, p. 186.

24. C. B. F. Kingcombe, *A Willingness to Die* (Stroud: Tempus, 1999), p. 31.

25. Meikle, *Reconstructing Faces*, p. 130.

26. *Ibid.*, p. 130.

27. *Ibid.*, p. 184.

28. *Ibid.*

29. IWM: Interview Doe.

30. Meikle, *Reconstructing Faces*, p. 179.

31. TNA: AIR 2/6317 Facially Disfigured RAF Personnel – Proposed Scheme for Employment during Convalescence.

32. Doe, *Bob Doe, Fighter Pilot*, p. 38.

33. IWM: Interview Doe.

34. Doe Logbook.

35. Doe, *Bob Doe, Fighter Pilot*, p. 59.

36. Allen, *Fighter Squadron*, p. 122.

37. *Ibid.*,, pp. 122–6.

38. TNA: AIR 27/598 66 Squadron ORB.

39. Laddie Lucas, *Thanks for the Memory; Unforgettable Characters in Air Warfare, 1939–1945* (Guildford: Grub Street), p. 78.

40. TNA: AIR 27/598 66 Squadron ORB.

41. Bungay, *The Most Dangerous Enemy*, p. 346.

42. Holland Interview Bob Doe.

43. TNA: AIR 50/26 Doe Combat Report; RAF Museum Hendon: Intelligence Reports 66 Squadron.

44. Doe Logbook.

45. Lucas, *Thanks for the Memory*, p. 77.

46. *Ibid.*

47. *Ibid.*

48. Doe, *Bob Doe, Fighter Pilot*, p. 59; Doe Logbook.

49. Lucas, *Thanks for the Memory*, p. 77.

50. TNA: AIR 27/598 66 ORB.

51. Doe Logbook.

52. IWM: Interview Doe; Doe Logbook

53. Shapland, *The Memories Linger On*, p. 5.

54. Doe Logbook.

55. *The Times* 1 August 1941.

56. CA: Char 20/25/8 Letter 4 Aug 1941 from Lady Carr to Churchill.

57. TNA: AIR 27/936 130 Squadron ORB.

58. Doe Logbook.

59. TNA: AIR 27/936 130 Squadron ORB.

60. Allen, *Fighter Pilot*, pp. 165–178; TNA: AIR 27/598 66 Squadron ORB.

61. TNA: AIR 27/936 130 Squadron ORB.

62. TNA: AIR 27/2126 Letter from AVM AOC 10 Group 27 March 1941.

63. TNA: AIR 41/71 Flying Training Vol. II Organisation Part III Operational Training.

64. *Ibid.*

65. Doe Logbook.

66. TNA: AIR 41/71 Flying Training Vol. II Organisation Part III Operational Training.

67. Doe Logbook.

68. TNA: AIR 28/344 ORB of RAF Station Hawarden.

69. TNA: AIR 41/71 Flying Training Vol. II Organisation Part III Operational Training.

70. TNA: AIR 29/683 57 OTU ORB; AIR 16/798 Synthetic Trainer.

71. H. L. Thompson, *New Zealanders with the Royal Air Force (Vol. I)* (Wellington: Historical Publications Branch, 1953), p. 241; Christopher Shores and Clive Williams, *Aces High: A Tribute to the most Notable Pilots of the British and Commonwealth Forces in WWII* (London: Grub Street, 1994), pp. 275–6.

72. Wynn, *Men of the Battle of Britain*, pp. 269 & 351.

73. Eddie Sparkes, *Mumblings*, http://www.users.zetnet.co.uk/sparkes/ [accessed July 2012]

74. Doe Logbook.

75. Sparkes, *Mumblings*.

76. TNA: AIR 2/6001 Medical Care of Flying Personnel in War.

77. Doe Logbook.

78. Pickering pers. com.

79. *The Times* 25 May 1942.

80. Pers. com.

81. Wynn, *Men of the Battle of Britain*, p. 177.

82. Doe Logbook.

83. TNA: AIR 29/683 57 OTU ORB; Doe Logbook.

84. Sparkes, *Mumblings*. Letter home dated Thursday 1 March 1943 on arriving at 57 OTU. 85. Interview Keith Lawrence.

86. IWM: Interview Doe; Doe Logbook.

87. Interview Keith Lawrence.

88. Sparkes, *Mumblings*.

89. *Ibid*.

90. Doe Service Record.

91. TNA: AIR 16/800 Fighter Leaders School.

92. TNA: AIR 16/800 17 April 43 Air Marshall Leigh Mallory to Under Sec of State.

93. TNA: AIR 16/800 Fighter Leaders School.

94. Kingcombe, *A Willingness to Die*, p. 143.

95. TNA: AIR 16/800 Fighter Leaders School letter 30 August 1943.

96. TNA: AIR 16/800 Fighter Leaders School.

97. John Adair, *Action Centred Leadership* (Gower Press, 1973).

98. AMP 202 (1948) *Leadership: Some Notes for the Guidance of Royal Air Force Officers*. With grateful thanks to Group Captain Jupp.

99. TNA: AIR 2/6001 Medical Care of Flying Personnel in War.

100. *Ibid*.

101. TNA: Air 27/909 118 Squadron ORB.

102. TNA: AIR 2 8110 Air/sea Rescue Dinghies.

103. TNA: AIR 27/217 613 ORB 540 August 1943.

104. My thanks to Dr Henrik Skov Kristensen, Head Curator, the Frøslev Camp Museum for this information. Email dated 20 May 2014.

7 India and Squadron Leadership

1. IAM: Interview Doe; Doe Logbook.

2. Email from Tim Elkington 4 April 2013; IWM: Interview Doe.

3. Doe, *Bob Doe, Fighter Pilot*, p. 67.

4. Henry Probert, *The Forgotten Air Force: The Royal Air Force in the War against Japan, 1941–1945* (London: Brasseys, 1995), p. 94.

5. Probert, *The Forgotten Air Force*, p. 127.

6. Air Historical Branch (AHB): Michael Seth-Smith, 'The Abandoned Earl', unpublished biography, p. 111.

7. Probert, *The Forgotten Air Force*, pp. 136–37.

8. *Ibid.*, p. 149.

9. *Ibid.*, p. 148–51.

10. Doe, *Bob Doe, Fighter Pilot*, p. 71; Doe Logbook.

11. Shri S. C. Gupta, *History of the Indian Air Force, 1933–45* (Delhi: Combined Inter-Services Historical Section India & Pakistan, 1961), p. 177.

12. See Probert, *The Forgotten Air Force*.

13. TNA: CAB 66/21/34 Sec of State for India. India War Effort 30 Jan 1942.

14. *Ibid.*

15. TNA: CAB 65/34/26 War Cabinet Conclusions.

16. TNA: CAB 66/26/37 War Cabinet 22 July 1942.

17. Probert, *The Forgotten Air Force*, p. 148.

18. Norman Franks and Paul Richey, *Fighter Pilot's Summer* (London: Grub Street, 1993), p. 203.

19. Franks and Richey, *Fighter Pilot's Summer*, p. 203.

20. *Ibid.*

21. Probert, *The Forgotten Air Force*, p. 153.

22. TNA: AIR 23/2214 IAF Administration, Policy and Command 17 February 1944.

23. RAF Leadership booklet 1948.

24. TNA: AIR 27/155 10 IAF Squadron ORB.

25. TNA: AIR 2/5007 RAF in India Health Reports.

26. TNA: AIR 29/494 IAF Inspectorate.

27. *Ibid.*

28. *Ibid.*

29. TNA: AIR 27/155 10 Squadron IAF.

30. TNA: AIR 29/481 1 IAF Exhibition Unit.

31. TNA: AIR 29/494 IAF Inspectorate.

32. *Ibid.*

33. TNA: AIR 29/481 1 IAF Exhibition Unit.

34. TNA: AIR 27/155 10 IAF Squadron ORB.

35. Sparkes, *Mumblings*.

36. Doe, *Bob Doe, Fighter Pilot*, p. 68.

37. TNA: AIR 27/155 10 IAF Squadron ORB.

38. *Ibid.*; Doe Logbook.

39. TNA: AIR 27/155 10 IAF Squadron ORB; IWM Interview Doe.

40. TNA: AIR 27/155 10 IAF Squadron ORB.

41. Sparkes, *Mumblings*.

42. TNA: AIR 27/155 10 IAF Squadron ORB.

43. *Ibid.*

44. Doe, *Bob Doe, Fighter Pilot*, pp. 70–1.

45. IWM: Interview Doe.

46. TNA: AIR 27/155 10 IAF Squadron ORB.

47. *Ibid.*; Sparkes, *Mumblings*.

48. Sparkes, *Mumblings*.

49. TNA: AIR 27/155 10 IAF Squadron ORB.

50. *Ibid.*

51. Doe, *Bob Doe, Fighter Pilot*, p. 72; Doe Logbook.

52. TNA: AIR 27/155 10 IAF Squadron ORB.

53. Doe, *Bob Doe, Fighter Pilot*, p. 72; TNA: AIR27/155 No 10 IAF Squadron ORB.

54. Sparkes, *Mumblings*.

55. TNA: AIR 27/155 10 IAF Squadron ORB.

56. *Ibid.*

57. AIR 23/2214 Deputy AOC-in-C, Air Marshal Air Marshal Sir Guy Garrod, 7 November 1943.

58. *Ibid.*

59. Doe Logbook.

60. TNA: AIR27/155 No. 10 IAF Squadron ORB; Doe Logbook.

61. IWM: Interview Doe.

62. Probert, *The Forgotten Air Force*, p.162.

63. W/O Clegg memoirs, http://homepage.ntlworld.com/colin.clegg1/page712.html. [accessed 20 March 2014].

64. Doe, *Bob Doe, Fighter Pilot*, p. 72.

65. Doe Logbook.

66. Martin Francis, 'Men of the Royal Air Force, the Cultural Memory of the Second World War and the Twilight of the British Empire', in *Gender, Labour, War and Empire: Essays on Modern Britain*, ed. P. Levine & S. Grayzel (London: Palgrave Macmillan, 2009), 179–96, pp. 186–8.

67. P. C. Lal, *My Years with the IAF* (New Delhi: Lancer, 1986), pp. 36–7.

68. Doe, *Bob Doe, Fighter Pilot*, p. 72.

69. *Ibid.*

70. Sparkes, *Mumblings.*

71. TNA: AIR 27/155 10 IAF Squadron ORB.

72. *Ibid.*

73. *Ibid.*

74. *Ibid.*

75. *Ibid.*

76. *Ibid.*

77. *Ibid.*

78. *Ibid.*

79. Probert, *The Forgotten Air Force*, p. 193.

80. *Ibid.*, p. 194.

81. *Ibid.*, p. 168.

82. *Ibid.*, p. 167.

83. *Ibid.*, pp. 170–171.

84. Gupta, *History of the Indian Air Force, 1933–45*, p. 24.

85. TNA: AIR 27/155 10 IAF Squadron ORB. The ORB quotes, 'This is discussed at some length in the appendix.' Unfortunately the appendix is missing.

86. TNA: AIR 27/155 10 IAF Squadron ORB; Rana T. S. Chhina, *The Eagle Strikes: The Royal Indian Air Force 1932 to 1950* (New Delhi: Ambi Knowledge Pvt Ltd, 2006), pp. 76–7.

87. TNA: AIR 23/2184 ACM Peirse private correspondence with HH the Nawab of Bhopal. Note: On partition he elected to keep Bhopal within India.

88. TNA: AIR 27/155 10 IAF Squadron ORB.

89. *Ibid.*

90. Doe Logbook; TNA: AIR 27/155 10 IAF Squadron ORB.

91. Doe Logbook.

92. Doe Service Record.

8 The Battle over the Burmese Jungle

1. Anon., *Wings of the Phoenix: The Official Story of the Air War in Burma* (London: HMSO, 1949), p. 107–8.

2. Anon., *Victory in Burma* (British Information Services, 1945).

3. Probert, *The Forgotten Air Force*, p. 253.

4. *Ibid.*, p. 228.

5. AHB: Seth-Smith, 'The Abandoned Earl', p. 137.

6. Gupta, *History of the Indian Air Force, 1933–45*, p. 155.

7. TNA: AIR 23/1939 AVM Bandon Despatch: Report on air training.

8. Gupta, *History of the Indian Air Force, 1933–45*, p. 155.

9. Doe Logbook.

10. TNA: AIR 27/155 10 Squadron IAF ORB; IWM Interview Doe.

11. TNA: AIR 27/155 10 Squadron IAF ORB.

12. *Ibid.*

13. *Ibid.*

14. *Ibid.*

15. TNA: AIR 26/495 HQ no. 904 Wing Cox's Bazar.

16. TNA: AIR 27/155 10 Squadron IAF ORB.

17. Doe, *Bob Doe, Fighter Pilot*, p. 74.

18. TNA: AIR 27/155 10 Squadron IAF ORB.

19. AHB: Seth-Smith, 'The Abandoned Earl', p. 35.

20. TNA: AIR 27/155 10 Squadron IAF ORB.

21. *Ibid.*

22. Probert, *The Forgotten Air Force*, p. 255.

23. Doe Logbook.

24. Neville Gill interview, http://www.bharat-rakshak.com/IAF/ History/1940s/Neville.html#Smoke [accessed 8 June 2013]

25. TNA: AIR 27/155 10 Squadron IAF ORB.

26. Probert, *The Forgotten Air Force*, p. 213.

27. TNA: AIR 23/2429 Lecture Notes 'Walking out of the Jungle' 1944.

28. *Ibid.*

29. TNA: AIR 2/5032 RAF Rescue Services, Jungle and Desert Rescue.

30. Probert, *The Forgotten Air Force*, p. 319.

31. Doe, *Bob Doe, Fighter Pilot*, p. 73.

32. TNA: AIR 27/155 10 Squadron IAF ORB.

33. *Ibid.*

34. *Ibid.*

35. TNA: WO 172/9551 81st West African Division RA War Diary.

36. TNA: WO 172/9551 81st West African Division RA War Diary; Doe Logbook.

37. Sparkes, *Mumblings*.

38. TNA: AIR 27/155 10 Squadron IAF ORB; AIR 27/1919 9 Squadron IAF ORB; Chhina, *The Eagle Strikes*, p. 201.

39. *Ibid.*

40. IWM: Interview Doe.

41. TNA: AIR 27/155 10 Squadron IAF ORB; IWM: Interview Doe.

42. TNA: AIR 27/155 10 Squadron IAF ORB.

43. Chhina, *The Eagle Strikes*.

44. Seth-Smith, 'The Abandoned Earl', pp. 135–7.

45. TNA: AIR 27/155 10 Squadron IAF ORB.

46. *Ibid.*

47. AHB: Seth-Smith, 'The Abandoned Earl', p. 135.

48. Probert, *The Forgotten Air Force*, p. 212–3.

49. TNA: AIR 27/155 10 Squadron IAF ORB.

50. *Ibid.*

51. AHB: Seth-Smith, 'The Abandoned Earl', p. 130.

52. TNA: AIR 27/155 10 Squadron IAF ORB.

53. AHB: Seth-Smith, 'The Abandoned Earl' book radio broadcast.

54. Doe *Bob Doe, Fighter Pilot*, p. 73.

55. TNA: AIR 27/155 10 Squadron IAF ORB.

56. *Ibid.*

57. Doe, *Bob Doe, Fighter Pilot*.

58. AHB: Seth-Smith, 'The Abandoned Earl'.

59. TNA: AIR 27/155 10 Squadron IAF ORB.

60. *Ibid.*

61. *Ibid.*

62. *Ibid.*

63. TNA: AIR 23/1939 Bandon despatch.

64. *Ibid.*

65. TNA: AIR 27/155 10 Squadron IAF ORB.

66. *Ibid.*

67. *Ibid.*

68. TNA: AIR 23/1939 Bandon despatch.

69. TNA: AIR 27/155 10 Squadron IAF ORB.

70. IWM: Interview Doe.

71. TNA: AIR 27/156 10 Squadron IAF ORB.

72. Doe, *Bob Doe, Fighter Pilot*, p. 78.

73. TNA: AIR 27/156 10 Squadron IAF ORB.

74. *Ibid.*

75. *Ibid.*

76. *Ibid.*

77. *Ibid.*

78. *Ibid.*

79. *Ibid.*

80. *Ibid.*

81. *Ibid.*

82. *Ibid.*

83. Chhina, *The Eagle Strikes*, p. 220.

84. TNA: AIR 23/1939 AVM Bandon Despatch; Probert, *The Forgotten Air Force*, p. 277.

85. TNA: AIR 27/156 10 Squadron IAF ORB.

86. *Ibid.*

9 Post-War RAF and 25th Anniversary of the Battle of Britain

1. AIR 27/156 10 Squadron IAF ORB.

2. Probert, *The Forgotten Air Force*, p. 274.

3. TNA: AIR 27/156 10 Squadron IAF ORB.

4. *Ibid.*

5. IWM: Interview Doe.

6. IWM: Interview Doe.

7. Doe, *Bob Doe, Fighter Pilot*, p. 82.

8. Doe Service Record.

9. *Ibid.*

10. Probert, *The Forgotten Air Force*, p. 302.

11. Spink Sale Catalogue London 25 November 2010, p. 21.

12. Ron Howe recollections of 9 Squadron RIAF via email from Mick Howe 24 May 2012; Thomas, 'Memories of 8 Squadron', http://www.bharat-rakshak.com/IAF/History/1940s/TJThomas.html [accessed 24 May 2014]

13. Probert, *The Forgotten Air Force*, p. 298.

14. *Ibid.*, p. 297.

15. *Ibid.*, p. 300.

16. TNA: AIR 24/1743 ACSEA Ceylon.

17. Doe, *Bob Doe, Fighter Pilot*, p. 89.

18. *Ibid.*, pp. 87–94.

19. TNA: AIR 20/986 Combined Operations Formation of Training School.

20. *Ibid.*

21. *Ibid.*

22. Doe, *Bob Doe, Fighter Pilot*, p. 95.

23. Gee disliked her Christian name of Gladys.

24. IWM: Interview Doe; TNA: AIR 20/8987 Royal Aux AF: Planning and Training.

25. Doe Service Record.

26. Campion, *The Good Fight*, pp. 140–45.

27. TNA; AIR 2/9909 Publicity, Allegations by Commander Noel Gaylor.

28. Doe, *Bob Doe, Fighter Pilot*, p. 98.

29. Doe, *Bob Doe, Fighter Pilot*, p. 98.

30. Doe Service Record; Note AVM David Atcherley was lost at sea on a flight to Nicosia in June 1952; *Bob Doe, Fighter Pilot*, p. 102.

31. Pers. com. Sir Erik Bennett, June 2013; *The Times* 19 October 1950 and 11 December 1950.

32. http://news.bbc.co.uk/onthisday/low/dates/stories/november/20 [accessed 24 September 2014]

33. Doe, *Bob Doe, Fighter Pilot*, p. 102; Doe Logbook.

34. Sir Erik Bennett interview; Ron Dick, 'Flying First Generation Jet Fighters in the RAF', *Proceedings of the Royal Air Force Historical Society*, 27 (2002), 41–58, p. 57.

35. Doe Logbook; Doe, *Bob Doe, Fighter Pilot*, p. 102; Dick, 'Flying First Generation Jet Fighters'.

36. D. Dicken interview; Dick, 'Flying First Generation Jet Fighters', p. 56.

37. D. Dicken interview.

38. Doe Service Record.

39. TNA: AIR 29/2314 Central Gunnery School ORB.

40. Doe Service Record.

41. *Ibid.*

42. TNA: DEFE 32/7 Chiefs of Staff Committee: Secretary's standard file; Philip Ziegler, *Mountbatten: The Official Biography* (London: William Collins & Son, 1985), pp. 578–89.

43. Doe, *Bob Doe, Fighter Pilot*, pp. 116–7.

44. Ashton, Nigel John, 'A Microcosm of Decline: British Loss of Nerve and Military Intervention in Jordan and Kuwait, 1958 and 1961', *The Historical Journal*, 40(4) (December 1997), 1069–83, p. 1079; David Lee, *Flight from the Middle East: A History of the Royal Air Force in the Arabian Peninsular and Adjacent Territories, 1945-1972* (London: HMSO, 1980), pp. 165–170; Jones, Ben, 'The Persian Gulf and British Defence Policy, 1956-71', *Air Power Review*, 15(2) (2012), 53–80, pp. 54–6.

45. Ashton, 'A Microcosm of Decline', p. 1075; Lee, *Flight from the Middle East*, p. 172; Jones, 'The Persian Gulf and British Defence Policy', p. 61.

46. Doe, *Bob Doe, Fighter Pilot*, pp. 117.

47. *Ibid.*, pp. 117–8.

48. Ashton, 'A Microcosm of Decline', p. 1082; Jones, 'The Persian Gulf and British Defence Policy', p. 61.

49. TNA: DEFE 32/7 Chiefs of Staff Committee: Secretary's standard file.

50. Doe, *Bob Doe, Fighter Pilot*, p. 116.

51. Doe Service Record.

52. Ziegler, *Mountbatten*, pp. 590–592.

53. *Independent* 2 April 1993, obituary.

54. TNA: DEFE 10/390 JIGSAW Minutes of meetings.

55. *Ibid.*

56. *Ibid.*

57. http://www.independent.co.uk/news/obituaries/capt-bill-jewell-6162996.html [accessed 3 September 2014]

58. Doe, *Bob Doe, Fighter Pilot*, p. 119.

59. Doe Service Record.

60. TNA: AIR 20/11288 Battle of Britain week, 1965: Service of Thanksgiving.

61. TNA: AIR 8/2420 Department of Chief of Air Staff: Battle of Britain 25th Anniversary; Christopher Shores and Clive Williams, *Aces High: A Tribute to the most Notable Pilots of the British and Commonwealth Forces in WWII* (London: Grub Street, 1994).

62. TNA: AIR 8/2420 Department of Chief of Air Staff: Battle of Britain 25th Anniversary.

63. TNA: AIR 2/11288 Battle of Britain week, 1965: Service of Thanksgiving.

64. TNA: AIR 2/11288 26th July 1965 Roberts to MacDonell.

65. *Ibid.*

66. TNA: AIR 20/11289 Air Commodore A. R. D. MacDonell 3 August 1965

67. TNA: AIR 20/11289 J. E. Carruthers PS to Minister (RAF) 3 August 1965.

68. TNA: AIR 20/11288 Confidential minute from Roberts to Dir. Gen Personal Services.

69. TNA: AIR 20/11289 Roberts.

70. TNA: AIR 20/11288 Minute from Roberts.

71. TNA: Air 20/11289 P. P. Villa 30 September to HQ Fighter Command.

72. AIR 20/11289 J. M. Templeton editor 15 October 1965.

73. AIR 20/11289 Roberts to MacDonell 23 September 1965.

74. Doe Service Record.

SELECT BIBLIOGRAPHY

Primary Sources

The National Archives

AIR 2/1630 Recruitment of pilots in national emergency: selection boards 1935–1939

AIR 2/2075 Wartime entrants: commissions, conditions of service, 1937–47

AIR 2/4904 RAF Fighter Command: contribution to medical history of war

AIR 2/5007 RIAF in India: health report

AIR 2/5032 RAF rescue services, jungle and desert rescue

AIR 2/6001 Medical care of flying personnel in war

AIR 2/6160 Disabled personnel

AIR 2/6317 Facially disfigured personnel

AIR 2/6876 Coloured personnel in RAF

AIR 2/8591 Aircrew who refuse or are unfit to fly: disposal policy 1940–1942

AIR 2/9909 Publicity, allegations by Commander Noel Gaylor

AIR 8/2420 25th anniversary Battle of Britain

AIR 16/798 Synthetic trainer Hawarden

AIR 16/800 Fighter Leaders School, Milfield

AIR 20/8992 RAF recruiting: policy 1939–53

AIR 20/986 Combined Operations formation of training school

AIR 20/8987 Royal Aux AF: planning and training

AIR 20/10269 Plastic surgery in RAF II

AIR 20/11288 25th anniversary Battle of Britain

AIR 20/11289 Battle of Britain 25th anniversary

AIR 23/1939 AVM Earl of Bandon despatch

AIR 23/2184 ACM Peirse private correspondence with HH the Nawab of Bhopal

AIR 23/2429 ACSEA 1944 Lecture notes on walking out of the jungle

AIR 23/2307 Park letter re: India awards

AIR 23/2214 Deputy AOC-in-C, Air Marshal Sir Guy Garrod, 1943

AIR 23/3427 ACSEA Light aircraft and jungle warfare

AIR 24/1743 HQ ACSEA Ceylon

AIR 25/182 1940 Group 10 ORB
AIR 25/184 1940 Group 10 appendices
AIR 26/495 HQ 904 Wing Cox's Bazar
AIR 32/14 History of flying training
AIR 32 /15 History of flying training

Squadron Operations Record Books
AIR 27/139 9 Squadron IAF
AIR 27/155 10 Squadron IAF
AIR 27/156 10 Squadron IAF
AIR 27/598 66 Squadron
AIR 27 /907 118 Squadron
AIR 27/909 118 Squadron
AIR 27/936 130 Squadron
AIR 27/1439 234 Squadron
AIR 27/1441 234 Squadron
AIR 27/1453 238 Squadron
AIR 27/1455 238 Squadron
AIR 27/1583 273 Squadron
AIR 27/2102 609 Squadron
AIR 27/2117 613 Squadron
AIR 27/2119 613 Squadron
AIR 27/2126 616 Squadron
AIR 27/2409 32 Squadron
AIR 27/2607 32 Squadron

Station Operations Record Books
AIR 28/344 Hawarden
AIR 28/448 Leconfield
AIR 29/488 Uxbridge
AIR 28/545 Middle Wallop
AIR 28/729 St Eval (include Fighter Sector)
AIR 28/732 St Eval
AIR 28/733 St Eval
AIR 28/888 Warmwell
AIR 28/1598 Church Fenton

Misc. Unit Operations Record Books
AIR 29/29 Fighter Command School of Tactics Charmy Down
AIR 29/481 1 IAF Exhibition Unit
AIR 29/494 IAF Inspectorate
AIR 29/547 9 Air Observer School Penrhos
AIR 29/558 6 Flying Training School Little Rissington
AIR 29/605 Central Gunnery School
AIR 29/606 Central Gunnery School
AIR 29/619 16 EFTS Redhill

AIR 29/683 57 OTU Hawarden
AIR 29/684 OTU Hawarden
AIR 29/2314 Central Gunnery School

Combat Reports and Casualty Files
AIR 50/26 Doe Combat Report 2 June 1941
AIR 50/89/73 Doe Combat Reports 15 August 1940 to 5 September 1940
AIR 50/89/22 Doe Combat Reports 5 September 1940
AIR 50/89/35 Doe Combat Reports 7 September 1940
AIR 50/91 Doe Combat Reports 30 September 1940 and 3 October 1940
AIR 50/89/88 Mortimer-Rose Combat Report 15 August 1940
AIR 50/89/18 O'Brien Combat Report 21 August 1940
AIR 50/89/26 Harker Combat Report 5 September 1940
AIR 81/200 Gout Casualty File
AIR 81/1444 Cecil Hight Casualty File

Cabinet Papers
CAB 66/21/34 Sec of State for India. India War Effort 30 Jan 1942
CAB 65/34/26 War Cabinet Conclusions
CAB 66/26/37 War Cabinet 22 July 1942

Chiefs of Staff
DEFE 10/390 Joint Inter-Service Group for Study of All Out Warfare (JIGSAW): Minutes of Meetings
DEFE 32/7 Chiefs of Staff Committee: Secretary's standard file

Education
ED 161/11756 1900-71 Walton on Hill, Banstead C. of E. School
ED 21/40436 Jan 1928 to Dec 1933 Walton on Hill, Banstead C. of E. School

Army
WO 172/9551 81st West African Division, Royal Artillery War Diary

Other Archives
Air Historical Branch
Michael Seth-Smith, 'The Abandoned Earl', unpublished biography, p. 111.

Army Air Museum, Middle Wallop
Letter from W. Blake to Captain J. R. Cross 3 August 1982

Bentley Priory
Letter from Sigurd Hey 25 January 1985

Churchill Archive
Churchill correspondence with *News of the World*
CHAR 8/551 2 Feb 1937–22 Jun 1937
CHAR 8/629 21 Feb 1939–28 Oct 1939
CHAR 8/551 1 Jan 1935–2 Dec 1935
CHAR 8/533 21 Jan 1936–24 Jun 1937
CHAR 20/25/8 Lady Carr to WSC

Imperial War Museum
Interview Recording 26964 RFT Doe 2004
Interview Recording 28605 Judy Chard 2008
Interview Recording 26966 Joe Roddis 2006

*News International Archive (*News of the World *Archive)*
Staff card R. F. T. Doe

RAF Museum Hendon
Plans of air bases, St Eval, Warmwell
X005-3084 Recording R. F. T. Doe
Intelligence Reports 66 Squadron

Surrey History Centre, Woking
Electoral Rolls 1938 Parish of Walton on the Hill
Leatherhead Central School Registers
794 Walton Heath Golf club Records
8928/2/1/1 LCS Play Programme

Newspapers and Magazines
The Times
Illustrated London News
London Gazette
Western Daily Press
Gloucester Echo
Cornishman
Aberdeen Journal
Flight

www.ancestry.co.uk
British Army Service Records James Thomas Doe
WW1 Medal rolls Index Cards James T. Doe

www.bharat-rakshak.com
Neville Green memoirs and much more

www.users.zetnet.co.uk/sparkes/
Eddie Sparkes, *Mumblings*

www.griffonmerlin.com/ww2_
James Holland Interview with Bob Doe

Interviews
Sir Erik Bennett
A. B. 'Dickie' Dicken
Tim Elkington
Terry Kane
Keith Lawrence
Tony 'Pick' Pickering

Unpublished
H. A. Fenton, 'Aquarius: The Man Who Held the Watering Pot'
A. C. Williamson, 'Co-Operation between the British Army and the Royal Air Force in South-East Asia: 1941–45', unpublished PhD (Cambridge, 2002)

Secondary Sources

Anon., *Leadership: Some Notes for the Guidance of Royal Air Force Officers* (Air Ministry Publication 202, 1948).
Anon., *Wings of the Phoenix: The Official Story of the Air War in Burma* (London: HMSO, 1949).
Addison, Paul & Crang, Jeremy. A. (eds), *The Burning Blue: A New History of the Battle of Britain* (London: Pimlico, 2000).
Alexander, Kristen, *Australia's Few and the Battle of Britain* (Sydney: NewSouth Publishing, 2014).
Allen, H. R., *Fighter Squadron: A Memoir 1940–1942* (London: Harper Collins, 1982).
Andrew, F. R., *History of RAF Perranporth 1941–45* (Perranporth, 1995).
Ashton, Nigel John, 'A Microcosm of Decline: British Loss of Nerve and Military Intervention in Jordan and Kuwait, 1958 and 1961', *The Historical Journal*, 40(4) (December 1997), 1069–83.
Bainbridge, Cyril & Stockdill, Roy, *The News of the World Story* (London: Harper Collins, 1993).
Baines, Dudley & Johnson, Paul, 'In Search of the Traditional Working Class: Social Mobility and Occupational Continuity in Interwar London', *Economic History Review*, 52(4) (1999), 692–713.
Barclay, George, *Angels 22: Self Portrait of a Fighter Pilot* (London: Arrow Books, 1976).
Bennett, G. H., 'The RAF's Free French Fighter Squadrons: The Rebirth of

French Airpower, 1940-44', *Global War Studies: The Journal for the Study of Warfare and Weapons, 1919–1945*, 7(2) (2010), 62–102.

Bennett, G. H., '"The Scars of War" – Displacement, Dislocation and the Aircrew of the Forces Aériennes Françaises Libres 1940–44: Towards a Quantitative and Qualitative Analysis', *War & Society*, 33(3) (August 2014), 194–207.

Bishop, Patrick, *Fighter Boys: Saving Britain 1940* (London: Harper Perennial, 2004).

Bungay, Stephen, *The Most Dangerous Enemy: A History of the Battle of Britain* (London: Aurum, 2000).

Campion, G., *The Good Fight: Battle of Britain Propaganda and the Few* (Basingstoke: Palgrave Macmillan, 2009).

Chhina, Rana T. S., *The Eagle Strikes: The Royal Indian Air Force 1932 to 1950* (New Delhi: Ambi Knowledge Pvt Ltd, 2006).

Crang, Jeremy. A., 'Identifying the "Few": The Personalisation of a Heroic Military Elite', *War & Society*, 24(2) (2005), 13–22.

Dawson, Leslie, *Wings over Dorset: Story of Aviation in the South* (Wincanton: Dorset Publishing, 1989).

Devitt, Peter, '"Repeat, Please!" Poles and Czechoslovaks in the Battle of Britain', *Proceedings of the Royal Air Force Historical Society*, 49 (2010), 35–57.

Dick, Ron, 'Flying First Generation Jet Fighters in the RAF', *Proceedings of the Royal Air Force Historical Society*, 27 (2002), 41–58.

Doe, Bob, *Bob Doe, Fighter Pilot* (Tunbridge Wells: Spellmount, 1991).

English, Allan D., 'A Predisposition to Cowardice? Aviation Psychology and the Genesis of "Lack of Moral Fibre"', *War & Society*, 13(1) (1995), 15–34.

Fopp, Michael, 'The Battle of Britain – 70 Years On', *Proceedings of the Royal Air Force Historical Society*, 50 (2011), 6–30.

Francis, Martin, *The Flyer: British Culture and the Royal Air Force, 1939–1945* (New York: Oxford University Press, 2008).

Francis, Martin, 'Men of the Royal Air Force: The Cultural Memory of the Second World War and the Twilight of the British Empire', in P. Levine & S. Grayzel (eds), *Gender, Labour, War and Empire: Essays on Modern Britain* (London: Palgrave Macmillan, 2009), pp. 179–96.

Franks, Norman & Richey, Paul, *Fighter Pilot's Summer* (London: Grub Street, 1993).

Freeman-Cuerden, Caroline, *Veteran's Voices: Coventry's Unsung Heroes of the Second World War* (History Press, 2005).

Freudenberg, Matthew, *Negative Gravity: A Life of Beatrice Shilling* (Charlton Publications, 2003).

Garside, W. R., 'Juvenile Unemployment and Public Policy between the Wars', *Economic History Review*, 30(2) (1977), 322–39.

Goss, Chris, *Brothers in Arms* (Crecy Publishing, 1994).

Goss, Chris, *The Luftwaffe Bombers Battle of Britain* (Crecy Publishing, 2000).

Goss, Chris, 'Who Shot Rolf?', *Britain at War* 2013.

Gupta, Shri S. C., *History of the Indian Air Force, 1933–45* (Delhi: Combined Inter-Services Historical Section India & Pakistan, 1961).

Harvey, A. D., 'The French Armee de L'Air in May-June 1940', *Journal of Contemporary History*, 25(4) (1990), 447–65.

Heath, Linda, *Of Good Report: The Story of the Leatherhead Schools* (Leatherhead: Leatherhead and District Local History Society, 1986).

Hemingway, Kenneth, *Wings over Burma* (London: Quality Press, 1944).

Higham, Robin, 'Flying for the Royal Air Force in South East Asia Command: Legacies and Realities', *Proceedings of the Royal Air Force Historical Society*, 47 (2010), 70-85.

James, John, *The Paladins* (London: Futura, 1990).

James, T. C. G., *The Battle of Britain* (London: Frank Cass, 2000).

Jefford, C. G. (ed.), *Royal Air Force Reserve and Auxiliary Forces* (Oxford: Royal Air Force Historical Society, 2003).

Jefford, C. G., 'Accidents – Investigation, Institutions and Attitudes 1919-1945', *Proceedings of the Royal Air Force Historical Society*, 37 (2006), 35-55.

John, Vivian, 'Order of Battle of Salonika Army', *The New Mosquito*, 12 (2005).

Jones, Ben, 'The Persian Gulf and British Defence Policy, 1956-71', *Air Power Review*, 15(2) (2012), 53-80.

Jones, Edgar, 'LMF: The Use of Psychiatric Stigma in the Royal Air Force during the Second World War', *Journal of Military History*, 70(2) (2006), 439-58.

Joseph, C. J. B., 'Brand, Sir (Christopher Joseph) Quintin (1893-1968)', *Oxford Dictionary of National Biography* (Oxford: Oxford University Press, 2004).

Kingcombe, C. B. F., *A Willingness to Die* (Stroud: Tempus, 1999).

Lal, P. C., *My Years with the IAF* (New Delhi: Lancer, 1986).

Lee, David, *Eastward: A History of the Royal Air Force in the Far East, 1945-1972* (London: HMSO, 1984).

Lee, David, *Flight from the Middle East: A History of the Royal Air Force in the Arabian Peninsular and Adjacent Territories, 1945-1972* (London: HMSO, 1980).

Lockyer, Eleanor M., *Memories of Chilbolton Airfield, 1940-41* (Andover, n.d.).

Lovegrove, Gill, *The RAF and St Eval* (St Eval: Parish, 2009).

Lucas, Laddie, *Wings of War* (London: Hutchinson, 1983).

Lucas, Laddie, *Thanks for the Memory: Unforgettable Characters in Air Warfare 1939-1945* (London: Grub Street, 1989).

Mansell, A., 'Flying Start: Educational and Social Factors in the Recruitment of Pilots of the RAF in the Interwar Years', *History of Education*, 26(1) (1997), 71-90.

Mansell, A., 'The Origins of Aircrew Who Fought in the Battle of Britain', *Proceedings of the Royal Air Force Historical Society*, 34 (2006), 67-79.

Mason, F. K., *Battle over Britain* (London: McWhirter Twins, 1969).

Mayhew, E. R., *The Reconstruction of Warriors: Archibold McIndoe, the Royal Air Force and the Guinea Pig Club* (London: Greenhill, 2004).

McCarthy, John, 'Aircrew and "Lack of Moral Fibre" in the Second World War', *War & Society*, 2(2) (1984), 87-101.

Meikle, Murray C., *Reconstructing Faces: The Art and Wartime Surgery of Gillies, Pickerill, McIndoe and Mowlem* (Otago: Otago Univeristy Press, 2013).

Orange, Vincent, *Park: The Biography of Air Chief Marshall Sir Keith Park* (London: Grub Street Press, 2001).

Overy, Richard, *The Air War 1939-1945* (2005 edn; Washington: Potomac Books, 1980).

Overy, Richard, *The Battle of Britain* (London: Penguin, 2000).

Pollock, Mary, 'The Solving of a Mystery', *Hampshire Magazine* April 1997.

Prasad, Bisheshwar, *History of the Indian Air Force, 1933–45* (Delhi: Combined Inter-Services Historical Section India & Pakistan, 1961).

Probert, Henry, *The Forgotten Air Force: The Royal Air Force in the War against Japan, 1941–1945* (London: Brasseys, 1995).

Ramsey, Winston G. (ed.), *The Battle of Britain: Then and Now* (Old Harlow, Essex: Battle of Britain International, 2011).

Saunders, Andy, *Finding the Foe: Outstanding Luftwaffe Mysteries of the Battle of Britain and Beyond Investigated and Solved* (London: Grub Street Publishing, 2010).

Shapland, Jean, *The Memories Linger On: A Collection of Reminiscences of Wartime RAF ST Eval* (Cornwall, 1989).

Sherwood, Tim, *Coming into Land: A Short History of Hounslow, Hanworth and Heston Aerodromes, 1911–1946* (Hounslow: Heritage Publications, 1999).

Shores, Christopher, *Air War for Burma: The Allied Air Forces Fight Back in South-East Asia 1942–1945, Bloody Shambles* (London: Grub Street, 2005).

Shores, Christopher and Williams, Clive, *Aces High: A Tribute to the most Notable Pilots of the British and Commonwealth Forces in WWII* (London: Grub Street, 1994).

Somerfield, Stafford, *Banner Headlines* (Shoreham: Scan Books, 1979).

Steinhilper, Ulrich & Osborne, Peter, *Spitfire on My Tail: A View from the Other Side* (Bromley: Independent Books, 1990).

Terraine, John, *The Right of the Line: The Royal Air Force in the European War, 1939–1945* (London: Hodder and Stoughton, 1985).

Todd, Selina, 'Young Women, Work and Leisure in Interwar England', *Historical Journal*, 48(3) (2005), 789–809.

Walpole, Nigel, *Dragon Rampant: The Story of No. 234 Fighter Squadron* (London Colney: Merlin Massara, 2007).

Wells, Mark K., *Courage and Air Warfare: The Allied Aircrew Experience in the Second World War* (London: Frank Cass, 2000).

Wilkinson, W. A., *One Pilot's War: The Battle of Britain and Beyond* (Windsor: Windsor Books Ltd, 2010).

Willis, John, *Churchill's Few: The Battle of Britain Remembered* (London: Michael Joseph, 1985).

Wood, Derek, *The RAF and the Far East War 1941–1945* (Brighton: Royal Air Force Historical Society, 1995).

Wynn, Kenneth, *Men of the Battle of Britain: A Biographical Directory of the Few* (Norwich: Gliddon Books, 1999).

Yuhas, Theodore Frank, 'Development of Education for Adolescents in England', *History of Education Journal*, 51 (1953), 30–33.

Ziegler, Philip, *Mountbatten: The Official Biography* (London: William Collins & Son, 1985).

LIST OF ILLUSTRATIONS

55. 224 Group order of battle, showing 10 Squadron at the front. (Courtesy of the Air Historical Branch)
56. Accident to a 10 Squadron Hurri-bomber. (Author's collection)
57. 32 Squadron Vampires in Egypt. (Author's collection)
58. 32 Squadron travelling Ops Wagon at Deversoir. (Courtesy of Check Collison)
59. Bob in his 32 Squadron jet. (Author's collection)
60. Bob, Gee, Susan and Helen in Egypt. (Author's collection)
61. A favourite occupation, Liar Dice. (Author's collection)
62. Another winning game of cricket in Egypt; 32 Squadron cricket team. (Courtesy of Check Collison)

INDEX